HOW TO
WRITE
SONGS
on Keyboards

RIKKY ROOKSBY

HOW TO WRITE SONGS ON KEYBOARDS

RIKKY ROOKSBY

To Lawrence G. James, mentor and friend, on the occasion of his retirement

A BACKBEAT BOOK

First edition 2005

Published by Backbeat Books

600 Harrison Street

San Francisco, CA 94107, US

www.backbeatbooks.com

An imprint of The Music Player Network CMP Media LLC

Published for Backbeat Books by Outline Press Ltd,

2A Union Court, 20-22 Union Road, London SW4 6JP, England

www.backbeatuk.com

ISBN 13: 978-0-87930-862-9

ISBN 10: 0-87930-862-1

EDITOR: Paul Quinn

DESIGN: Paul Cooper Design

Printed by Colorprint Offset Ltd (Hong Kong)

05 06 07 08 09 5 4 3 2 1

Contents

Preface

The pianoforte is the most important of all musical instruments: its invention was to music what the invention of printing was to poetry.

George Bernard Shaw

Sit yourself down at the piano
Just about in the middle,
Put all your fingers on the black notes anyway you want to.

Graham Nash, 'Black Notes'

I need to touch music as well as think it, which is why I have always lived next to a piano.

Igor Stravinsky

He who plays the piano keeps sane.

Italian proverb

The simplest way to write a song is to put some chords together and then sing some words on top. This book – from the same stable as the best-selling *How To Write Songs On Guitar* – shows you how to find and link chords on a keyboard. It explains how to play chords with simple shapes, and how to get inspiring new sounds by altering these shapes on the basis of physical patterns rather than theory. It reveals which chords go well with each other and how to find them on a keyboard. It describes how to construct the renowned 'three-chord trick'. Section by section, *How To Write Songs On Keyboards* introduces the four, five and six-chord song, basic structure, hit-making techniques like the turnaround, and many other tips to get more from your creative ideas.

You don't need to read music. Everything is laid out in easy-to-read diagrams. You also don't need to be a keyboard player. The beauty of using a keyboard for songwriting is that just pressing a few keys can get you started. This book is ideal for guitar players looking to expand their creativity by exploring a new instrument. If you regularly compose songs on guitar you can find you're going around the same chords all the time, sometimes without realising it. Writing music on a different instrument is a good way to stimulate new ideas. Some ideas natural to one instrument won't occur to you on another.

Songs of a kind you never knew you could write are waiting among the shapes and progressions in these pages.

Rikky Rooksby, 2005

The first thing to point out is that *How To Write Songs On Keyboards* is not a book about how to play keyboards.

It will not tell you how to read keyboard music, nor how to hold your hands correctly, nor how to practise scales. It won't tell you how to get your left and right hands to work independently of each other, or any of the other techniques covered in a keyboard tutor book. If you want to concentrate on building technique to play piano music, look for one of the many instruction courses available. *How To Write Songs On Keyboards* is a book with a different focus: the keyboard as a source of song ideas. It does something new.

It's a book about creativity. And it's as much for guitarists and singers as it is for keyboard players.

So it doesn't matter whether you already play keyboards and would like to write a song, or if you usually play guitar and fancy getting new ideas from another instrument.

Music is about inspiration and feeling. Unfortunately these are not always easy things to come by. A songwriter with even a small amount of experience soon realises that although it would be terrific to be guaranteed a classic song every time you sat at the keys, or picked up the guitar, it doesn't happen that way. I'm often asked if there is anything a songwriter can do to summon inspiration. Well, one method is to try writing a song on a different instrument to your usual one.

Why keyboards?

From time to time most songwriters want to compose a different type of song from the kind they usually write. Changing instrument is a way of doing this. You might think lack of technique would be limiting on an unfamiliar instrument, and that's true up to a point. But unlike many instruments, getting notes from a keyboard is easy – even a cat walking over the keys can do it. Compare the ease of pressing a key to the effort involved in trying to produce a single note from a saxophone or flute, or playing even a half-barre F chord on the guitar when you're a beginner.

With some instruments you have to practise hard to get technically good enough to make a pleasing sound. Woodwind players have to learn how to breathe, how to direct air, how to handle the reed. String players have to learn to bow, and to accurately pitch notes on a fingerboard where there are no frets. In this sense at least guitarists have it easy – they know exactly *where* to put their fingers to get an F♯ major chord. But that still leaves the problem of making sure those fingers are correctly positioned so they don't create a buzz or stop an adjacent string from sounding. And if, as is true with F♯, the chord requires several strings to be held down with a single finger – a barre – that can take months to get right, even if your guitar has a decent 'action' so the strings are not too far off the fingerboard. So on the guitar an F♯ chord is something most beginners can't play. But anyone can go to a piano – whether it's electronic, a battered old 'upright', or a baby grand – and hold down an F♯ major, as long as they know which keys to press. On a keyboard it's no harder than holding down a C major.

For the purposes of this book a 'keyboard' means any instrument with a piano-like keyboard of at least two complete octaves (ie 16 white keys in width), preferably three octaves (24 white keys in width). This could be an acoustic piano, an electric or digital piano, an organ, or a modern synthesiser/workstation.

Regardless of the tone(s) the instrument produces, the notes are laid out flat in front of you in white and black keys. This layout has its own special qualities in terms of the way it

A fistful of notes

"Each generation, from Scott Joplin forward, has found its own ways of playing with those 12 notes. The possibilities *are* endless."

Lamont Dozier

Here's what you need to know about finding notes on the keyboard. Western music uses 12 notes, labelled A, B, C, D, E, F, G, with an additional five modifications to these seven, the five sharp/flat notes (there's no sharp/flat note between B and C, or between E and F). Since there are only 12 notes, there are only 12 keys to familiarise yourself with – that's the distance from the white key to the left of the first black key (C) to the white key after the last black key (B) (see diagram).

This is an important point. No matter how wide your keyboard, it consists of repetitions of the same 12 notes. A keyboard can look intimidating, sitting down at it for the first time – a full-size piano, for instance, has 88 keys. But the thing to remember is that you are not trying to learn 88 different keys. You just need to learn the notes contained in a single 'octave' of 12 keys. Each group of 12 keys is the same – a keyboard repeats this physical block of 12 keys as many times as its width dictates.

The smallest interval (or distance) in pitch between any of these notes is called a semitone (ie half a tone).

Each key on the keyboard (white or black) is a semitone, just as the frets on a guitar are a semitone apart.

The white keys are given the letters A, B, C, D, E, F and G. Notice that the white keys B & C, and E & F, are next to each other, but all the others have a black key in-between them. This is because B-C and E-F are only a semitone apart. The white keys C-D, D-E, F-G, G-A, and A-B, are all a tone apart. Which means there's room to squeeze a note in-between them. That's where the five black keys come in.

The five black keys are called sharps (♯) and flats (♭). Each black key can be thought of as either the lower note plus a semitone (A to A♯) or the higher note minus a semitone (B to B♭). So each of the black notes has two names: C♯/D♭, D♯/E♭, F♯/G♭, G♯/A♭, A♯/B♭. Whether a note is thought of as a sharp or flat will depend on musical context – it's easier to consider a note flat in one context and sharp in another.

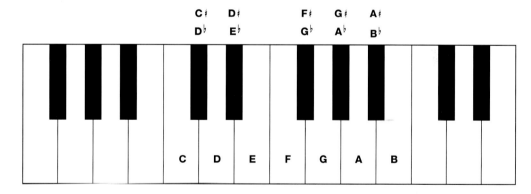

Note names

The notes F♯/G♭, G♯/A♭, and A♯/B♭ form the group of three black keys you see together on the keyboard. The two black keys in an isolated pair are C♯/D♭ and D♯/E♭. The contrast of white with black, plus the pattern of three black keys alternating with two, helps the player know quickly where he or she is on the keyboard.

Depending on the width of your keyboard each of these 12 notes is available in more than one place (in different octaves), lowering in pitch as you move left on the keyboard and rising as you move right. This means you can play one note in as many octaves as your keyboard will allow. So for instance you can play a low-sounding bass C or a very high C, and several in-between.

PIANO PEDALS

Acoustic pianos are equipped with at least two foot pedals. The one on the left (the 'soft' pedal) has the effect of muting the keyboard so that it doesn't sound as bright and resonant. In grand pianos this is achieved by shifting the hammers so they make less full contact on the strings (the 'una corda' effect, which gives this pedal its alternative name), but in upright pianos it simply reduces the impact of the hammers, so the sound they produce is quieter.

The pedal on the right is for sustain. It's technically called the 'damper', though this name can cause confusion, because its effect is to *release* the piano's natural dampeners. It's also sometimes (inaccurately) called the 'loud' pedal. Hold it down with your right foot and strike any note. The note rings for a long time because the pedal has removed all damping from the strings. Before the note fades completely, lift your foot from the pedal. The note will suddenly be cut off.

On grand pianos, and some better-quality or more modern uprights, there will be a third pedal in-between these two. This is traditionally the sostenuto, which allows the sustain effect to be targeted by releasing the dampers only on particular notes (so for example a chord can be sustained while the notes of a melody are not), as opposed to the normal sustain pedal where it's all-or-nothing. In some modern uprights this middle sostenuto pedal is replaced by a 'practice' pedal – an extreme version of the soft pedal, which reduces the piano's volume level still further for private practice.

The right (sustain) pedal is very helpful for beginners on the keyboard. To start with you will not necessarily be able to change chords fast enough to create a seamless sound. To avoid losing the sense of the chords progressing from one to another you can use the sustain pedal. Keep the pedal down, hit your first chord, then go to the second. Although you will have taken your fingers off the keys, the first chord will go on sounding. Just before you strike the second chord, lift your foot off the pedal. This will kill the first chord, but now you are ready to hit the second – there will be hardly any gap between the two.

On an electronic keyboard or synth there are usually menus that allow you to increase the sustain of a chord so that it will hang for a short while, long enough to change to the next chord (in a synth's 'ADSR envelope' functions you can change the 'attack, decay, sustain or release' of notes).

On synths some of the preset sounds themselves will feature quite long sustains and a reverb that means you can lift your hands off the keyboard and the chord will continue briefly as you move to the next. This is good for slow songs but not for medium-to-fast ones. Synths will also let you split a keyboard so that the left end has one sound and the right has another. Some have an arpeggiator that will play the notes of a chord one at a time at various speeds and in various orders. Clearly such options are there for you to exploit as songwriting tools, but they are not the focus of this book, which is centred on the business of harmony itself.

GETTING STARTED: TRIADS

The basic chords in song harmony are majors and minors. It only takes three notes to make a simple major or minor chord. This kind of three-note chord is called a 'triad'. The majority of the examples in this book are triad-based because they are technically easy to play (and this is, after all, a book for people who *don't* play keyboards as well as for those that do). A triad can be played using one hand, or its notes distributed between two.

How to find a major triad

• Notice that the black keys are grouped in twos and threes. The C key is the key just before the paired black keys. Choose a C roughly in the middle of your keyboard. This C is the 'root' note of the chord of C major, which gives the chord its name.

- Count up four keys (including all black and white keys) and hold that key down. This is the note E, and it's called the '3rd' of the chord – because it's the third note in the C major scale (C-D-E-F-G-A-B). Play the two notes together with your thumb on the C and longest (middle) finger on the E.
- Count up three more keys (black and white) from the E and, with your little finger, add the note G, which is the '5th' of the chord. You should now be holding down three white keys (C-E-G) that make a C major chord.

How to find a minor triad
- Hold down the C white key. This C is also the 'root' note of C minor.
- Count up three keys (black and white) and hold that black key down. This is the note E♭, and is the '3rd' of the C minor chord. Play the two notes together, with your thumb on C and longest/middle finger on E♭.
- Count up four more keys (black and white) and add the note G, the 5th of the chord, with your little finger. You now have the chord of C minor.

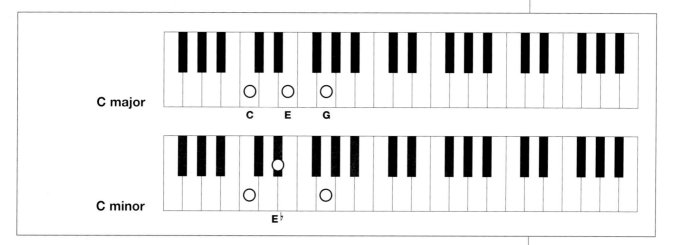

Notice that in comparison to C major, C minor sounds sad. This is the main expressive effect of the contrast between minor chords and majors. Major chords, when compared to minors, sound happy. This emotional contrast is vital to songwriting.

A ONE-FINGER CHANGE

TECHNIQUE 1

The aim of Sections 1 and 2 of this book is to give you shapes and finger-movements that will spark off song ideas and interesting chord sequences. Here's the first of these, based on the movement of a *single finger* within a chord. Play the C major chord four times in a steady rhythm and then move your middle finger down a key: it turns into C minor. Play that four times, then do the same thing with the chords of F major and F minor (see p16). When you have tried it yourself, listen to Track 1 on the CD that comes with the book to make sure you played the correct shapes.

CD TRACK
1

CD TRACK 1 Eight-bar idea in C

| C | \ | \ | \ | Cm | \ | \ | \ | C | \ | \ | \ | Cm | \ | \ | \ |

| F | \ | \ | \ | Fm | \ | \ | \ | F | \ | \ | \ | Fm | \ | \ | \ |

15

Most of the examples in this book assume a 4/4 time signature, since this is the most common in popular music. It means there are four beats in a bar. The slashes represent the chord played on a beat (the vertical lines indicate the bar-lines, separating one bar from the next). It could be any rhythmic pattern, that doesn't matter; as long as there are four beats. Minor chords on these examples are symbolised by a letter with an 'm' after it.

THE MAGIC NUMBERS 4 AND 3

The *gaps* between the notes of the chords are measured either by three keys or four keys. Major chords have the pattern 4+3 (which means after the root note you count four keys to find the next note, then three to complete the triad); minor chords have the pattern 3+4. You can work out how to play any major or minor chord simply by applying this formula.

Just remember:

Don't count the piano key you're on when you go three up or four up.
Don't forget the black keys – they count just as much as the white ones.

TO FIND A MAJOR CHORD ON ANY NOTE:

• Choose your root note, white or black.
• Count up four keys, add that note.
• Count up another three keys, add that note.
• Strike all three notes together.

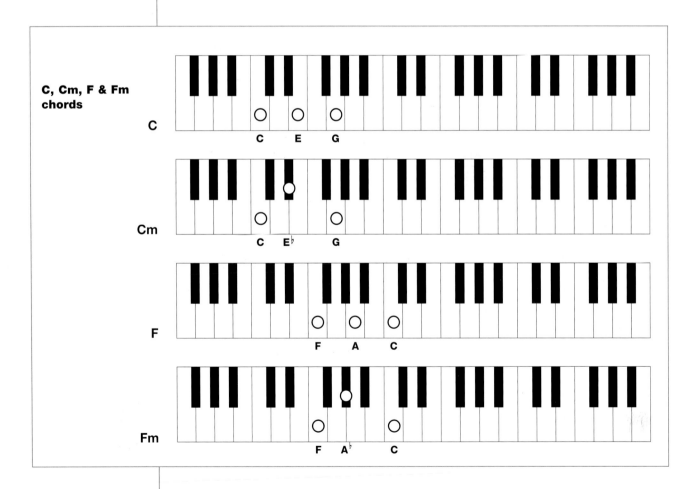

C, Cm, F & Fm chords

TO FIND A MINOR CHORD ON ANY NOTE:

• Choose your root note, white or black.
• Count up three keys, add that note.
• Count up four keys, add that note.
• Strike all three notes together.

Remember: 4+3 = major, 3+4 = minor

WHITE-KEY CHORDS – THE BEGINNER'S FRIENDS

Three major and three minor chords can be played just on the white keys. They are C, F and G, and Am, Dm and Em. (All other chords will require one or more black notes.) These six chords all sound great together, so they are an effective place to start when you first try playing at the keyboard. In previous pages you've had diagrams for C and F, so here are the diagrams for G, Am, Dm and Em.

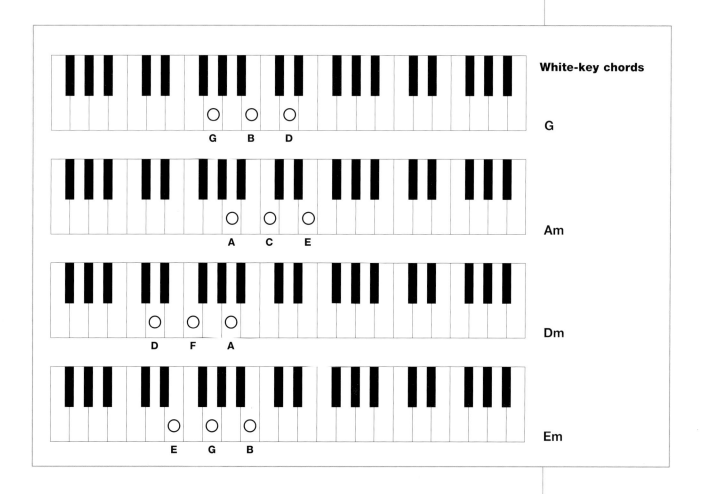

TECHNIQUE 2

THREE CHORDS FROM ONE – INVERSIONS

As we've seen, three notes make a simple major or minor chord. All of the chords so far have been described in what's called root position, and with the notes in sequence, 1st-3rd-5th (1-3-5). But you don't always have to finger the notes in this order. Major or minor triads can take three forms, depending on which of the three notes is lowest. If the middle note (the 3rd) is the lowest, it's called a first inversion. If the top note (the 5th) becomes the lowest note, it's called second inversion.

The three top diagrams on p19 are all C major chords, but each has a subtly different sound. (Right-hand inversions are shown in this book with a lower-case letter after a slash.)

MAKING A FIRST INVERSION:

(Note for guitarists: inversions are generally much easier to work out and play on keyboards than they are on guitar.)

• Hold down a C triad.
• Let go of the C key. Hold the E with your thumb and count up three keys to G. Hold that with your first finger.
• Count up five keys from the G. This brings you to the white note C an octave above the one you started on. Hold this note with your little finger.
• Play this chord (E-G-C): a first-inversion C major.

MAKING A SECOND INVERSION:

• Hold down a C triad.
• Let go of the C and E keys and hold the G down with your thumb.
• Count up five keys from the G. This brings you to the white note C an octave above the C you started on. Hold this note down with your first finger.
• Then count up four keys from C to get the next E.
• Play this chord, G-C-E: a second-inversion C major.

You might be wondering to yourself: what use are these additional shapes? Well, putting aside their individual sounds, they are often essential in order to make your right-hand chord changes easier and fluent. If you play guitar you know about easy changes, and instinctively choose shapes near to each other for this reason. The same thing applies on a keyboard, and this is important for beginners because it makes life a lot easier.

Let's take a simple white-key chord sequence with the chords of C, F and G.

CD TRACK 2 Eight-bar idea in C

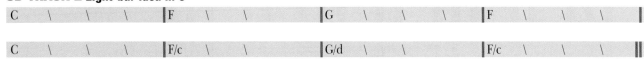

CD TRACK 2

In diagrams i-iii on p19 the chords are given in root position. Notice that you have to shift your hand up to get the F and G – it's a jump to go from C to F this way. Now try diagrams iv-v for the second-inversion F/c and G/d chords. This requires much less movement from the C. As you go from C to F/c your thumb stays on the C key. When you go to the G/d chord your thumb has only gone one key up from where it was. This way of arranging the notes of these chords makes the changes physically easier and sound smoother. Since C and F chords have the note C in common it makes sense to leave that note where it is and only move the notes you have to. That's why right-hand inversions are useful.

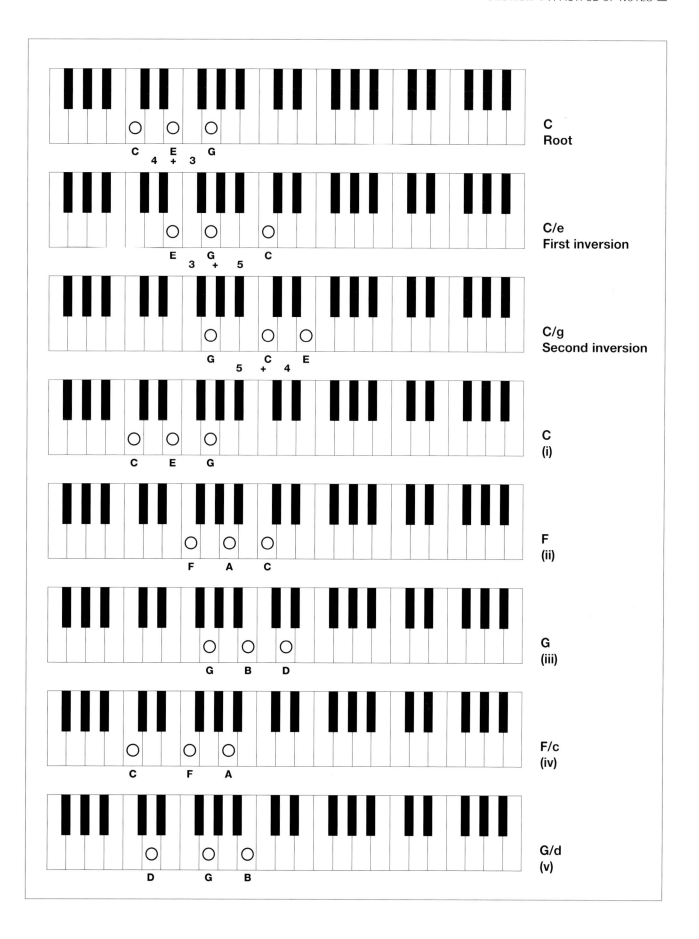

TECHNIQUE 3

THE MINOR INVERSION

We can transform the minor triad in the same way.

MAKING A MINOR FIRST INVERSION:
- Hold down a Cm triad.
- Let go of the C key, hold the E♭ with your thumb, then count up four keys to G and hold that down with your first finger.
- Count up five keys from the G. This brings you to the white note C an octave above the one you started on. Hold this note with your little finger.
- Play this chord (E♭-G-C), a first-inversion Cm.

MAKING A MINOR SECOND INVERSION:
- Hold down a C triad.
- Let go of the C and E♭ keys and hold the G down with your thumb.
- Count up five keys from the G. This brings you to the white note C an octave above the one you started on. Hold this note with your first finger.
- Count up three keys from C to get E♭.
- Play this chord (G-C-E♭), a second-inversion Cm.

CD TRACK

3

CD TRACK 3 Eight-bar idea in C

| C | \ | \ | \ | Cm | \ | \ | \ | F/c | \ | \ | \ | Fm/c | \ | \ | \ |

| G/d | \ | \ | \ | Gm/d | \ | \ | \ | C/e | \ | \ | \ | Fm | \ | C/e | \ |

Here's an example of the minor second inversion in action. These inverted minors are slightly more awkward to play than the root minor chords. But again, there is less jumping around than if you tried to play all the chords in this example in root shapes.

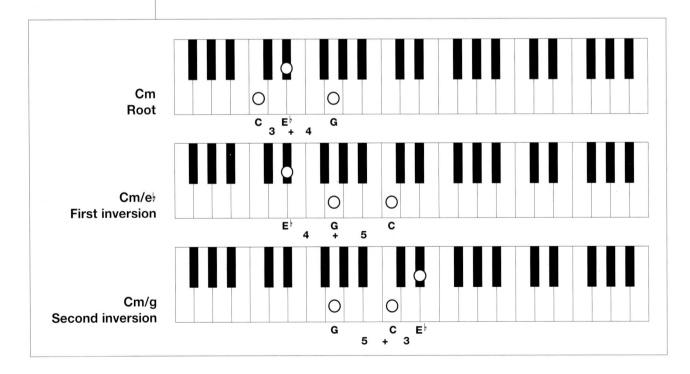

20

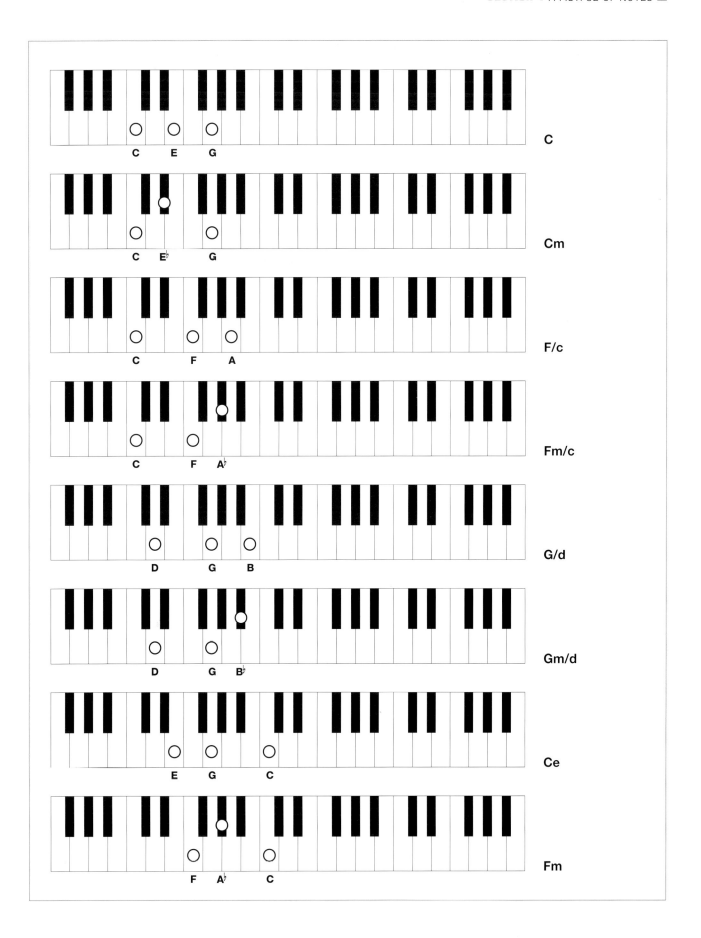

TECHNIQUE 4

WHITE-KEY MINORS

Here's a sequence that presents the three white-key minor chords, with their root position shapes and inversions. Bars 1-4 involve more movement of the right hand than bars 5-8 where the inversions tie the shapes closer to each other. The thumb stays on the note A for the change in bars 5-6 and only moves up to the next white key for the Em/b in bar 7.

CD TRACK 4 Eight-bar idea in Am

Am	\	\	\	Dm	\	\	\	Em	\	\	\	Dm	\	\	\
Am	\	\	\	Dm/a	\	\	\	Em/b	\	\	\	Dm/a	\	\	\

Writing with just these three minor chords would create a song with strong feelings of sadness and gloom. Exactly how sad and how gloomy would depend on additional factors, such as the effect of the melody, the speed, the instruments used in the arrangement and, perhaps most important, the lyric. A songwriter often matches this kind of minor-chord progression to words which express themes of loss, unhappiness, lack of hope, despair, etc. Minor-chord sequences are also good for expressing unfulfilled desire, so they are often heard in love songs.

Another option is to put the lyric and the music slightly at variance. Try writing a lyric which is not overtly sad to sing over these minor chords. The music will shade an emotion under the words which the words themselves would not produce alone. This approach can lend the words a fascinating tension.

CD TRACK 4

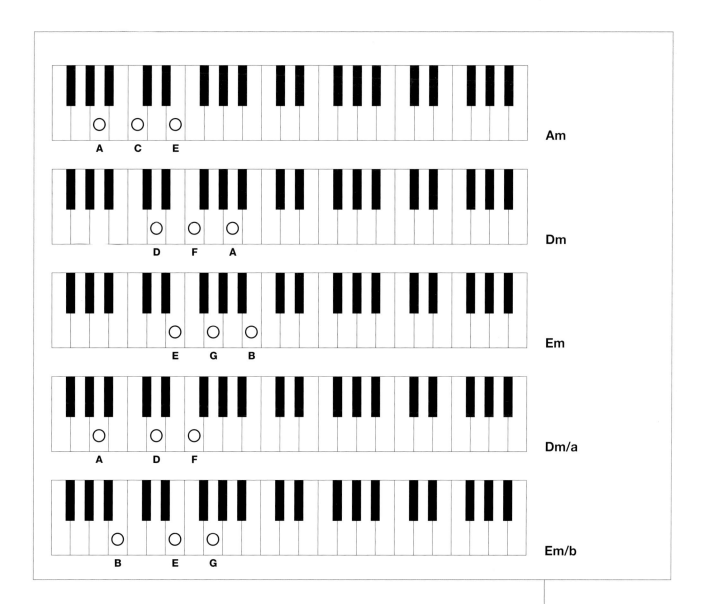

CD TRACK
4

TECHNIQUE 5

START FROM A FIRST-INVERSION SHAPE

On CD Tracks 1-4 the chord shape in bar 1 has been a root chord. But we could start on an inversion and that would offer other possibilities for organising smooth hand movements between chords. Let's say we decide not to start on a root C but on a first-inversion C. In Track 5 a first-inversion C moves comfortably to a root F. The little finger holding the C at the top doesn't need to move. The same thing happens if we start from a Dm first inversion and move to a first-inversion Em and then root Am.

CD TRACK 5 **Eight-bar idea in C**

C/e	\	\	\	F	\	\	\	C/e	\	\	\	F	\	\	\

Dm/f	\	\	\	Em/g	\	\	\	Am	\	\	\	Dm/a	\	C/g	\

Notice how the C/e moves satisfyingly to the F with a kind of musical logic. This is a very common chord change, involving two major chords a perfect 4th (five semitones) apart. Songwriters have often used this change to carry an entire verse. The Em/g to Am is the minor equivalent.

CD TRACK

5

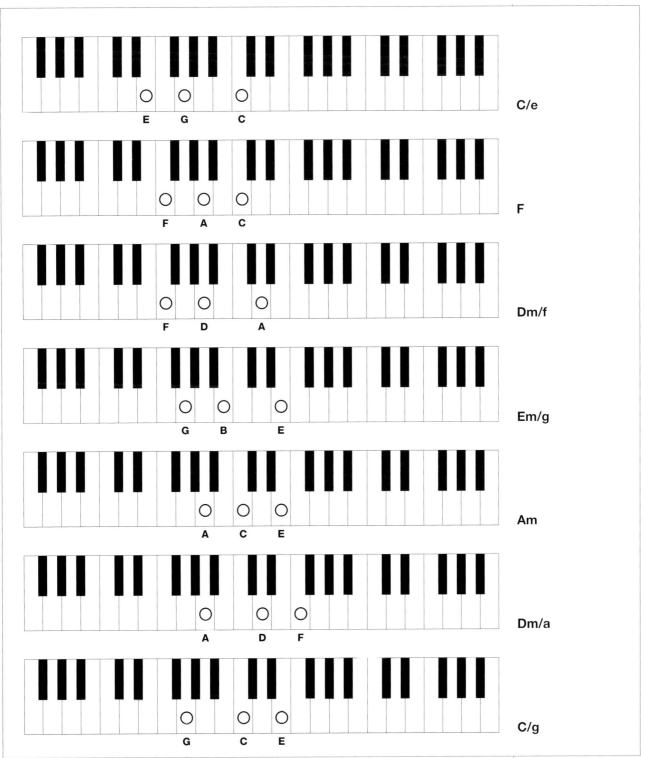

C/e
E G C

F
F A C

Dm/f
F D A

Em/g
G B E

Am
A C E

Dm/a
A D F

C/g
G C E

CD TRACK
5

■ **how to write songs on keyboards**

TECHNIQUE 6 — **START FROM A MINOR FIRST INVERSION**

This is what it would sound like if the initial chord were a first-inversion Cm proceeding to the Fm and Gm chords heard on Track 3. Doing this involves using black keys in all three chords.

CD TRACK 6 Eight-bar idea in Cm

| Cm/e♭ \ \ \ | Fm \ \ \ | Gm \ \ \ | Cm/g \ \ \ |

| Cm/e♭ \ \ \ | Fm \ \ \ | Gm/d \ \ \ | Cm \ \ \ |

The first-inversion Cm proceeds comfortably to the root Fm and Gm, and from there to a second-inversion Cm. This is an easier way to play the sequence than if you started holding down a root Cm chord.

As with CD Track 4, this exclusively minor-chord sequence creates a sombre mood. You will tend to find that you won't write a whole song with just minor chords very often. Most songs are either all major chords or mostly major with a sprinkling of one or two minor chords. Surrounded by major chords, even a single minor chord can have a powerful effect.

CD TRACK
6

26

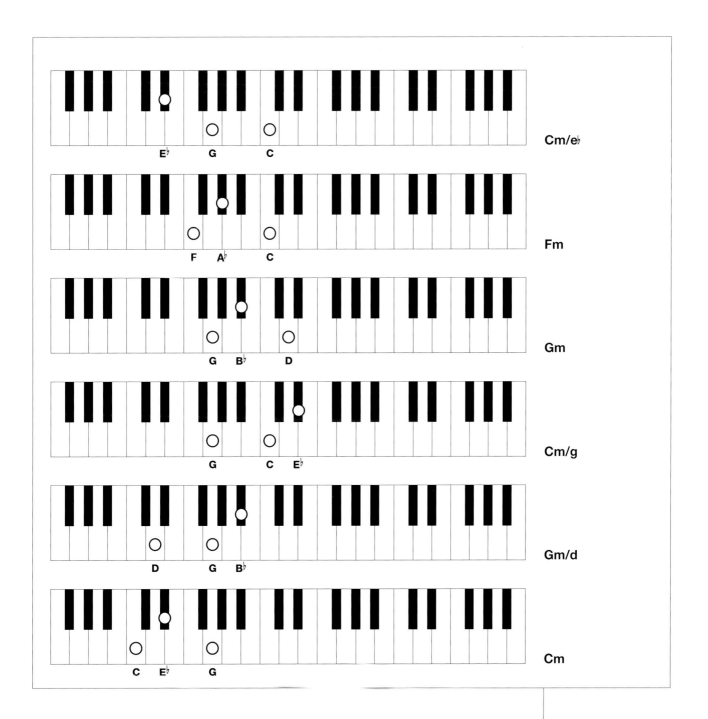

Cm/e♭

Fm

Gm

Cm/g

Gm/d

Cm

CD TRACK
6

| TECHNIQUE 7 | # START FROM A SECOND INVERSION |

You can also work out easy, effective hand movements if you start a progression on a second-inversion shape. This example links together the C-F-G idea of Track 2 with the Am-Dm-Em of Track 4 to make an eight-bar phrase suitable for any part of a song. Notice how the thumb stays on the same note going from C/g to G, and how only the thumb moves when going from F to Am/e:

CD TRACK 7 Eight-bar idea in C

C/g	\	\	\	G	\	F	\	C/g	\	\	\	G	\	F	\
Am/e	\	\	\	Dm/f	\	Em	\	Am/e	\	Dm/f	\	Em	\	C/e	\

As shown here, ending on a C/e chord, this eight-bar progression has a natural sense of completion. I would be inclined to use it as a chorus. If you wanted to make a verse out of it try substituting a G chord for the C/e in bar 8, or even replace bars 7-8 altogether with a reprise of bars 1-2.

CD TRACK

7

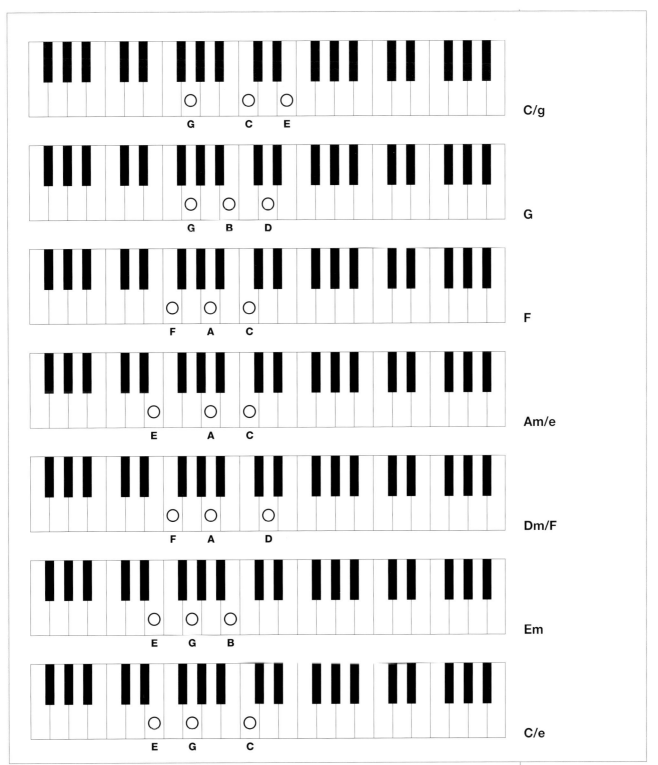

TECHNIQUE 8 | # START MAJOR, MOVE DOWNWARD

Most of the examples we've tried so far have involved moving chords to the right, up in pitch. But we could also move to the left, downward in pitch, with the same use of inversions to reduce the amount of hand movement needed to link the chords. Take this example:

CD TRACK 8 Four-bar idea in C

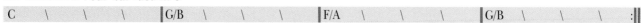

| C | \ | \ | \ | G/B | \ | \ | \ | F/A | \ | \ | \ | G/B | \ | \ | \ :‖ |

If root-position chords were used, the change from C to a root G would either involve a jump to the right or an almost as big jump to the left, to the G root chord in the octave to the left of the starting C chord (see C-G 'jump' diagram). Inversions make the changes smoother. The key to the immediate left of the C key is B. This is the note we would find lowest in a first-inversion G chord (B-D-G). So the thumb goes down one key, the first finger goes down from E to D, and the little finger stays still on G. To get the F we just move this entire first-inversion shape down to the next white key, A (A-C-F is a first-inversion F).

If you listen closely to the CD track you will hear that the bass guitar line duplicates (and therefore reinforces) these inversions in bars 1-4, but in bars 5-8 (on the repeat) it plays root notes. The effect is slightly different. You could do the same thing on a keyboard if the left hand were to play bass notes. This would result in what in this book is termed a 'true' inversion. There is more on the subject of 'true' inversions in Section 9. We're not bringing the left hand into action for most of the book, just to keep things technically easy.

CD TRACK

8

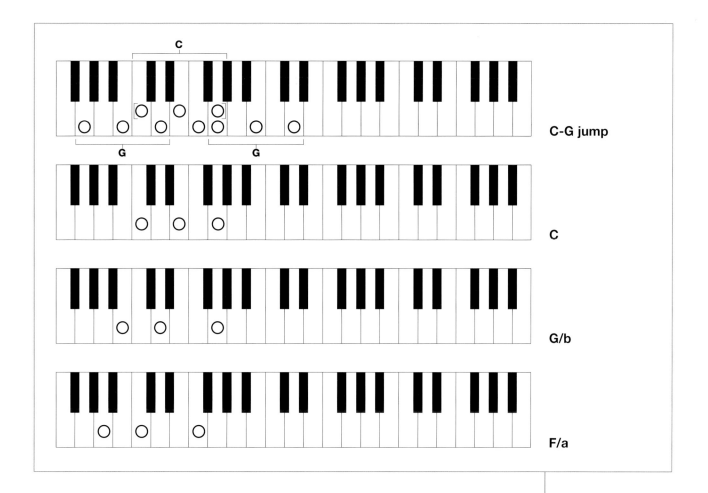

C-G jump

C

G/b

F/a

| TECHNIQUE 9 | ## START MINOR, MOVE DOWNWARD |

Here's the same sequence with the notes C, B, and A as the lowest notes but harmonising the A and B with Em and Dm second inversions (your thumb is on the same notes), and then in bars 5-8 there is an equivalent movement to that in Track 8, starting on a minor chord:

CD TRACK 9 Eight-bar idea in C

C	\	\	\	Em/b	\	\	\	Dm/a	\	\	\	Em/b	\	\	\

Am	\	\	\	Em/g	\	\	\	Dm/f	\	\	\	Em/g	\	\	\

Again, using all root chords would make for a lot of hand movements. Using the first-inversion shapes moving to the left makes the changes smoother in sound.

If you compare bars 1-4 with CD Track 8, where the chords were all major, the subtle but important change of tone is apparent. CD Track 9 has a more plaintive character than Track 8 because of the harmonising of the bassline with the minor chords in bars 2-4. Either set of chords is a perfectly valid way to put chords above the C-B-A-B bassline. Which one a songwriter uses depends on the emotion required and the lyric. One possibility is to alternate the exclusively major harmony of CD Track 8 with the minor one of bars 1-4 here to make an eight-bar section, and then add a repeat to get 16 bars in total. This would make a good verse. Alternatively, if a song has three verses, you could use the major version from CD Track 8 for verses 1 and 2, and then bars 1-4 above for verse 3, keeping the melody the same in all three.

CD TRACK
9

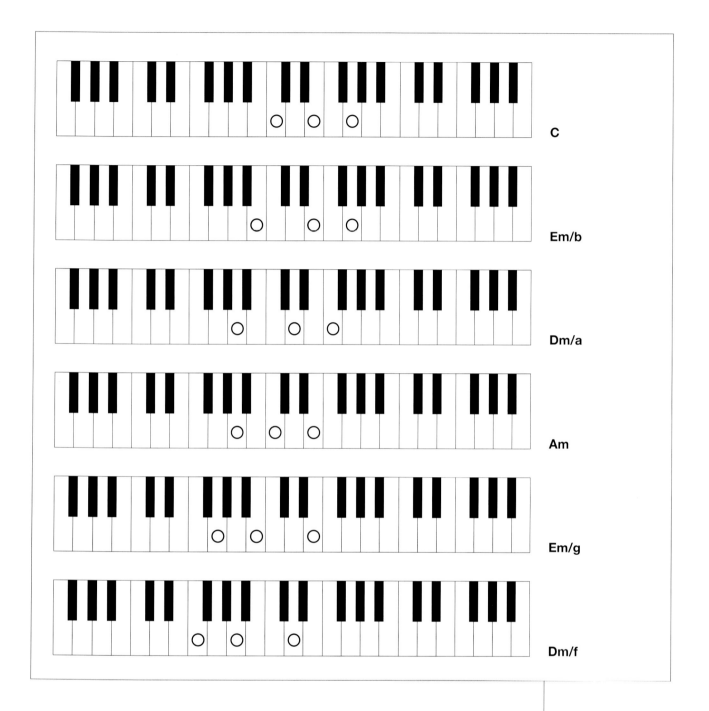

C

Em/b

Dm/a

Am

Em/g

Dm/f

CD TRACK
9

Ten easy moves

"It's where your hands go, where they're comfortable going … I never feel comfortable with, like, a straight triad – straight C major chord or F major – I'm always looking to make it something more, to expand it."

Burt Bacharach

The subtitle of Section 2 could be, "So who cares what the notes are? I'm having fun with this". This section showcases ten simple physical movements, usually involving one or two fingers being moved from a major or minor triad, which will get ideas going for songs. These create a large number of new chords for you, some of which have more than one possible name, though at this stage you don't need to worry about names – Section 8 reveals more if you want to find out about them. What counts at this point is purely their sound.

You may feel you're in the dark, but let your fingers dance towards some good ideas. The aim is to demonstrate that by sitting at a keyboard, holding a triad and then adjusting it by way of finger movement, you can create musical effects that lend themselves to song ideas.

As a songwriter you are always on the lookout for inspiration. Inspiration is the vital spark, that indefinable magic which gives a song an extra dimension. Unfortunately, the reality is that inspiration will not always come when you want it. It cannot be turned on and off like a tap. Experienced songwriters have so much knowledge and grasp of the craft of songwriting that they can knock you out a song pretty much to specification in a short space of time. But there is no guarantee that such a song will sound inspired. Consequently, songwriters (and creative people in all fields) develop habits and activities that encourage inspiration to come to them. These are not always going to be successful, but sometimes they will work. Playing a different musical instrument to the one you normally play is certainly one method.

If you're a guitarist using this book to explore a keyboard for the first time (as I hope many of you are) then you're doing just that. In a creative sense, lack of technical expertise can sometimes be an advantage. If you can't play keyboards proficiently you can't sit at the piano rattling off impressive scales and arpeggios – which is good, because they aren't really the gist of a song. The fact that you may not know the names of the chords you make when you press your fingers to the keys doesn't matter when your prime aim is creativity. You can record and annotate them later. What counts is the pure sound. If you can move your fingers and find a sequence of chords that stirs your feelings and brings snatches of lyric to your mind, that's what counts. Inspiration will have struck and a song is in the making.

So turn the page and let's try out some of these potentially inspiring hand movements.

| TECHNIQUE 11 | # LITTLE FINGER RISES IN HALF STEPS |

First we're going to have some fun with the C and Dm triads that you played in Section 1. From the C chord your little finger moves up one key at a time, in semitones. You then do the same movement on the Dm chord. This motion results in a suspenseful chord sequence whose tension lends itself to songs of high drama. This is the kind of sequence employed in certain kinds of action film in the cinema and on television.

CD TRACK 11 Eight-bar idea in C, half-step rising

C	\	C+	\	C6	\	C7	\	C	\	C+	\	C6	\	C7	\	

Dm	\	Dm♯5	\	Dm6	\	Dm7	\	Dm	\	Dm♯5	\	Dm6	\	Dm7	\	‖

You can do this with any major or minor chord. In either case, if you hold the chord in root position in the right hand, with the notes in 1-3-5 order, it is always the note under the outside finger which moves upward. This effect is one way of creating change within a single chord rather than actually changing to an entirely different chord. It's important to know how to do this when writing songs, because sometimes your melody or lyric may work better if there isn't too much chord movement underneath.

Experiment with moving any of the other notes in a simple triad by semitone steps and listen for the range of effects that can result.

CD TRACK

11

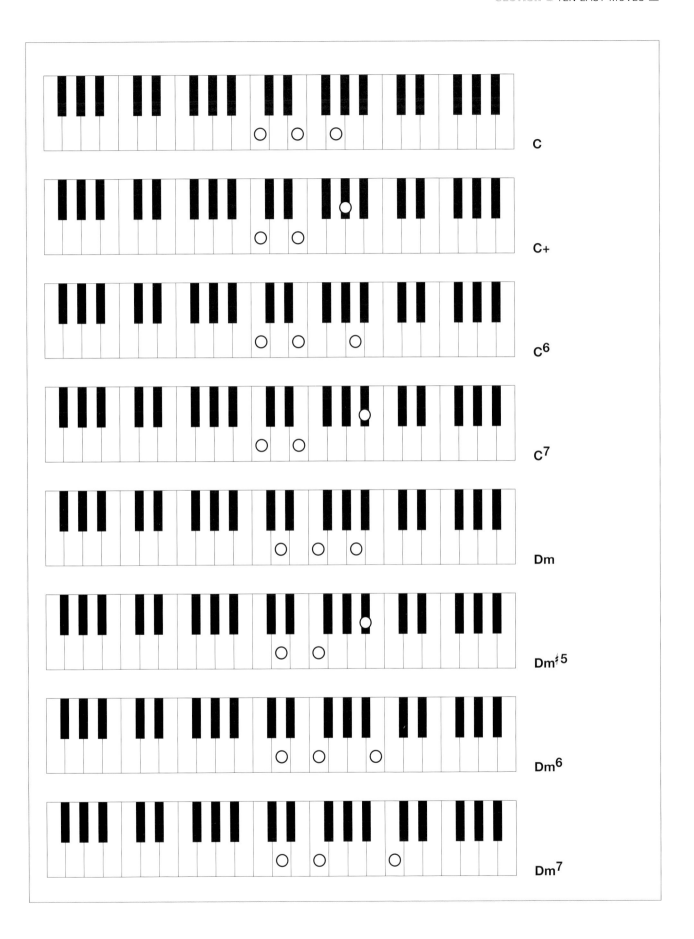

| TECHNIQUE 13 | **MOVING THE THUMB DOWN** |

Having messed about with the little finger at the top of the chord, we can now apply the same technique to the thumb that's holding the root note. Once again we'll work from a C chord and a Dm. In bars 1-4 the thumb moves down in semitones; in bars 5-6 it moves down a tone from the note D to C and then in semitones to B and B-flat. This progression has a little of the edginess of track 11 but a broader, more expansive feel.

CD TRACK 13 Eight-bar idea in C, thumb down in half and whole steps

| C | \ | \ | \ | Cmaj7/B | \ | \ | C7/B♭ | \ | \ | \ | A9 | \ | \ | \ | |
| Dm | \ | \ | \ | Dm7/C \ | \ | \ | Dm6/B \ | \ | \ | B♭maj7 \ | \ | \ | \ | ‖ |

If you made this sequence the basis of the verse it would be a good idea to repeat it, so that the length was 16 bars. This would give the listener the chance to appreciate the chord changes again, which is useful since there is quite a lot happening. The approach to treating chords by adjusting one note at a time will yield many ideas and is easier on a keyboard than on guitar. On guitar this technique often causes awkward fingerings: typically, a guitar-playing songwriter will get a great idea for a chain of one-note adjusted chords only to quickly run into fingering problems which make it hard to keep the adjustments going. This is much less likely to happen on a keyboard.

CD TRACK

13

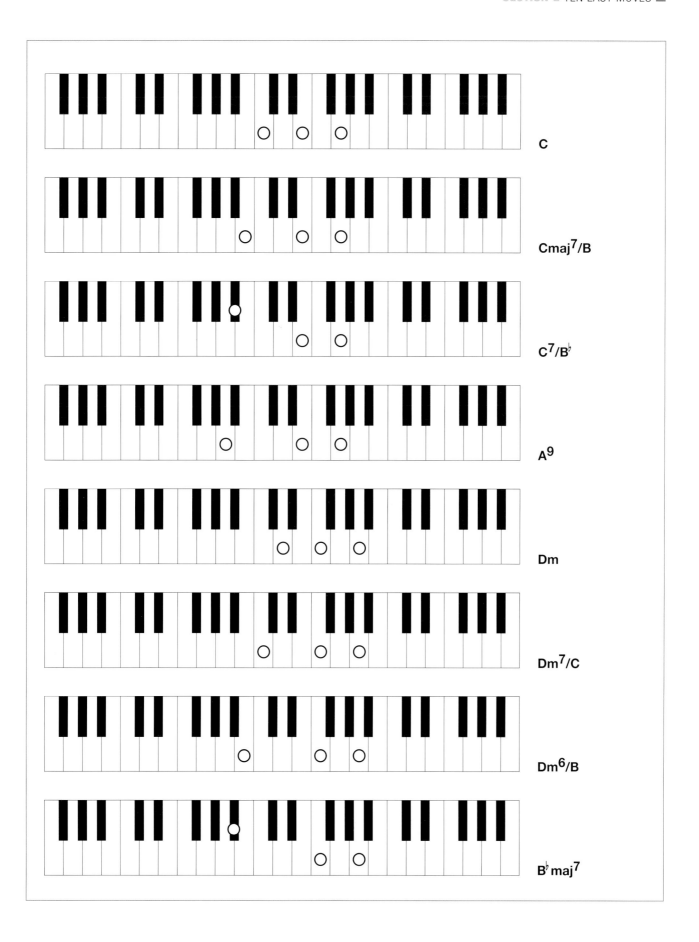

C

Cmaj^7/B

C^7/B$^\flat$

A^9

Dm

Dm^7/C

Dm^6/B

B$^\flat$ maj^7

TECHNIQUE 14

THUMB UP AND DOWN ON A MINOR

Here's another thumb movement that is simple to do and musically effective. It could make an idea in itself, or it could be a way of decorating a root minor chord anytime you land on one in a sequence. In bars 1-2 you'll hear a Dm triad, then the thumb goes up a tone (two keys), returns to Dm and then falls a tone (two keys). In bar 4, when this idea is repeated, the final chord is changed to an alternative one: the thumb only goes down a semitone (one key) to C♯ instead of the C heard before.

CD TRACK 14 Thumb up and down in half and whole steps

| Dm \ | Dmadd9 | \ | Dm \ | Dm7/C \ | Dm \ | Dmadd9 \ | Dm \ | Dm/maj7/C♯ \ | :‖ |

Notice that the Dm7/C doesn't sound as tense as the Dm/maj7/C♯. The former is a much more common chord type. Minor 7s are heard all the time in songs. They are popular because they dilute the sadness of a simple minor chord and so stop the minor chords in a song from overwhelming it with gloom. The min/maj7 is rarer and crops up in a narrower spectrum of emotions in songs. It can represent something in a lyric which is more urgently a problem or concern. You can read more about it in Technique 67.

Technique 14's colourful way of treating a minor chord in particular lends itself to link or intro passages where there may not be any singing.

CD TRACK

14

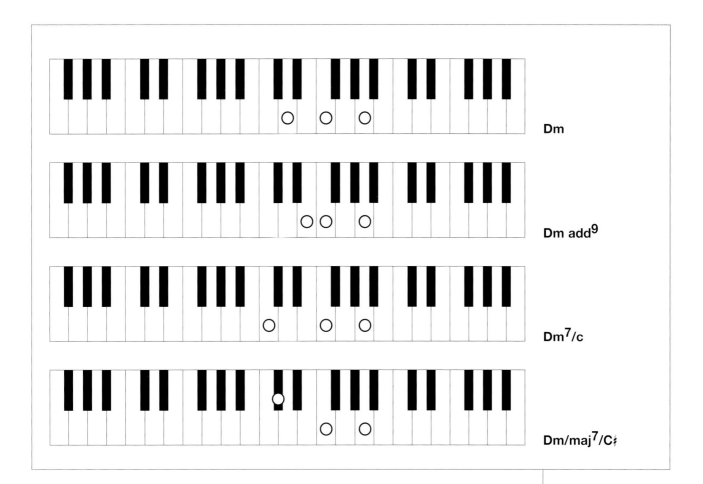

Dm

Dm add⁹

Dm⁷/c

Dm/maj⁷/C♯

CD TRACK
14

TECHNIQUE 15

THUMB UP AND DOWN ON A MAJOR

You can try the same thumb-up-and-down movement on a root major chord. track 15 has the thumb moving up a tone, returning to C and then going down a semitone. The same idea is repeated in bars 5-8 on a D chord (notice *not Dm*), with the thumb down a tone in bar 6 and a semitone in bar 8.

CD TRACK 15 Thumb up and down in half and whole steps

C	\	Cadd9 \	C	\	Cmaj7/B \	C	\	Cadd9 \	C	\	Cmaj7/B \	

D	\	Dadd9 \	D	\	D7/C \	D	\	Dadd9 \	D	\	Dmaj7/C♯ \	

The Dmaj7/C♯ has the same notes as F♯m second inversion – it is missing its root note – but the bass guitar supplies a D. So in this context we hear these three notes as a Dmaj7/C♯.

CD TRACK

15

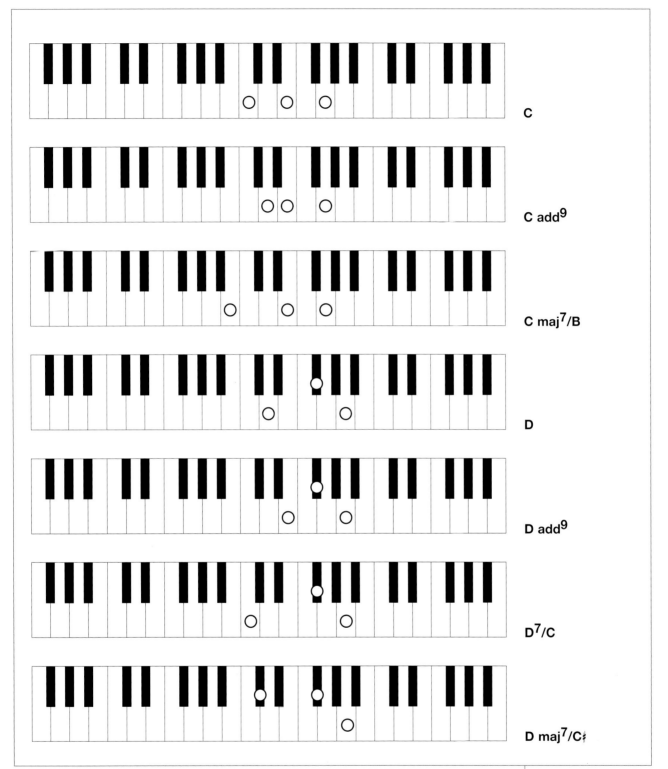

C

C add^9

C maj^7/B

D

D add^9

D^7/C

D maj^7/C♯

CD TRACK
15

TECHNIQUE 16

MIDDLE FINGER UP AND DOWN (SUSPENSIONS)

Having had some fun moving the little finger and thumb of a triad up and down to get new chord effects, what about the finger in the middle? When you start moving this you hear a classic songwriting idea that expresses tension and release. In bars 1-2 here the middle finger of the triad moves up a semitone (one key), returns to C and then drops down a tone (two keys). In bars 5-6 this idea is applied to a root minor chord, in this case Em. On a minor chord there are two possible ways of doing this: either you move the same distances as with the major, or reverse them, so the thumb goes up a tone (two keys) and drops a semitone (one key). Let your ear guide you initially.

The technical name for this effect is a suspension.

CD TRACK 16 Eight-bar idea in C, middle finger up and down in C

C	\	Csus4	\	C	\	Csus2	\	C	\	Csus4	\	C	\	Csus2	\

Em	\	Esus4	\	Em	\	Esus2	\	Em	\	Esus4	\	Em	\	Esus2	\

These kinds of changes are another way to stay on a single chord for a number of bars but make it interesting and create a feeling of anticipation for the next section. You can read more about suspended chords in Techniques 69 and 70.

CD TRACK

16

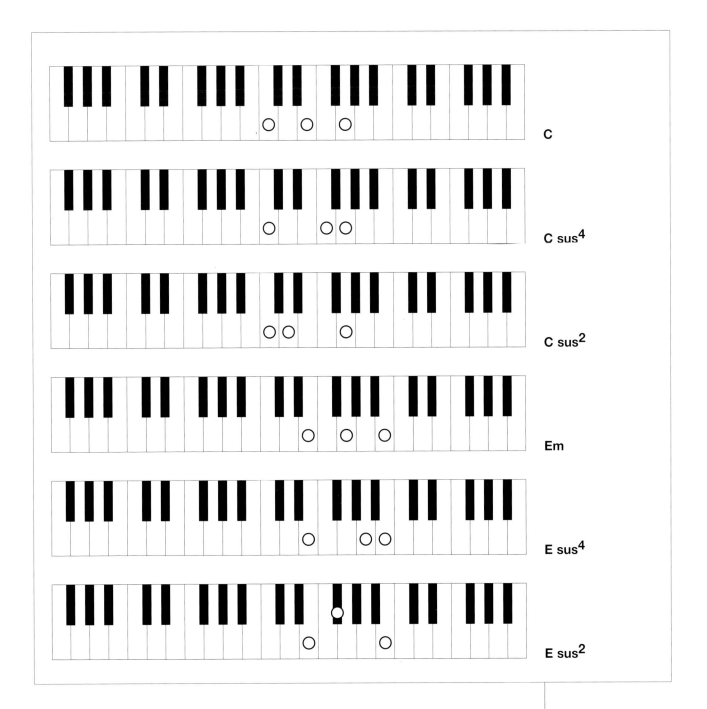

MOVING TWO FINGERS

So far we've only moved one finger of the triad at a time. But what about moving two? You'd need to move the middle and top finger of the chord up together (keeping the thumb where it is), bring them back to the triad, then bring them both in to the left. This procedure is applied to C (bars 1-2), Am (bars 3-4), F (bars 5-6) and G (bars 7-8). The other chord names you see are really only decorations of the main chord (as I've said, sometimes chords can be described in more than one way, but that goes beyond our concerns here). A simple, well-known sequence of C, Am, F, G can be transformed like this. You might use this decorated form for an intro or links in a song, and play the straight four-chord version for a verse.

CD TRACK **17**

To understand how many keys are involved in these movements, here's a breakdown. The numbers refer to the number of keys, the first number being the middle finger, the second number the little finger. Remember each pair sound together, not one after the other.

- For a major chord: +1+2 (going up), -2-2 (going down)
- For a minor chord: +2+1 (going up), -1-2 (going down)

CD TRACK 17 Moving two fingers in C

| C | \ | F/C | \ | C | \ | C11 | \ | Am | \ | Dm/F | \ | Am | \ | Am11 | \ | |
| F | \ | G7/F | \ | F | \ | F11 | \ | G | \ | C/G | \ | G | \ | G11 | \ | |

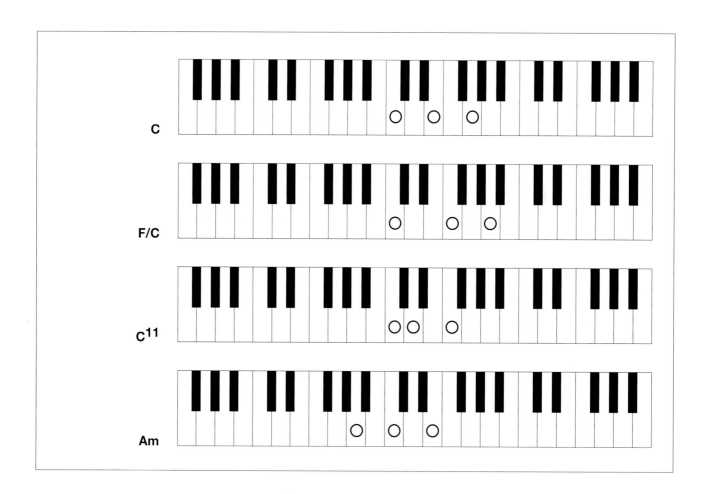

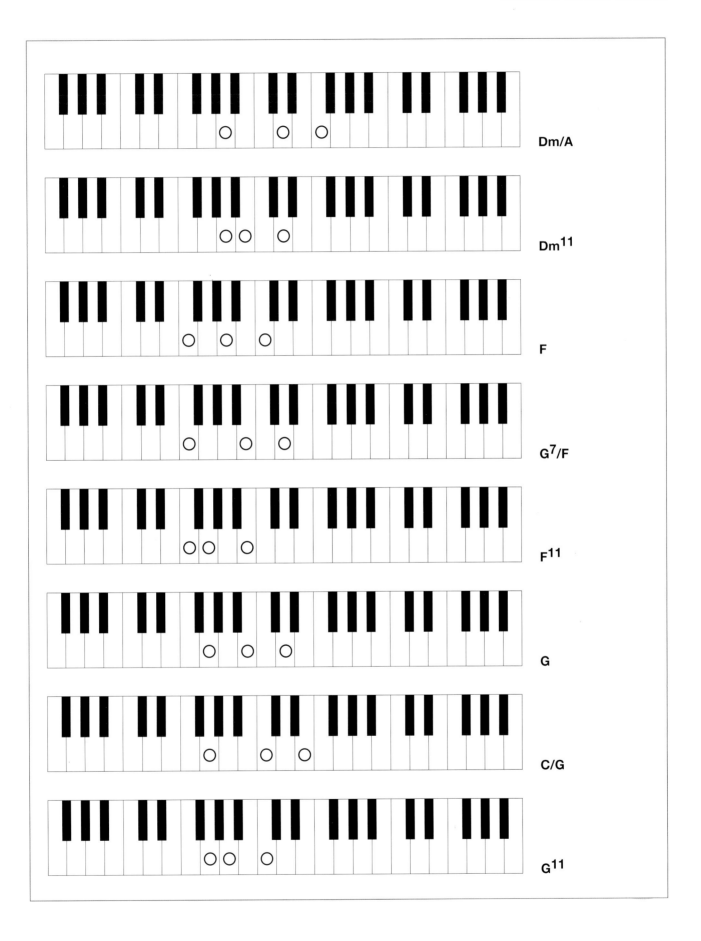

Dm/A

Dm^{11}

F

G^7/F

F^{11}

G

C/G

G^{11}

THE 'CRAB' MOVE

Crabs are renowned for their scuttling sideways motion. This is the image that comes to my mind when I play this sequence of moves. The thumb makes a move down, then the upper two notes that were left behind move down to join it. The thumb moves down again, the upper notes move down again. In the musical key of C major this entire progression – which is based on C, Am, F, Dm – takes place on the white keys. It's so easy to do even a beginner at the keyboard will soon find he or she can do it, and soon with both hands at once. This sequence has been used in many classic songs.

CD TRACK 18 Thumb down, the 'crab' move in C

| C | \ | Em/B | \ | Am | \ | C/G | \ | F | \ | Am/E | \ | Dm | \ | F/C | \ | :‖ |

There are several reasons for the popularity of this sequence. The descending bass, making its way methodically down the notes of the major scale, has a logic and force which is compelling. At the same time the sequence moves between steady root position chords and less grounded inversions, and also between major chords and minor chords. The combination of these factors creates a flow of musical stimuli to which we respond with a happy/sad mixture of emotions. These will be further guided and defined by the melody and the lyric.

The classic melodic trick with such a descending sequence is to make it move slowly upwards in opposite direction to the bass and chords.

CD TRACK
18

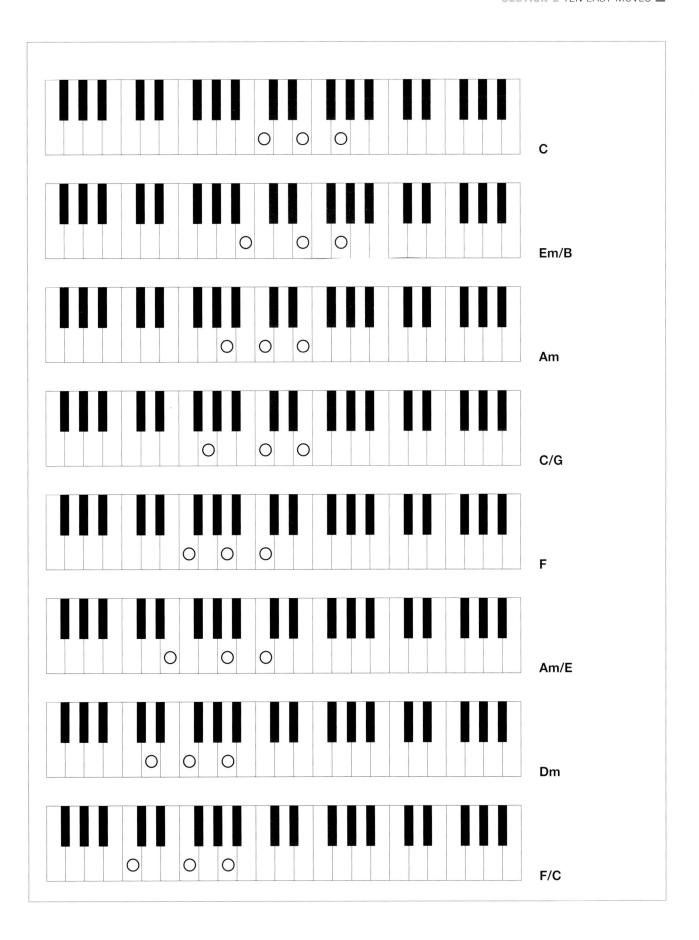

C

Em/B

Am

C/G

F

Am/E

Dm

F/C

TECHNIQUE 19

A LEFT-HAND MOVE

Talking of two hands, it's time to bring in the left hand and see if you can get the hang of doing something simple with it. This is another songwriting trick, and a great way of finding new chords if you play around with it.

Let your right hand hold a first inversion C triad. Your left hand holds the first C immediately below the triad in pitch. This means that the overall sound of the four notes is a root chord, not an inversion, because the left hand C creates a foundation for the notes in your right hand. You play the triad on the beat and after each bar your left hand moves down to a different bass note. Every time this happens the sound of the C triad changes. The altering bass note colours it differently. These chords have complex names of their own but for simplicity's sake they are notated just as a C with a different bass note.

Notice that bars 7-8 are different to 3-4, and that the C/F♯ is by far the most arresting chord of the sequence. This is because the F♯ is essentially unrelated to the C chord – but a songwriter could weave magic with that unrelatedness.

CD TRACK 19 LH bass note under a static C chord

C	\	\	\	C/A	\	\	\	C/F	\	\	\	C/D	\	\	\

C	\	\	\	C/A	\	\	\	C/F♯	\	\	\	C/F	\	\	\

This example raises the broader issue of harmonic freedom and how much latitude and innovation a songwriter can permit in their work. This very much revolves around the question of who is the intended audience. If you write songs purely for your own pleasure, to express your experiences, feelings and thoughts, then essentially you can use whatever chords you like. Your songwriting will be shaped by your own taste, the limits of your musical knowledge and songcraft, and your own self-criticism (or lack of it). The issue of the potential conflict between artistic ambition (I want to use these strange-sounding chords) and commercial necessity (the wider audience might not know how to respond to your strange chords) does not arise. But if you want to make popular music you have to take into account how much strange harmony your target audience can respond to. It's not that odd chord changes can't express emotions, it's just that they don't express *familiar* emotions for the majority of people, and the bigger the audience the simpler and more familiar the emotions have to be.

CD TRACK
19

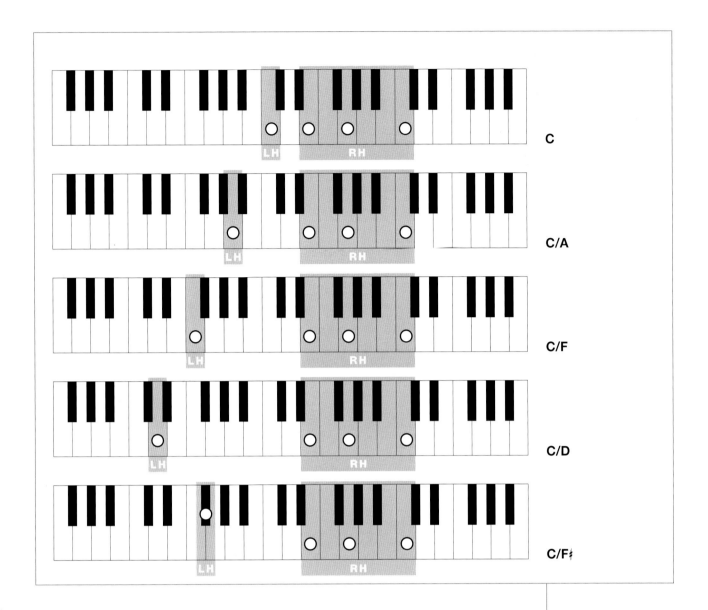

C

C/A

C/F

C/D

C/F♯

CD TRACK
19

TECHNIQUE 20 — A LEFT-HAND 5TH AND A BASS 'CRAB'

Finally, let's try a similar idea to track 19 but hold down two notes with the left hand. This shape is called a '5th' and the overall chord organisation in this example follows 'option 5' discussed in Technique 10. The left hand moves this 5th down to A, then F, then D. The right hand holds a root C triad for three bars before changing to a second inversion F in bar 4. The D+A in the left hand makes this sound like a Dm. Bars 5-8 create a variation on this progression. The D9/F♯ chord requires that the left-hand 5th changes to a wider interval (of a 6th) before returning to the 5th. Notice also a small change in the right hand on the Dm9 chord.

CD TRACK 20 LH 5th

C	\	\	\	Am	\	\	\	Fmaj9	\	\	\	Dm7	\	Dm9	Dm7
C	\	\	\	Am	\	\	\	D9/F♯	\	\	\	F	\	Fmaj7	F

Tracks 19 and 20 show how powerful harmonic effects soon arise from the simplest of hand movements on the keyboard. You don't need to know the names of these chords or how they are formed theoretically. Just sit down and try these movements. Think shapes, not theory.

With this in mind, in the next section we'll look again at some of the basic material from Section 1, this time from a different angle – not as shapes on the keyboard, but as musical combinations that songwriters use.

CD TRACK
20

60

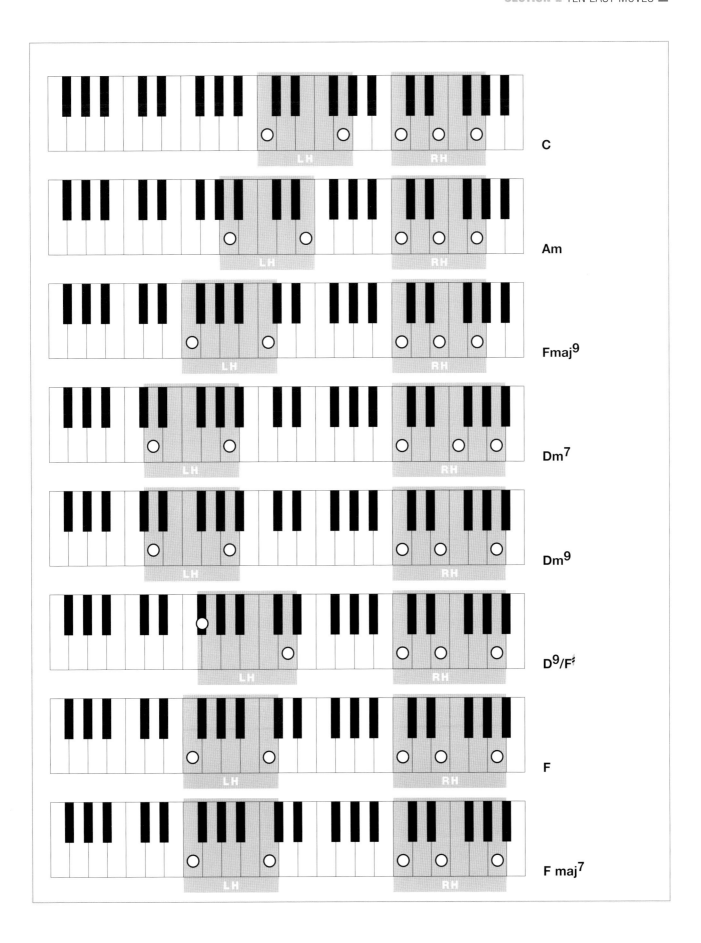

Write a song with three chords

"I've found that in writing music over the years it's often really cool to cut your [number of] chords in half ... leave all your melody the same but really space out what's behind it."

Paul McCartney

This section explores the 'three-chord song'. But not just any three chords: there are three special chords that sound great together. First thing to do is find out where we get these three special chords from... The chord sequence in a song supports and colours the melody and words, and the chords a song uses, its melody and sense of musical key, are generally derived from the major scale.

There are other types of scale, but none as important to songwriting as this one. The major scale is a sequence of eight notes. The gaps between these notes make the pattern of intervals: tone, tone, semitone, tone, tone, tone, semitone. You can hear this by striking the white key C and then playing the white keys going up until you reach C again (C-D-E-F-G-A-B-C). You can play a major scale from any note by moving up the keys in the distances of 2-2-1-2-2-2-1.

SEVEN MAGIC NUMBERS

Putting aside the eighth note (which is the same letter name as the first) the scale has seven *different* notes. The chords built on these are numbered in Roman numerals: I, II, III, IV, V, VI and VII. It's not important to know at the moment *how* chords are formed. These seven chords fit together and generate the impression of a musical key – we'll look at all seven in the course of *How To Write Songs On Keyboards*. The Roman numerals signify possible tonal 'roles' that a chord of a given pitch and type can play. A single chord like C major can play the 'role' of I, IV or V, depending on which musical key (and scale) the music is in.

Those three magic chords we're looking for occur on the 1st, 4th and 5th notes of the scale. So these chords are referred to as I, IV and V regardless of their *pitch* name (A, C, D, F♯, B♭ etc). To play a specific I, IV and V it's necessary to choose a scale/musical key, which will assign these Roman numeral chords a pitch. Since this book is partly aimed at guitarists who are trying keyboards, let's stay with the key of C major, in which I, IV and V are easy shapes. In C major chord I is C, chord IV is F and chord V is G.

Scale degree	I	II	III	IV	V	VI	VII
Scale note	*C*	*D*	*E*	*F*	*G*	*A*	*B*
Chord	C			F	G		

Of the three chords, chord I is the most important. Each time a chord sequence returns to chord I the listener has a feeling of arriving 'home'. Songs often end on chord I, as this gives the strongest sense of completion. After chord I, the most important is chord V, which assists the creation of the 'return home' feeling when placed before chord I. Chord IV isn't such a stabilising force as chord V, but still important for supporting the scale and key

It is possible to write a song with only two chords, but not easy to do this successfully. You might think it would be *easier* to write a song with fewer chords, but the two-chord song always runs the risk of harmonic monotony. The ear tires of the pair of chords, and the effect is static. Two-chord songs depend on either a rivetting lyric and melody, a lot of energy, or a very imaginative arrangement.

TECHNIQUE 21

THE 'THREE-CHORD TRICK' (AND THE EIGHT-BAR)

Thousands of songs have been written using only three chords like this. Let's use them to try our hand at putting together some chord progressions of our own.

Here's the simplest of song fragments using three chords. You could repeat it to make a verse or a chorus. The Roman numeral reminds you what the chord's role is in the key of C. Chords I, IV and V in a major key are always major.

The shape that the chord takes in the right hand will continue to be indicated by a forward-slash followed by a lower-case letter ('true' LH inversions have a capital letter after the slash).

CD TRACK 21 Eight-bar idea in C, three-chord trick

I				IV				I				V			
C	\	\	\	F/c	\	\	\	C	\	\	\	G/d	\	\	\

IV				I				IV				V			
F/c	\	\	\	C	\	\	\	F/c	\	\	\	G/d	\	\	\

In popular music it's unusual to find chords changing on every beat; once or twice a bar is the typical rate. Set your own speed – play at a tempo that enables you to change chord but keep a regular beat.

For a short song this is a possible verse idea. Provided the tempo is slow enough it would be possible to sing a short line for each of bars 1-3. The vocal line could finish in bar four but leave several beats with no singing as a 'breather' before starting again.

The eight bars could be repeated to make a 16-bar verse.

CD TRACK
21

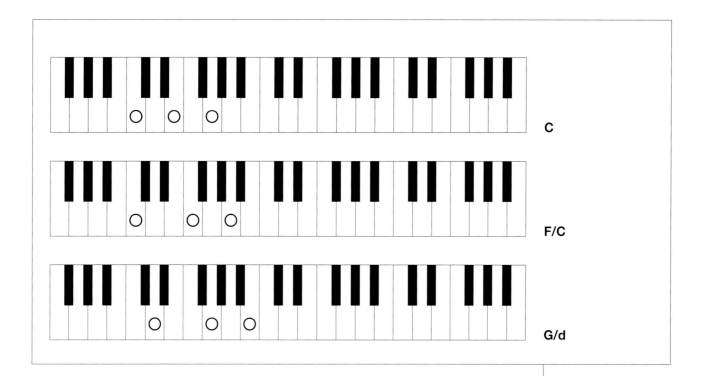

C

F/C

G/d

CD TRACK
21

65

TECHNIQUE 22 | THE BLUES AND THE 12-BAR

Song sections are dominated by the number four and its multiples eight, 12 and 16. The 12-bar structure is one of the most frequently-used in the history of popular music. It shaped a huge percentage of blues songs, and from blues it passed to 1950s rock'n'roll and the songs of Chuck Berry, Elvis Presley, Little Richard, Jerry Lee Lewis etc. From them it passed to 1960s pop and soul, re-establishing its blues roots during the British 'Blues Boom', and then the heavy, psychedelic rock that was influenced by the blues revival (Hendrix, Cream, Free, Led Zeppelin et al). In the 1970s it featured in everything from pop and glam-rock to punk, and it continues to be used to this day.

The 12-bar implies not only a verse length but a pattern for when chords I, IV and V will appear. CD Track 22 is a traditional example. Note that instead of being in 4/4 time, this is in 12/8 – it means there are still four beats in a bar but each divides into three, creating the distinctive 'swing' rhythm often heard in blues (and in some slower rock).

CD TRACK 22 12-bar in C

I				I				I				I			
C	\	\	\	F/c	\	\	\	C	\	\	\	C/e	\	\	\

IV				IV				I				I			
F	\	\	\	F	\	\	\	C/e	\	\	\	C/e	\	\	\

V				IV				I				V			
G	\	\	\	F	\	\	\	C/e	\	\	\	G	\	\	\

The 12-bar form is very flexible. It can be used for any part of a song – a verse, a chorus or a bridge – and you don't have to be writing a blues song either. It's so familiar that listeners recognise it and know where it is going, so the 12-bar can contrast with sections that are less formulaic and predictable. It also means the listener's expectations of what will happen can easily be overturned if you take a 12-bar as your foundation but alter it in some way.

In a traditional 12-bar blues the first line of a three-line verse is sung over bars 1-4. The line is then repeated over bars 5-8. A second answering lyric line is sung over bars 9-12. Notice how the *rate* of chord change (how often chords change) is slow.

By combining a 12-bar verse with an eight-bar chorus, the blueprint for a complete song is generated.

CD TRACK

22

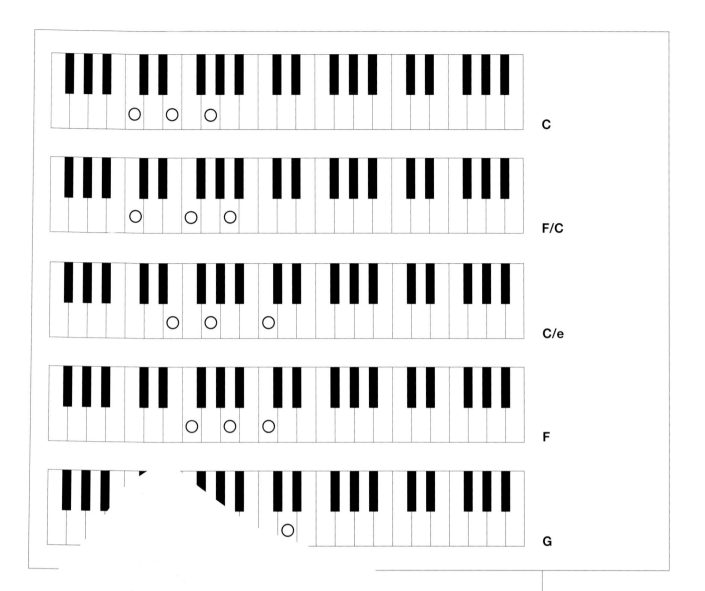

C

F/C

C/e

F

G

TECHNIQUE 23

THE 16-BAR SECTION

Along with the 12-bar, 16 bars is another very popular length for a song section. A 16-bar section can be handled in many ways, depending on the amount of repetition you allow within it. The most common options are:

• A four-bar phrase played four times.
• A four-bar phrase played three times with a different phrase for bars 9-12.
• A four-bar phrase played three times with a different phrase for bars 13-16.

The second of these is probably the most common in popular songwriting. In this next example, bars 5-8 and 13-16 are the same. CD Track 23 is in the musical key of G major, which means some of its chords use a black note, F♯ (you'll use it here whenever you play the chord of D).

CD TRACK 23 16-bar verse in G

I				IV				I				IV			
G	\	\	\	C/g	\	\	\	G	\	\	\	C/g	\	\	\

I				IV				I				V			
G	\	\	\	C/g	\	\	\	G	\	\	\	D/f♯	\	\	\

V				IV				IV				I			
G	\	\	\	C/g	\	\	\	C/g	\	\	\	G	\	\	\

I				IV				I				V			
G	\	\	\	C/g	\	\	\	G	\	\	\	D/a	\	\	\

CD TRACK
23

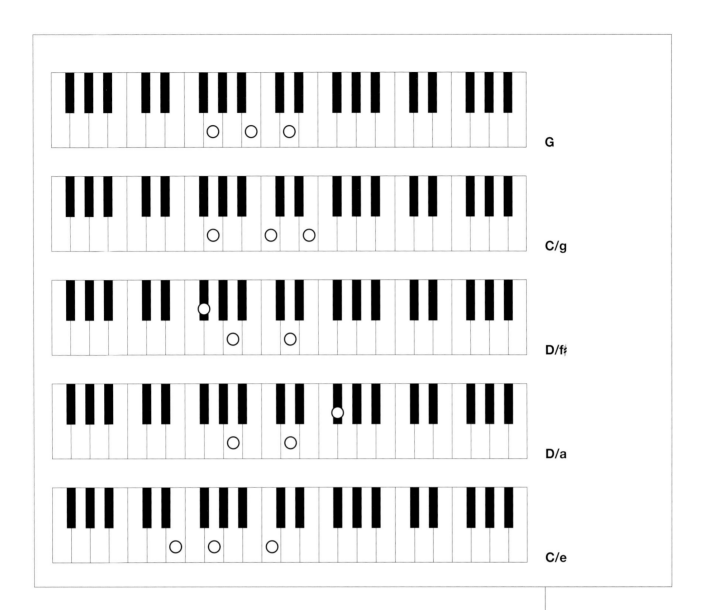

G

C/g

D/f♯

D/a

C/e

CD TRACK
23

| TECHNIQUE 24 | # CLASSIC SONG FORM |

Having met chords I, IV and V, and looked at four, eight, 12 and 16-bar sections, let's put some chords together for a whole song. This song template will have three chords and feature an intro, a verse, a chorus and a bridge. The assumption is that the song would proceed intro-verse-chorus-verse-chorus-bridge-chorus, but the sections are not repeated here, just to save space.

CD TRACK 24 Song in G

Intro

V	V	V	V
D/f♯ \ \	D/f♯ \ \ \	D/f♯ \ \ \	D/f♯ \ \ \

Verse

IV	V	I	IV
C/e \ \ \	D/f♯ \ \ \	G \ \ \	C/g \ \

IV	V	IV	V
C/e \ \ \	D/f♯ \ \ \	C/e \ \ \	D/f♯ \ \

Chorus

I	IV	V	IV	IV	V
‖: G \ \ \	C/g \ \ \	D/a \	C/g \	C/g \	D/a \ :‖

Bridge

IV	IV	I	I
C/g \ \ \	C/g \ \ \	G \ \ \	G \ \

IV	IV	I	V
C/g \ \ \	C/g \ \ \	G \ \ \	D/f♯ \ \

Note:
• The intro is entirely chord V.
• Chord I appears in only five bars out of 24 – it arrives in bar 3 and doesn't occur again in the verse. This means that when it *does* appear in bar 1 of the chorus, the arrival is more powerful and satisfying.
• The chorus is a four-bar phrase that repeats. Notice that in the chorus there are two chords in bars 3 and 4: this creates extra motion just where it might be handy – at the end of a phrase, as the music turns back to the beginning.
• For the bridge the music centres on chord IV for contrast. Notice how chord V at the end of the bridge will strongly lead back to either the verse or the chorus.

Even with a three-chord song, a lot can be learned about songwriting techniques. A songwriter develops an 'eye' and an ear for a sequence that sounds good, fits together well, and has a satisfying ebb and flow of tension, drama, feeling and balance. Many factors have to be weighed to get this, and more come into play when progressions become more complicated.

CD TRACK
24

RATE OF CHORD CHANGE

An important technique for refining a chord sequence is to consider the rate of chord change. Ask yourself how often the chords change. Does a chord always occupy a whole bar, two bars, or half a bar? If almost all the chords in a song last the same number of beats it might be a good idea to vary them – ensuring that the chord changes exhibit this variety is a shield against monotony. The fewer chords there are in a song, the more crucial it is to have such variety in the rate of chord-change. In a song where the general rate of change is one chord to a bar, the most useful alternatives are:

• Two in a bar (chords change on beats 1 and 3).
• Two in a bar (chords change on beats 1 and 4).
• One in a bar-and-a-half.
• One in two bars.
• Four in a bar (chords change on each beat).

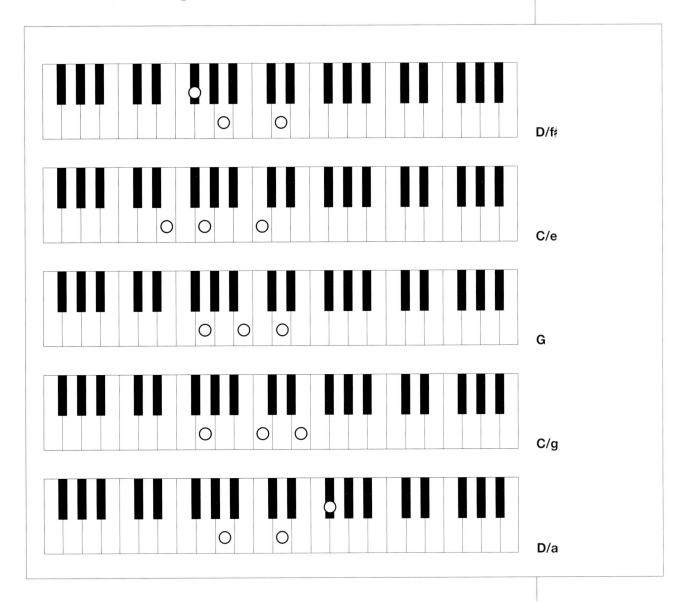

D/f♯

C/e

G

C/g

D/a

Write a song with four chords

"On guitar, to make some chords, your fingers have to go into acrobatics. On piano, you just move one note over … And changing a note on the bottom is easy, whereas on guitar it would be tricky, if not impossible."

Robbie Robertson

THREE CHORDS MEET THE MINOR

Four-chord songs are just as popular as three-chord ones. Before we look at how to construct one, let's see that table showing all seven chords in the key of C major, which was first presented in Section 3, but it now has the missing chord names filled in.

Scale degree	I	II	III	IV	V	VI	VII
Scale note	*C*	*D*	*E*	*F*	*G*	*A*	*B*
Chord	C	Dm	Em	F	G	Am	Bdim

So far we've only used chords I, IV and V. The easiest way to write a song with four chords is to add your choice of chord II or III or VI to the three majors. Notice that II, III and VI are all minor chords, which as we know sound sad in comparison to major chords: the opportunity to add a minor chord provides significant new 'colour' in the palette of harmony. (We'll leave aside chord VII for the moment as it falls into a category that's neither major nor minor.)

CD TRACK

26

Any of these minor chords can offer added potential to the sequences presented in Section 3. Still within the three-chord song format, try taking out either chord IV or V and replacing it with II, III or VI. In CD Track 26, chord V in C (G) is replaced by chord VI, Am. The contrast of the minor chord to the majors brings a new emotion to the music.

CD TRACK 26 **Adding a minor chord in C**

I				IV				I				VI				
C	\	\	\	F/c	\	\	\	C	\	\	\	Am/c	\	\	\	:‖

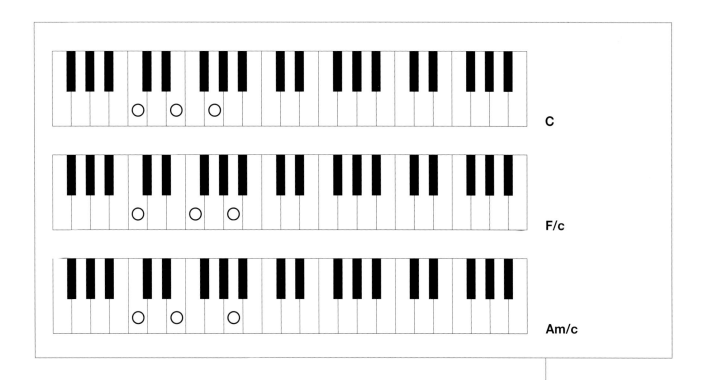

C

F/c

Am/c

TECHNIQUE 27 — AN EASY CHORD SUBSTITUTE

Every major chord has a 'relative' minor with which it has a special affinity. This is because they have two out of three notes in common. Think of these chords as 'twinned', with the minor having a melancholy quality.

The relative minor of C major is A minor. The chord of C is C-E-G and Am is A-C-E – only one note different. In the same way, Dm is the relative minor of F major (D-F-A, F-A-C) and Em is the relative minor of G major (E-G-B, G-B-D). So chords II and IV, and III and V are twinned in the same way as I and VI. In a major key this means:

• Chord VI is always the relative minor of I.
• Chord III is always the relative minor of V.
• Chord II is always the relative minor of IV.

To get certain effects it is possible to substitute a minor for its paired major, and vice versa. The melody receives a different colour at that moment, but won't sound wrong. This is a simple example of chord substitution, which has many beneficial results in songwriting. The first application is that you could substitute a Dm for an F, or an Em for a G, in any of the C major examples in Section 1. Try it and see how it sounds.

In terms of what happens on the keyboards, this change from major to relative minor can be achieved with a single finger movement. If you're holding a root major chord, move your little finger up two keys; if it's a first inversion, move the middle note up two keys; if a second inversion, move the thumb up two keys.

CD Track 27 is a sequence where the chords move to their relative minor or major. By using RH inversions there is a minimum of movement in the hand positions – they creep up step-by-step. Notice the rate of change is different in the last two bars.

CD TRACK 27 Major to relative minor changes in C

IV				II				V				III			
F/c	\	\	\	Dm	\	\	\	G/d	\	\	\	Em	\	\	\

VI				III		V		II		IV		I			
Am/e	\	\	\	Em	\	G/d	\	Dm	\	F/c	\	C	\	\	\

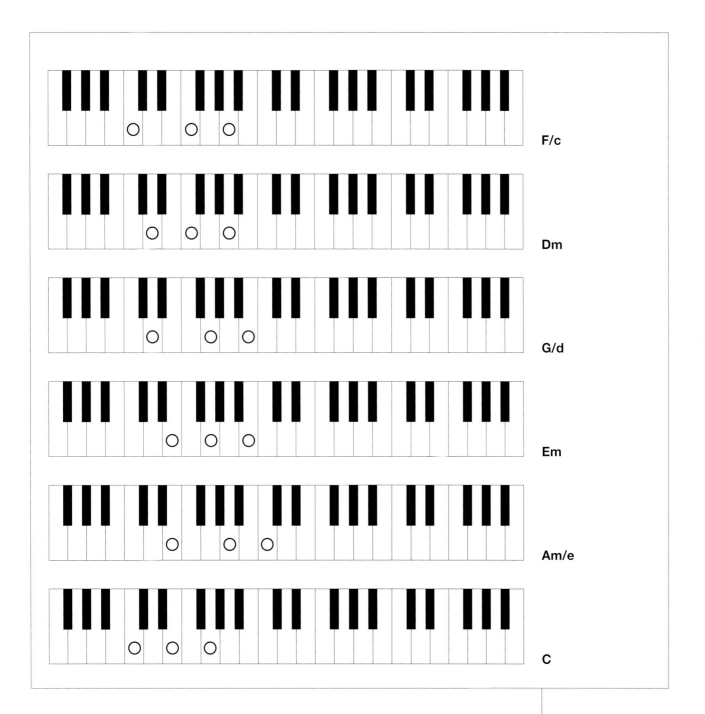

F/c

Dm

G/d

Em

Am/e

C

CD TRACK
27

TECHNIQUE 28

RH INVERSIONS AND RELATIVE MINORS

To reinforce the point about how little movement is required for this major-to-relative minor chord change, here's another example, this time in G. Here are the seven chords for G major:

Scale degree	I	II	III	IV	V	VI	VII
Scale note	*G*	*A*	*B*	*C*	*D*	*E*	*F♯*
Chord	G	Am	Bm	C	D	Em	F♯dim

Again, instead of trying to play all of these as root chords, using inversions shows how closely related these chords are. In bars 1-4 the progression kicks off from a root G and uses the same change from the root D and the root C. The arrow on the chord diagrams shows you which finger has moved. In bars 1-4 it's the finger at the top. In bars 5-8, where the changes lead off from a first inversion of the majors, it's the middle finger. In bars 9-12, where the changes lead off from a second inversion of the majors, it's the thumb.

CD TRACK 28 **Major-relative minor changes**

I		iVI		V		iIII		IV		iII		V					
G	\	Em/g	\	D	\	Bm/d	\	C	\	Am/c	\	D	\		\		\

iI		iiVI		iV		iiIII		iIV		iiII		V					
G/b	\	Em/b	\	D/f♯	\	Bm/f♯	\	C/e	\	Am/e	\	D/f♯	\		\		\

iiI		VI		iiV		III		iiIV		II		V					
G/d	\	Em	\	D/a	\	Bm	\	C/g	\	Am	\	D/a	\		\		\

In a song you would never use so many different shapes in a 12-bar progression like this. Any one of these three lines would be sufficient for a verse or a chorus idea. This is too overcrowded to be effective in a real song, but it shows you what changes are easy to make from the chords in each of their three different shapes.

CD TRACK

28

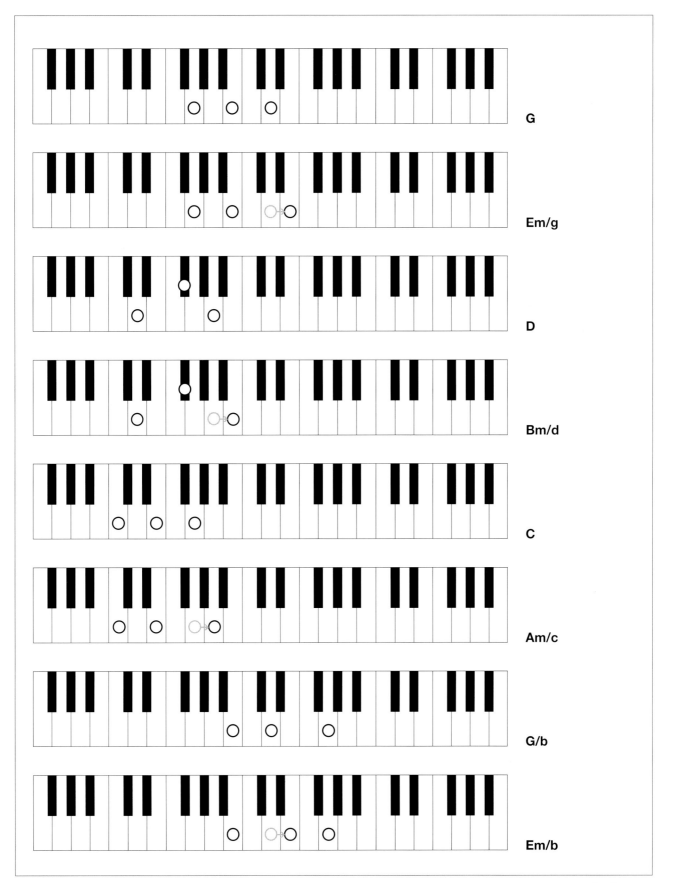

G

Em/g

D

Bm/d

C

Am/c

G/b

Em/b

continued over page

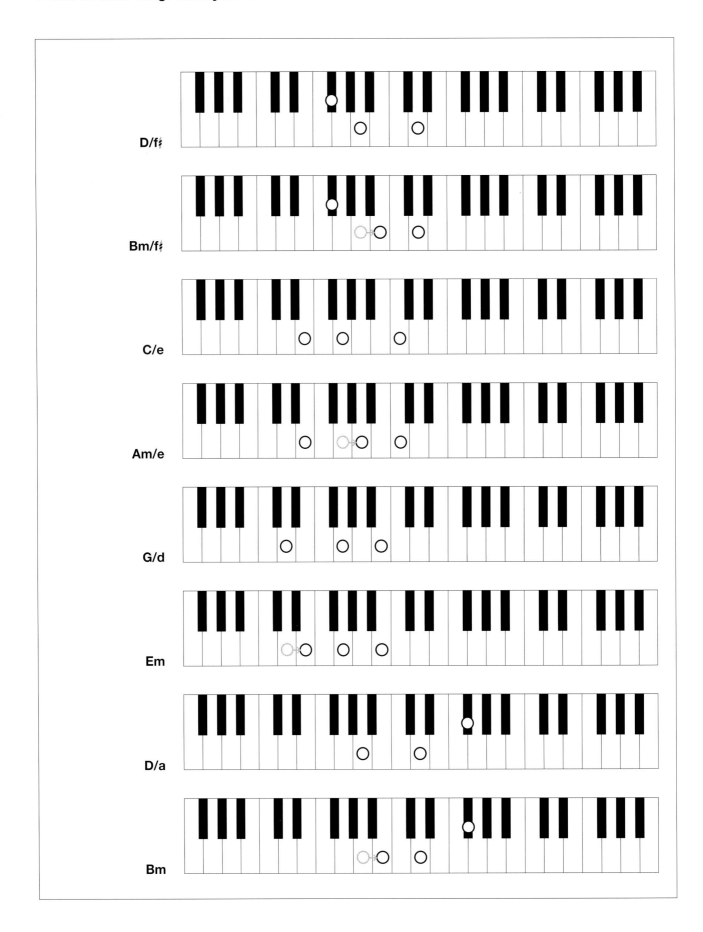

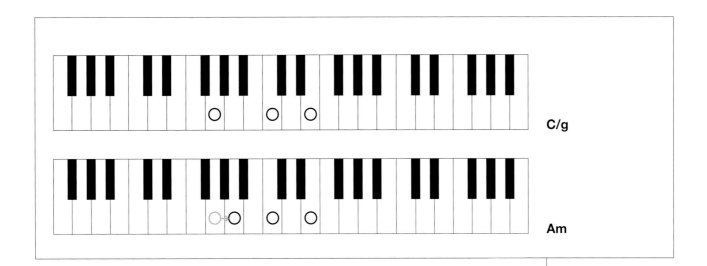

TECHNIQUE 29	# HOLD BACK THE FOURTH CHORD

As we've seen, substitution is one way to introduce a fourth chord. But a songwriter is free to pick one of the minor chords of the key and combine it with the three majors. On the basis of 'keeping your powder dry', one effective way to use this fourth chord is to hold it back until a significant moment. It could appear once in the middle of a sequence and thereafter could re-appear at the start or end of another section.

Since the 12-bar structure is so well-known by listeners, you can surprise them by putting in an extra (minor) chord. In CD Track 29, in a four-chord 12-bar the expected chord V in bar 9 is replaced by its 'sad twin', chord III. Not only is this expressive in itself but it usefully displaces chord V to bar 12.

CD TRACK 29 Four-chord 12-bar in C

I				IV				I				I			
C	\	\	\	F/c	\	\	\	C	\	\	\	C/e	\	\	\

IV				IV				I				I			
F	\	\	\	F	\	\	\	C/e	\	\	\	C/e	\	\	\

III				IV				I				V			
Em	\	\	\	F	\	\	\	C/e	\	\	\	G/d	\	\	\

CD TRACK
29

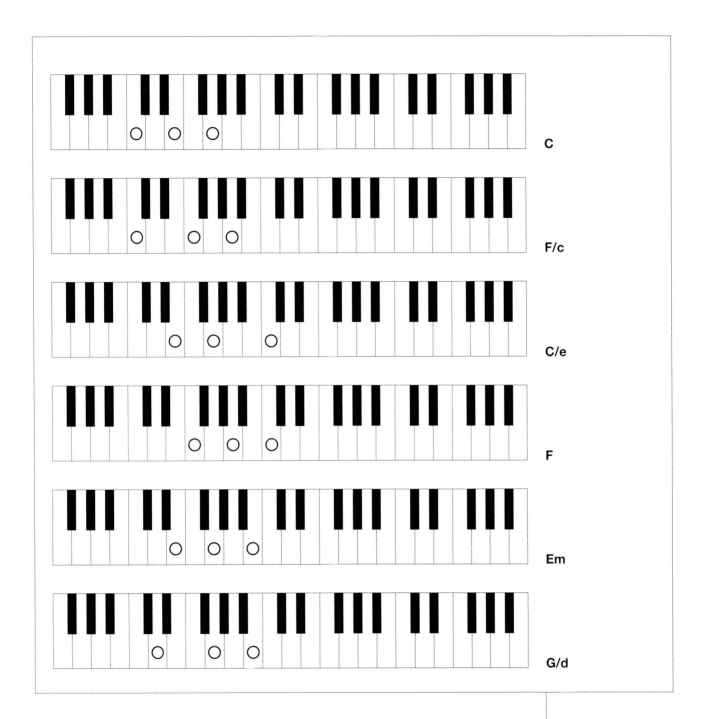

C

F/c

C/e

F

Em

G/d

CD TRACK
29

TECHNIQUE 30   FOUR CHORDS IN A 12-BAR VERSE

THE SECONDARY THREE-CHORD TRICK

Having access to the minor chords opens up the possibility of three-chord songs that, instead of using I, IV and V, have combinations such as I, II and IV, or I, III and V. I'd call a song written with any three from these six chords a secondary three-chord trick. Each has its own mood: those that omit chord V can sound less 'definite', less securely major. Of course chord I remains a fixture, since without it the song would no longer generate its musical key – but it is possible to withhold chord I in one section, or from the third of, say, three verses. This can be a powerful way to emphasise a statement or image in the lyric.

If verses 1 and 2 in your song have been optimistic but verse 3 is pessimistic, where there was, for example, a G chord for the equivalent two bars of tune in the early verses, chord VI (Em) could now substitute. The sadness of the minor chord would provide the right harmonic colour for the phrase. This also works in reverse: in a song primarily made of minor chords, the substitution of a major could be like a ray of light breaking in on a gloomy scene.

In CD Track 30 we are going to avoid using chord V of G major. Notice, therefore, there is no D chord in this sequence.

Four chords fit nicely into a 12-bar verse, so we'll use G, Em, C and Am (I, VI, IV and II). Notice in bar 13 the true first-inversion G chord replaces a root G that would have been too stable. Remember that a 'true' inversion can dilute the strength of chord I or chord V where they are present before a return of the root chord. In this sense, an inversion is a weaker version of displacing either of these chords. As before, the true inversion's bass note is played by bass guitar, so you don't have to worry about your left hand at this stage:

CD TRACK 30 *12-bar verse in G with chord VI*

I				IV				I		VI		IV			
G	\	\	\	C/g	\	\	\	G	\	Em/b	\	C	\	\	\

IV				iI				IV				iI			
C	\	\	\	G/B	\	\	\	C	\	\	\	G/B	\	\	\

iI				IV				VI				II			
G/B	\	\	\	C	\	\	\	Em/b	\	\	\	Am	\	\	\

BAR-SHARING

A further possibility with chord substitution is 'bar-sharing'. A bar with one major chord becomes a bar with two beats on the major chord and two on its relative minor. Or two bars of a major chord becomes one of the major and one of its relative minor. This can raise the emotional temperature when a section is repeated (like a later verse), especially if it contrasts with a predominant chord-rate of one to a bar. See bar 3 in CD Track 30.

CD TRACK

30

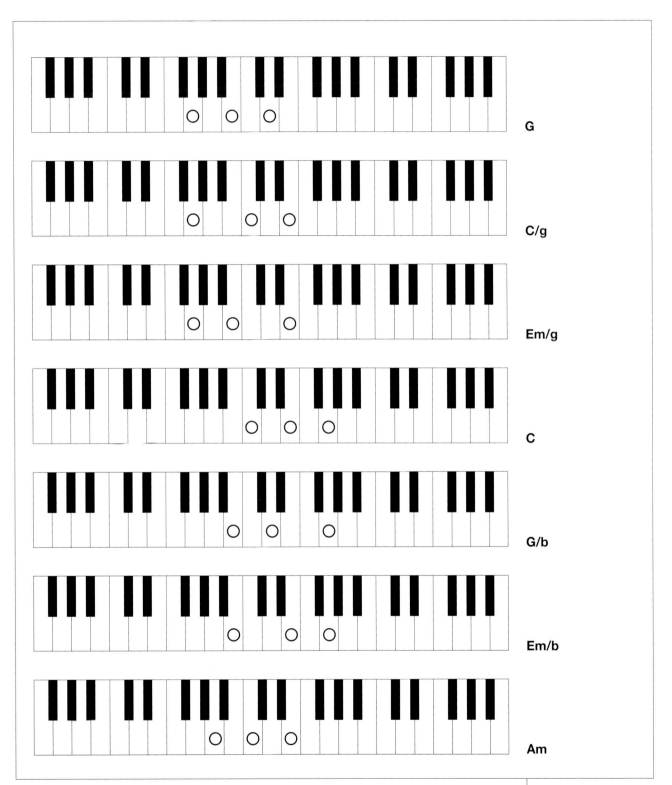

| TECHNIQUE 31 | # A VERSE/BRIDGE FOUR-CHORD SONG |

Let's now lay out a complete song structure that uses four chords, one of which is minor. It comprises only verses and bridges – the sort of song-form featured in many early Beatles songs. For variety let's have a new key, D major. Here are the chords:

Scale degree	I	II	III	IV	V	VI	VII
Scale note	D	E	F♯	G	A	B	C♯
Chord	D	Em	F♯m	G	A	Bm	C♯dim

A three-chord trick song in D major would have the chords D, G and A. To those three let's add one of its minors – chord III, F♯m.

CD TRACK 31 **Full verse/bridge four-chord song in D major**

Intro

V				V				V				IV			
A	\	\	\	A	\	\	\	A	\	\	\	G	\	\	\

Verse

I				IV				V				I			
D	\	\	\	G/d	\	\	\	A/e	\	\	\	D/f♯	\	\	\

IV				IV				V				iiV			
G	\	\	\	G	\	\	\	A	\	\	\	A/E	\	\	\

III				IV				I				V			
F♯m	\	\	\	G	\	\	\	D/f♯	\	\	\	A/e	\	\	\

Bridge

IV				IV				IV		V		IV			
G	\	\	\	G	\	\	\	G	\	A	\	G	\	\	\

IV				IV				III				V			
G	\	\	\	G	\	\	\	F♯m	\	\	\	A/e	\	\	\

NOTE:

- No chord I in the intro.
- Intro has the less common 3 + 1 bar pattern, instead of 4 bars on A. The change to G is more of a surprise.
- A second inversion chord V (A/E) does double service in bar 8. It adds more interest than just having two bars on A, and the E bass steps up to the F♯m chord in bar 9. An inversion usually emphasises the stable quality of a root chord when approached by step in this way.
- Notice how the bridge starts with two and a half bars on chord IV. The rate of chord change contrasts with the verse where no chord lasted this long.
- It's often good if the bridge avoids chord I – this makes it more of a contrast, which is its function.

CD TRACK
31

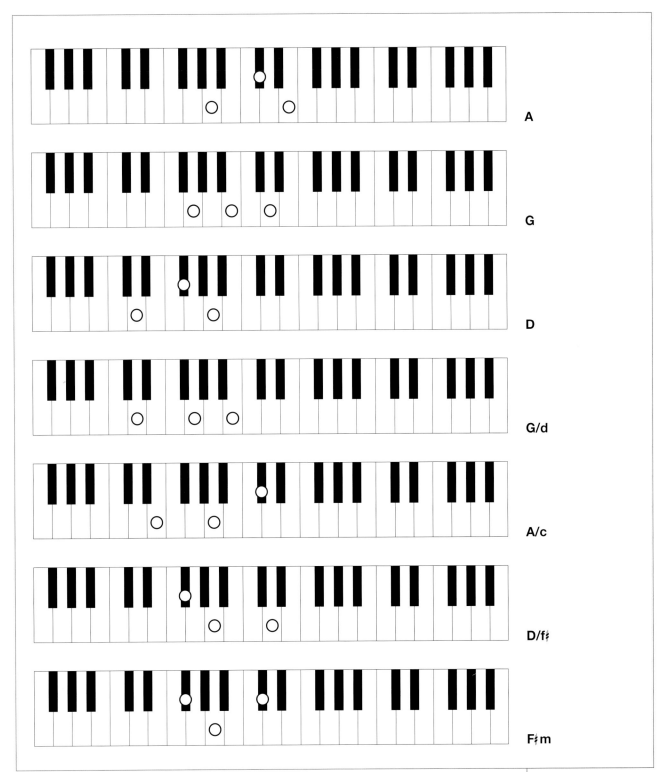

CD TRACK
31

Instant magic: four-chord turnarounds

"We wrote a lot of stuff together one-on-one, eyeball to eyeball. Like in 'I Want To Hold Your Hand', I remember when we got the chord that made the song. We were in Jane Asher's house, downstairs in the cellar playing on the piano at the same time. And we had, 'Oh you-u-u/ got that something...' And Paul hits this chord, and I turn to him and say, 'That's it! ... Do that again...'."

John Lennon

With the inclusion of a fourth chord, the turnaround technique (see Technique 25 in Section 3) gains in power. Many of the progressions in this section will remind you of famous songs and hits – that's because they've all been used many times, often at the 'hookiest' point in the song.

Four-chord turnarounds get their extra power not only from the increase of harmonic colour of this fourth, minor chord, but also because they take on the assertive symmetry of the number four. Many turnarounds are four chords, four beats each, in a four-bar phrase that may even be repeated four times...

To give you an idea how this technique might sound – and to demonstrate how popular it is – here are some famous songs that use four-chord turnarounds:

'Love Is All Around' (Troggs/Wet Wet Wet), 'Fall On Me' (R.E.M.), 'Show Me Heaven' (Maria McKee), 'Somebody' (Bryan Adams), 'Waiting For An Alibi' (Thin Lizzy), 'Let's Get It On' (Marvin Gaye), 'Bright Side Of The Road' (Van Morrison), 'I Can't Explain' (The Who), 'Runaround Sue' (Dion), 'Stand By Me (Ben E. King/John Lennon), 'Every Breath You Take' (The Police), 'All I Have To Do Is Dream' (Everly Brothers), 'Crocodile Rock' (Elton John), 'True Blue' (Madonna), 'Don't Dream It's Over' (Crowded House), 'More Than A Feeling' (Boston), 'Two Princes' (Spin Doctors), 'Talkin' 'Bout A Revolution' (Tracy Chapman), 'With Or Without You' (U2), 'So Lonely' (The Police), 'Beast Of Burden' (Rolling Stones), 'New York City Serenade' (Bruce Springsteen).

TECHNIQUE 32

THE 'BIG THREE' OF TURNAROUNDS

The 'primary' turnarounds are those that use the three major chords of a major key with one of the three minors: I-II-IV-V, I-III-IV-V or I-VI-IV-V. I call these the 'big three' turnarounds. The emotional effect is that bar 2 plunges us from a happy mood to a feeling of sadness, but this is re-adjusted in bar 3-4 by the major chords. This alternation between happy/sad-major/minor is very potent.

Here are those turnarounds in the key of C major, with right-hand inversion shapes to make the changes smooth:

CD TRACK 32 Primary four-chord turnarounds in C

I				II				IV				V			
C	\	\	\	Dm	\	\	\	F/c	\	\	\	G/d	\	\	C

I				III				IV				V			
C	\	\	\	Em/b	\	\	\	F/c	\	\	\	G/d	\	\	C

I				VI				IV				V			
C	\	\	\	Am/c	\	\	\	F/c	\	\	\	G/d	\	\	C

Each of these turnarounds has its own character. This is partly because of the different relationship between chord I and the succeeding minor chord. In the case of C (C-E-G) and Dm (D-F-A) there are no common notes to link the chords (you can see this on the keyboard – all three fingers have to move a key). But the chord pairs C and Em (E-G-B), and C and Am (A-C-E), have two notes in common.

The exact effect of a turnaround is modified by other factors such as where in the song it comes, what words are being sung over it, how slow or fast it is played, and how much force is applied. You can also vary the order of the four chords. This is discussed in more detail in *The Songwriting Sourcebook*.

CD TRACK

32

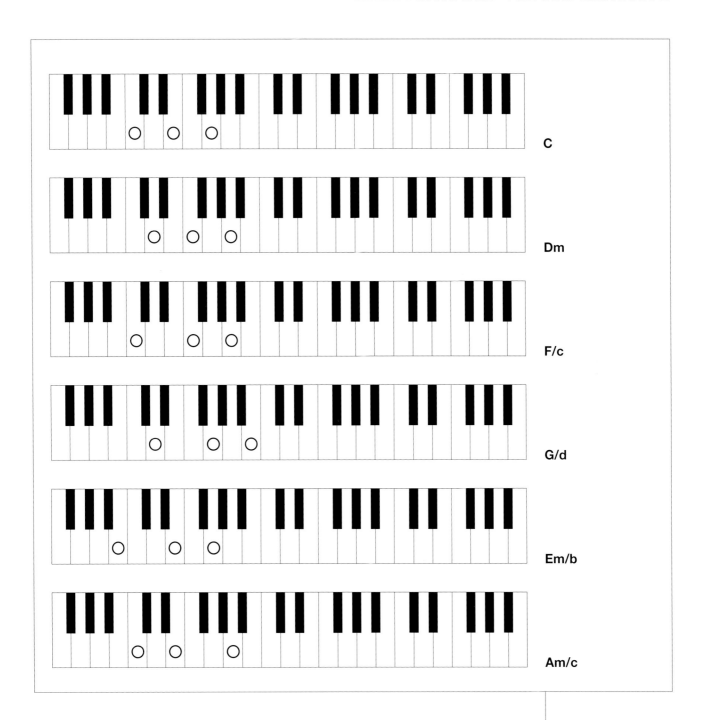

C

Dm

F/c

G/d

Em/b

Am/c

CD TRACK
32

TECHNIQUE 33 | A 'BIG THREE' TURNAROUND IN G

In the key of G major, the 'big three' turnarounds are: G, Am, C, D (I- II- IV-V); G, Bm, C, D (I-III-IV-V); and G, Em, C, D (I-VI-IV-V).

Altering the rate of chord change can make a turnaround give a different impression. In the next example (CD Track 33, which uses the I-II-IV-V in G), slowing the rate of chord change, or making it irregular, reduces the force of the turnaround's symmetry in bars 1-4. It's less predictable and 'four-square' if you only spend two beats on the Am. In bars 5-8 the changes come twice as fast.

CD TRACK 33 Primary four-chord turnaround in G

I				II	IV		V			
G	\	\	\	Am \	C/g \	C/g \	\	\	D/a \	\ \ :‖

I	II	IV	V	x4
‖: G \	Am/e \	C/e \	D/f♯ \	:‖

The first four bars of this technique could be a verse; the second line could make a chorus. Altering the rate at which the changes in a turnaround occur means the same turnaround could be used in different sections of the same song. But it's a good idea to break away from the turnaround at times otherwise it can lose its power.

CD TRACK
33

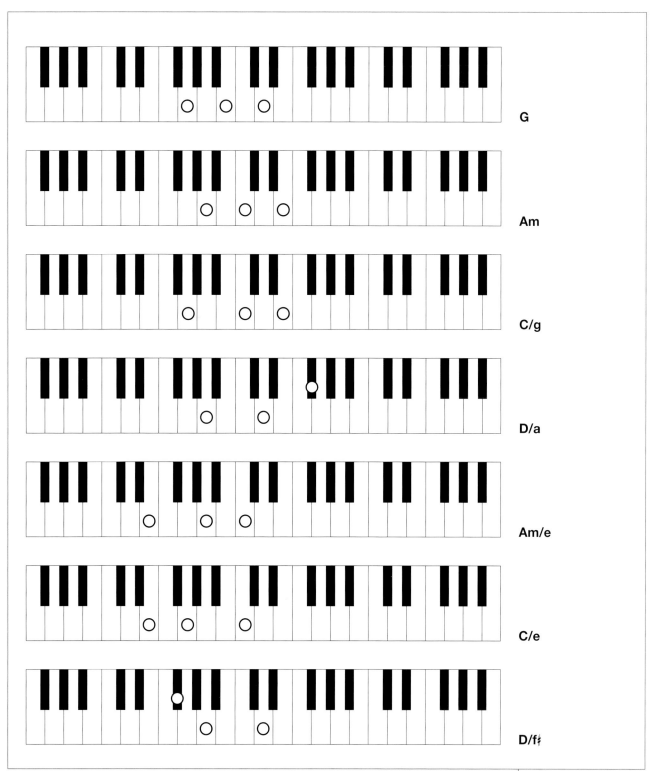

G

Am

C/g

D/a

Am/e

C/e

D/f♯

CD TRACK

33

TECHNIQUE 34 · A 'BIG THREE' TURNAROUND IN D

In the key of D major, the 'big three' turnarounds are D, Em, G, A (I-II-IV-V); D, F#m, G, A (I-III-IV-V); and D, Bm, G, A (I-VI-IV-V). Here's how they sound and look on the keyboard. Watch out for the Bm in bar 10 and the A in bar 12 placed two beats later than you might expect them.

CD TRACK 34 Primary four-chord turnarounds in D

I				II				IV				V			
D	\	\	\	Em	\	\	\	G/d	\	\	\	A/e	\	\	\

I				III				IV				V			
D	\	\	\	F#m/c#	\	\	\	G/d	\	\	\	A/e	\	\	\

I				VI			IV				V	
D	\	\	\		\	Bm/d	\	G/d	\	\	\	\ A/e \

Spending more or less than four beats on a chord is a handy way of adding variety and an element of surprise to a turnaround. This can be especially useful if you are writing a song with more than one turnaround in it. By this method you can give them more distinct identities. Such simple variations and irregularities can also be curiously touching.

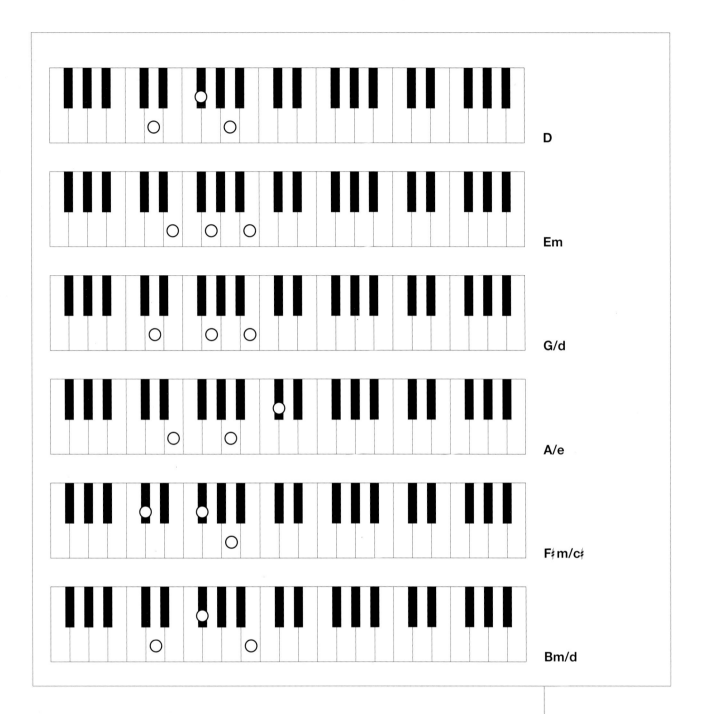

D

Em

G/d

A/e

F#m/c#

Bm/d

CD TRACK
34

TECHNIQUE 35

GET MORE FROM A TURNAROUND

A turnaround can also be subjected to 'displacement'. This means that the 'logical' order of the turnaround – starting on I and ending on V – is disrupted. You could also consider these as chord sequences in their own right, but I'm suggesting displacement is a way of thinking about manipulating a chosen turnaround. Displacement is when the order of chords in a turnaround remains the same but the whole thing is moved on a bar or more, with the chord(s) that 'fall off' the end (bar 4) taking up a new position at the beginning of bar 1. The order no longer lines up with chord I in bar 1, a minor chord in bar 2, IV in bar 3, and V in bar 4. This has a considerable effect on the sound of the sequence. Displaced turnarounds can also be affected by changing the rate of chord movement.

CD Track 35 takes the turnaround in G from Track 33, this time subjecting it to three stages of displacement (each is heard twice). The Em bar is there to separate the turnarounds from each other:

CD TRACK 35 Displaced form

II		IV		V		I			VI		
Am	\	C/g	\	|D/a	\	G	\	:||	Em/g	\	\	\

		IV		V		I		II			
|: C/g	\	D/a	\	|G	\	Am	\	:||	Em/g	\	\	\

V		I			II		IV			
|: D/a	\	G	\	|Am	\	C/g	\	:||

It's the same four chords, but you get three new sequences. Moving chord I from either the start or the end of the turnaround makes the progression flow more. Displacement reduces the stability of a turnaround and the feeling that every fourth bar is an end. Some of the displaced versions of the turnaround can be tonally ambiguous too. The first form of the example might be heard as being in the key of A minor. (There's more about minor key progressions in Section 7).

CD TRACK
35

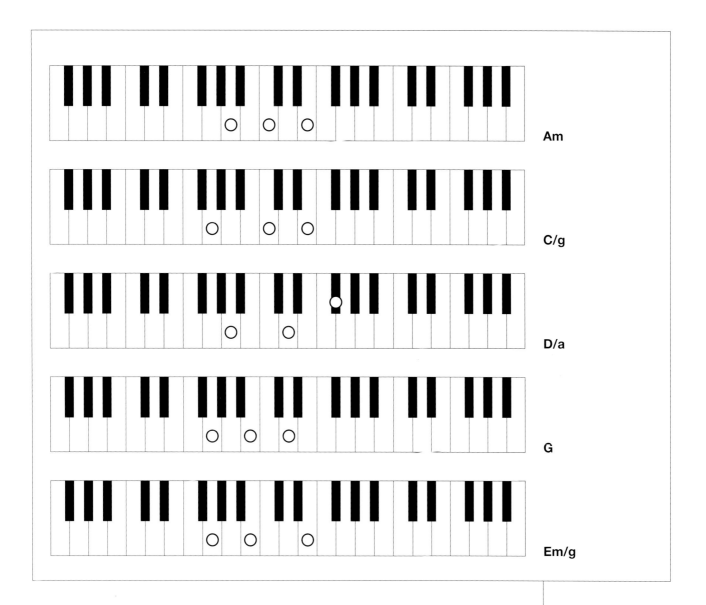

Am

C/g

D/a

G

Em/g

CD TRACK
35

TECHNIQUE 36

THE 'UP ESCALATOR'

Another way of handling the I-VI-IV-V turnaround is to create the 'escalator' effect by keeping the sequence in numerical order: I-IV-V-VI. This order can then be displaced in turn. Obviously the other two primary turnarounds – I-II-IV-V and I-III-IV-V – are already in escalating sequence. To enhance the effect in CD Track 36, the RH chords are all in root position. The sequence is presented first in C major and then a tone higher in the key of D major. This kind of transposition up a tone into a new key is often heard in the last choruses of a song.

CD TRACK 36 Escalator turnaround in C and D

Primary form

I	IV	V	VI	I	IV	V	VI
C \	F \	|G \	Am \	:|: D \	G \	|A \	Bm \	:||

The 'up escalator' progression can be heard in many classic Motown songs of the 1960s. In those it was frequently employed as a pre-chorus sequence, leading powerfully to the lyric and melodic hook of the whole song. For a classic pre-chorus play the chords II-III-IV-V in any key (in C major = Dm, Em, F, G). It works well at medium to fast tempos to generate excitement.

CD TRACK
36

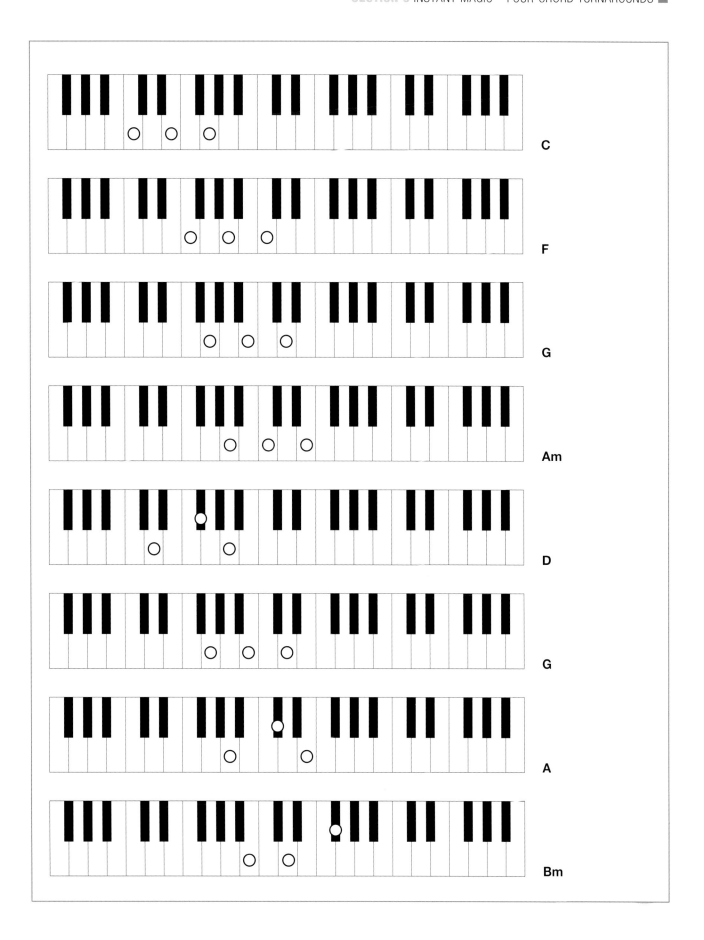

TECHNIQUE 37

THE 'DOWN ESCALATOR'

By reversing these turnarounds, a feeling of descent is created, like a trip on a down escalator. Descending turnarounds have a specific use at the end of a song, often with a slowing up of tempo, but they can also introduce contrary movement in any song section if it's desired. As the chords go downwards, the melody could rise.

There are two basic ways of guessing what this downward chord movement might bring to the emotion of a song. Either it is slightly depressing because it isn't rising up (literally uplifting), or comforting because it is returning home to chord I, the root chord. Other factors in the song, such as words, theme, arrangement and melody, will decide which it is.

CD TRACK 37 Descending turnarounds in D

V		IV		II		I			V	IV	III	I
A	\	G	\	Em	\	D	\	:‖:	A	G	F♯m	D/f♯ :‖

VI		V		IV		I		
‖: Bm	\	A	\	G	\	D	\	:‖

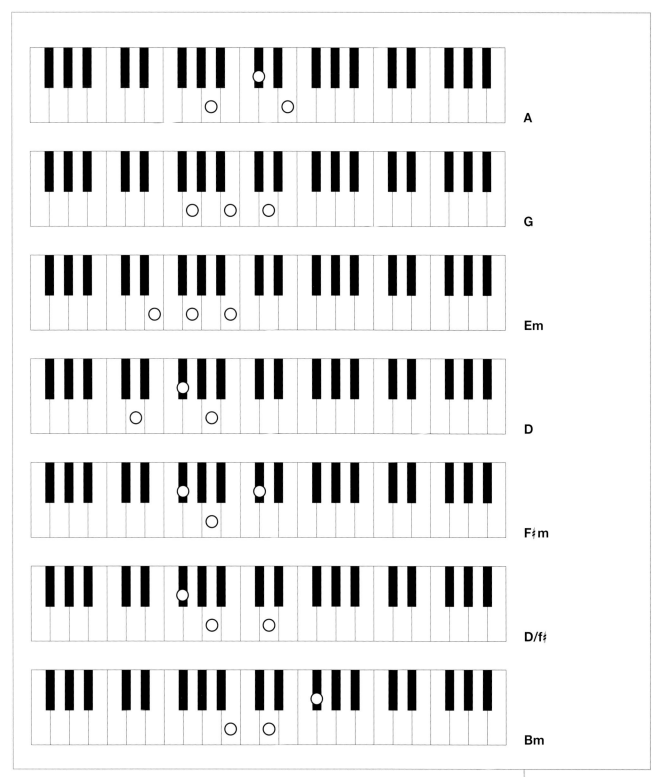

CD TRACK
37

TECHNIQUE 38

THE TURNAROUND MEETS THE INVERSION

By inverting some of the chords you can put a new slant on a turnaround, or 'blunt' it if it seems too slick or predictable. Invert chord I if you want the turnaround never to reach a point of rest. Invert chords IV or V if you want to give the turnaround extra motion. Invert the minor chord (II, III or VI) if you want it to have less 'presence', or replace it with the relevant inverted major if you want to keep the minor for another part of the song.

Note that the inversion bass note must be in the LH, not just the RH, otherwise the effect won't be heard. These must be 'true' inversions. As before, this is taken care of for you on the CD by the bass guitar. But to ensure you hear the effect, the RH shapes match the correct LH inversions.

A turnaround can have more than one inversion in it. But take care with the movement of the bass notes when you approach and leave an inverted chord.

CD Track 38 shows a first inversion Am in bars 1-4 which shares a bass note with the next chord. This weakens the sense of there being four different chords because iII (first inversion of chord II) sounds like a blurred version of IV.

Remember, as a general principle: if an inversion's bass note matches the root of one of the other chords, the turnaround will sound less like it has four chords in it.

The second four-bar example has the Em/G inversion's bass note already in place in the previous chord. Notice how the D/F♯ leads powerfully back to the G chord.

CD TRACK 38 Turnaround with first inversions in G

I				iII				IV				V			
G/b	\	\	\	Am/C \	\	\	\	C	\	\	\	D	\	\	\ :‖

I				iVI				IV				iV			
‖: G	\	\	\	Em/G	\	\	\	C/g	\	\	\	D/F♯	\	\	\ :‖

CD TRACK

38

102

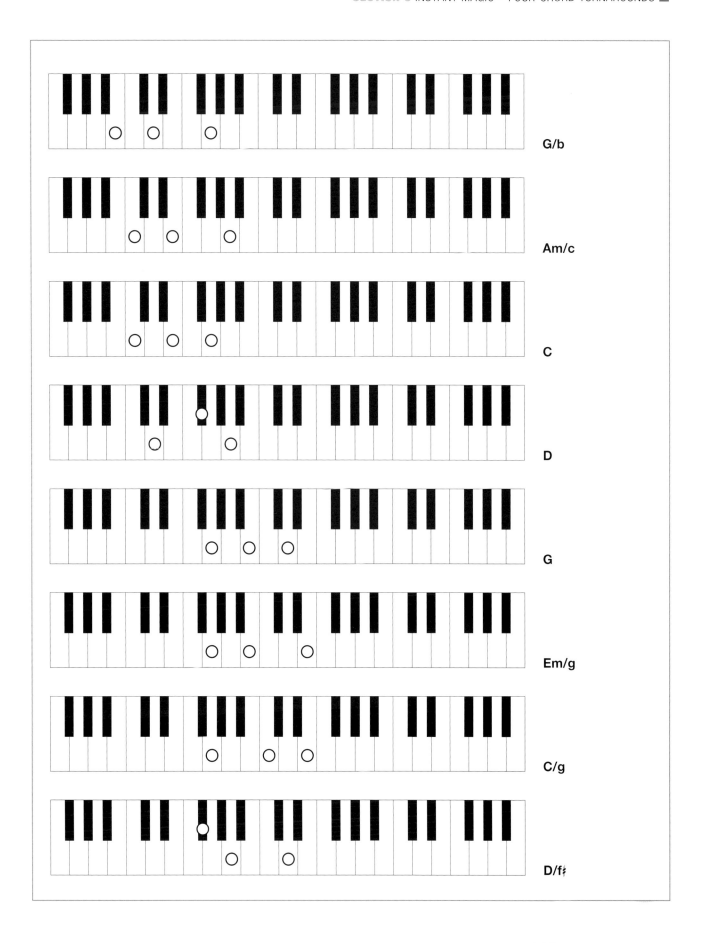

G/b

Am/c

C

D

G

Em/g

C/g

D/f♯

| TECHNIQUE 39 | # THE TURNAROUND MEETS THE SECOND INVERSION |

In CD Track 39, the bass note G that we associate with chord I (G) appears under a second inversion C, and the bass note E that we associate with chord VI (Em) appears under a second inversion Am. This effect is strengthened if it comes after a I-VI-IV-V change, as in CD Track 39, because an expectation has been created that the second chord of bar 3 will be Em. Remember, the crucial LH inversions are reinforced by the bass guitar and have a capital letter on the other side of the slash mark.

CD TRACK 39 Turnaround with second inversions in G

I		VI		IV		V		I		iiII		IV		V		
G	\	Em/g	\	C/G	\	D/a	\	G	\	Am/E	\	C/e	\	D/f♯	\	:‖

These kinds of descending sequences could be used as a pre-chorus in a slow ballad, but would not work so well in the same position in a fast song. They have a natural suitability for a song's closing bars and can give a powerful sense of ending. (For more about endings see Technique 79.)

CD TRACK
39

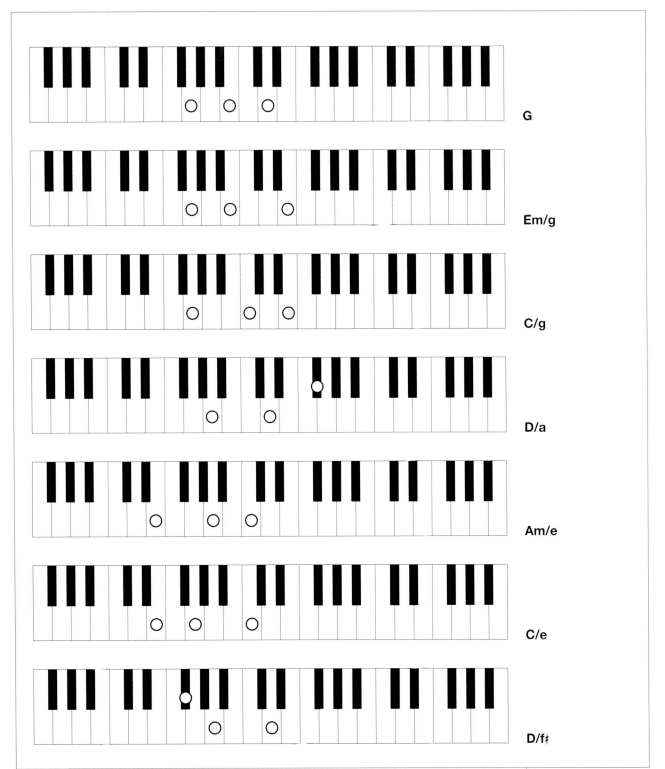

G

Em/g

C/g

D/a

Am/e

C/e

D/f♯

CD TRACK
39

TECHNIQUE 40

GOING UP AND GOING DOWN

Using an inversion is a good way of creating basslines that move by step. In this instance a I-III-IV-V sequence is given an overhaul by having a descending bassline underneath it. The iiIII and iIV refer to the fact that the bass guitar is playing F♯ and E under the Bm and C chords, creating true inversions. The chord patterns for the RH ensure that they rise.

CD TRACK 40 Turnaround with second inversion for a descending bassline

I				iiIII				iIV				V			
G/d	\	\	\	Bm/F♯ \	\	\		C/g	\	\	\	D/a	\	\	\ :‖

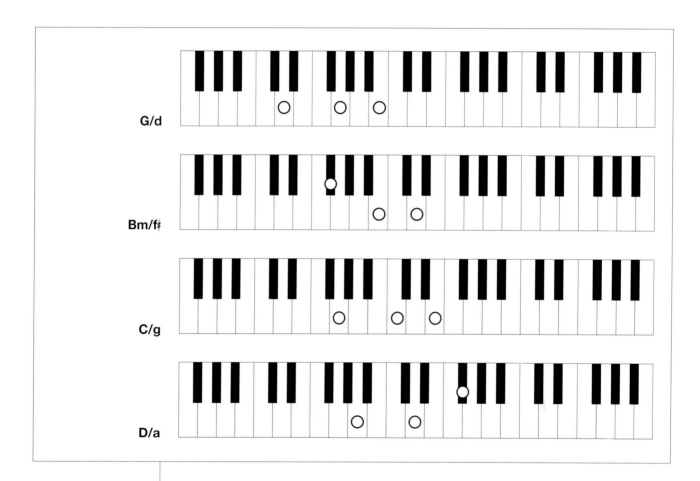

G/d

Bm/f♯

C/g

D/a

'TELESCOPING' A TURNAROUND

TECHNIQUE 41

A well-established songwriting trick is to use the same turnaround twice in a song but in the verse the chords change at a slower rate than the chorus. I call this 'telescoping'. The turnaround might use a rate of one chord every two bars through an eight-bar verse and then change to once a bar, or half a bar, during the chorus (the greater the discrepancy the less likely the listener will suspect the two sequences are the same). How the verse and chorus are arranged (how many instruments are playing and which instruments) can also help mask the similarity.

CD TRACK 41

Let's take a I-III-IV-V turnaround in D and see what happens when it's telescoped. The verse has one chord per bar but the chorus is one chord to two beats. The inversions in the verse help to contrast with the same progression in the chorus by providing an ascending bassline. The bass guitar makes the inversions 'true' in the verse and then plays root notes in the chorus.

CD TRACK 41 Telescoped turnaround in D major

Verse

I				iIII				iIV				iV			
D/a	\	\	\	F#m/A	\	\	\	G/B	\	\	\	A/C#	\	\	\ :||

Chorus

I		III		IV		V		
||: D/a	\	F#m/a	\	G/b	\	A/c#	\	:||

D/a

F#m/a

G/b

A/c#

107

TECHNIQUE 42 SECONDARY TURNAROUNDS

So far, all the examples have worked with the three primary turnarounds: I-II-IV-V, I-III-IV-V, and I-VI-IV-V. These three combine the key's three majors (I, IV and V) with one of the minor chords (II, III or VI). But there are many other possible turnarounds, even just drawing on chords I to VI. Any turnaround that omits chord IV or V, for example, can be categorised as a secondary turnaround. If only chords I through to VI are available, omitting IV or V will mean the necessary inclusion of two minor chords instead of one.

Here are two examples in G, one suitable as a verse, the other a chorus.

CD TRACK 42 Turnaround with no chord V in G

I	III	II	IV
G \ \ \	Bm/f♯ \ \ \	Am/e \ \ \	C/e \ \ \ :‖

I	III	IV	VI
‖: G \ Bm/f♯ \	C/g \ Em/g \ :‖		

Points about turnarounds
- Turnarounds make powerful hooks. They particularly suit choruses.
- An instrumental version of a turnaround chorus makes a great intro.
- Turnarounds are more effective at medium-to-quick tempos.
- Played with sufficient rhythmic accent a turnaround can become a riff.
- A displaced turnaround, which neither begins nor ends on chord I or V, is a good way of refreshing a predictable sequence such as I-VI-IV-V.
- A single turnaround can be refreshed by repeating it in a different key.

Cautionary points
Fine and handy as turnarounds are, they nevertheless should come, like cigarettes, with a health warning that reads, "Turnarounds are addictive and can seriously damage your songwriting". Turnarounds too easily become a quick fix and can make a songwriter musically lazy.

So remember
One turnaround in a song grabs the attention if used properly. If verse, chorus and bridge were all turnarounds, each would sound weaker.

If a song has more than one turnaround, only one should take the 'escalator' form. Use whatever technique you can to make them sound less similar.

Too much reliance on turnarounds makes your songs sound the same as each other (and a lot of other people's).

CD TRACK
42

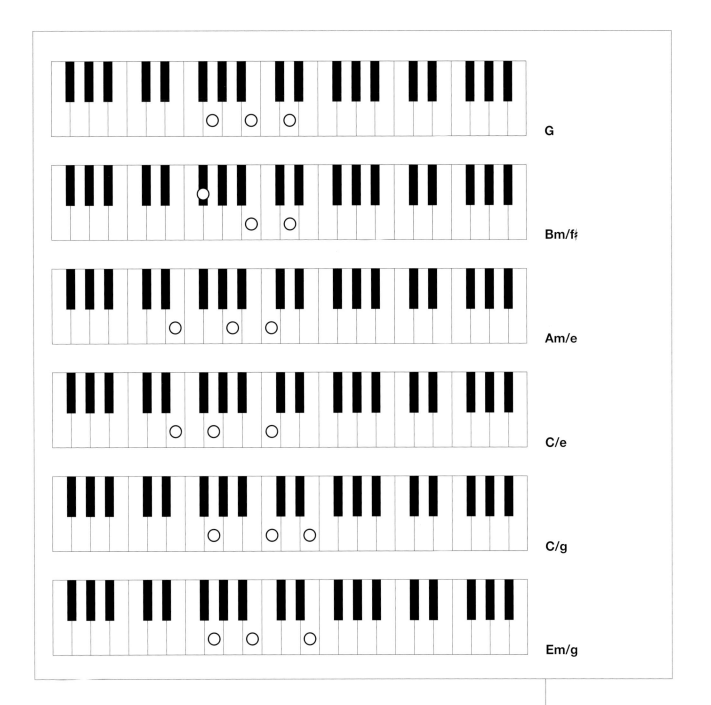

G

Bm/f♯

Am/e

C/e

C/g

Em/g

CD TRACK
42

Reaching for the five and six-chord song

"When you play piano, the chord structures of songs are so much different. You tend to put in more chords … a three-chord song on a guitar always sounds better than a three-chord song on a piano, for some reason. It's ludicrous. It has to do with the structure of the instrument."

Elton John

At the start of Section 4, three minor chords were added to the three majors used in Section 3. From this pool of six chords (and their inversions), four-chord turnarounds were constructed in Section 5. But songwriters regularly use any combination of these six chords. There are many songs with four, five or six chords and no turnaround. More chords (18 if you include the inversions) give more creative choice.

Here are some opportunities you can bear in mind when all six chords are available:

- The three minor chords can be distributed into separate sections – for example, II in the verse, III in the chorus, VI in the bridge.
- Sections can be entirely minor or major for contrast in mood.
- It's easier to have one section as a turnaround and the others not.
- Sequences do not have to be as repetitive.

A SIX-CHORD SONG IN C

TECHNIQUE 43

CD TRACK
43

Let's use these additional chords to lay out a typical song structure.

CD TRACK 43 Full song in C, six chords

Intro

I		V		I		V		
C	\	G/d	\	C	\	G/d	\	

Verse

IV				II				V			V				
‖: F/c	\	\	\	Dm	\	\	\	G/d	\	Am/e	G/d	\	\	\	:‖

IV				IV				iI				II		V	
F	\	\	\	F	\	\	\	C/E	\	\	\	Dm/f	\	G	\

Chorus

I				V				VI				IV			
C/e	\	\	\	F	\	\	\	G	\	\	\	Am/e	\	\	\

I				V				VI				IV			
C/e	\	\	\	F	\	\	\	G	\	\	\	F	\	\	\

Bridge

II		III	IV	V				II		III	IV	VI			
Dm	\	Em	F	G	\	\	\	Dm	\	Em	F	Am/e	\	\	\

II		III	IV	V				V				III			
Dm	\	Em	F	G	\	\	\	G	\	\	\	Em/g	\	Dm/f	\	‖

111

Note:

- The intro creates an expectation that the verse will start on chord I. It actually starts on chord IV.
- The verse withholds chord I in root position. Instead there is only a brief use of the first inversion C/E, where the bass guitar plays the note E.
- Notice the brief Am chord breaking up the rate of chord change in bar 3 of the verse.
- Chord III (Em) is reserved for the bridge as part of a II-III-IV-V 'escalator' turnaround. The second of three uses of this turnaround has a different fourth chord (Am instead of G).

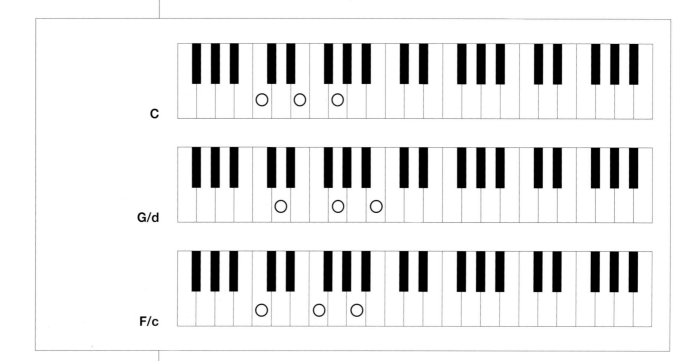

C

G/d

F/c

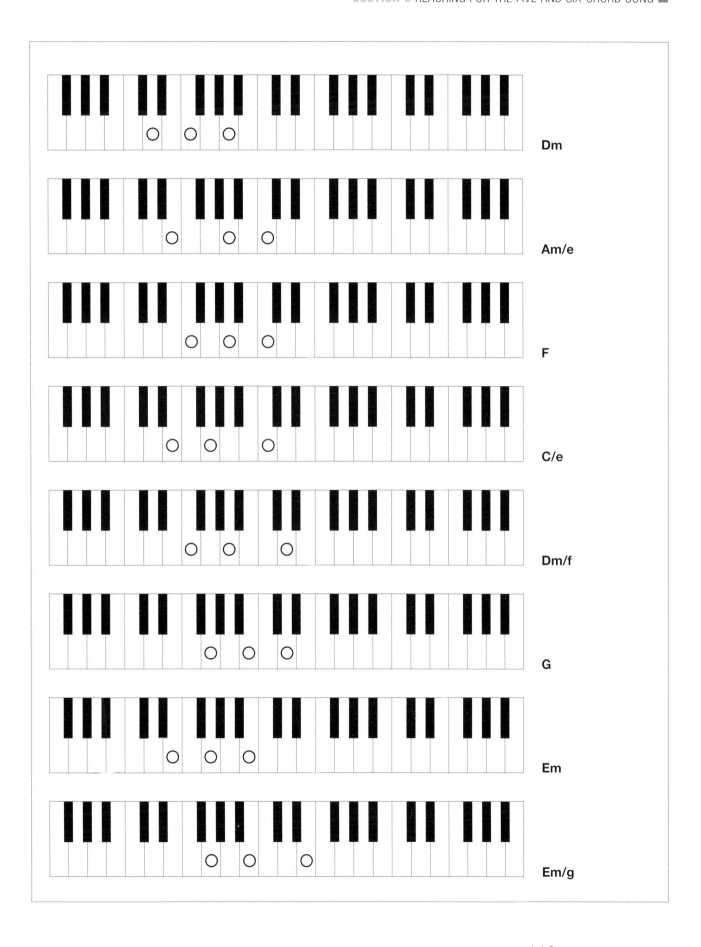

Dm

Am/e

F

C/e

Dm/f

G

Em

Em/g

HOW TO 'RE-DECORATE' A VERSE

Having all six of the chords we've discussed – the three majors and their relative minors – means you can use the technique of re-harmonising. This takes two forms. The first is chord substitution, where the melody will remain the same as a previous verse but the chords underneath will change from major to relative minor (or vice versa). In G major the substitutable pairs are G/Em, C/Am and D/Bm. This will often lend itself to a last verse and can add a new emotional slant to give a final verse more impact.

For example, imagine a verse that has this D major sequence:

Verse in D major

II				IV				I				V			
Em	\	\	\	G	\	\	\	D	\	\	\	A	\	\	:‖

To make this verse more interesting when it appears for the last time, you can use chord substitution, as in CD Track 44. In this case the relative minors (placed in brackets, to make them more obvious) take up only two beats.

CD TRACK 44 Verse 3 with reharmonised bars 2-3

II				IV				I				V			
Em	\	\	\	G	\	\	\	D/f♯	\	\	\	A/e	\	\	

II				IV		II		I		VI		V			
Em	\	\	\	G	\	[Em/g]	\	D	\	[Bm/f♯]	\	A/e	\	\	‖

This technique can be powerful if your lyric for verse 3 says something that will gain from having these brief touches of minor harmony where they are not expected. These extra chords, not heard in the earlier verses, can colour and strengthen the statement made in the lyric, and you probably won't need to adjust your melody.

CD TRACK
44

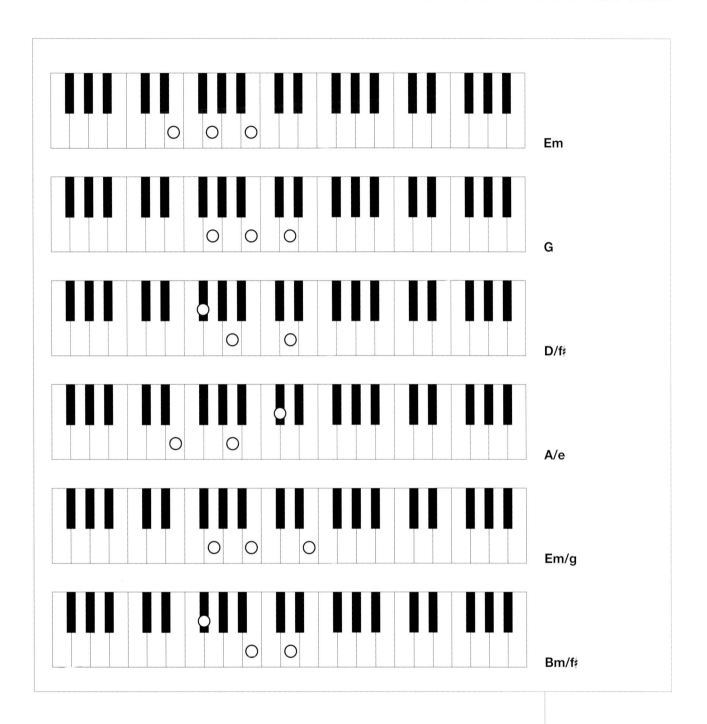

Em

G

D/f♯

A/e

Em/g

Bm/f♯

THE 'THREE-STROKE CLINCHER' CHORUS

The second type of re-harmonising involves changing chords that are not part of a relative pair.

This technique has a classic pop role on the final chorus of a song where the hook-line is re-harmonised and repeated. For the example used in CD Track 45 we will draw on C major, whose six main chords pair up C/Am, F/Dm and G/Em. Assume the earlier choruses went like this:

Chorus 1 & 2 in C major

IV				V				I				V			
F	\	\	\	G	\	\	\	C	\	\	\	G	\	\	\

IV				V				I				I			
F	\	\	\	G	\	\	\	C	\	\	\	C	\	\	\

A well-known technique, heard on some early Beatles hits, is to repeat the melody/lyric hook (which in this instance is the second line of the chorus) and re-harmonise it. Here Am replaces G in bar 4, a change repeated in the next line but with the additional alteration of C to Em in bar 7. A further refinement is to add Dm (chord II) for two beats after the last F in bar 9. This means the hook-phrase is sung three times but over different chords. It's an exciting and expressive way of postponing the end of the last chorus.

CD TRACK 45 Last chorus

IV				V				I				VI			
F	\	\	\	G	\	\	\	C/e	\	\	\	Am/e	\	\	\

IV				V				III				VI			
F	\	\	\	G	\	\	\	[Em/g]	\	\	\	Am/e	\	\	\

IV		II		V				I	
F	\	Dm/f	\	G	\	\	\	C	

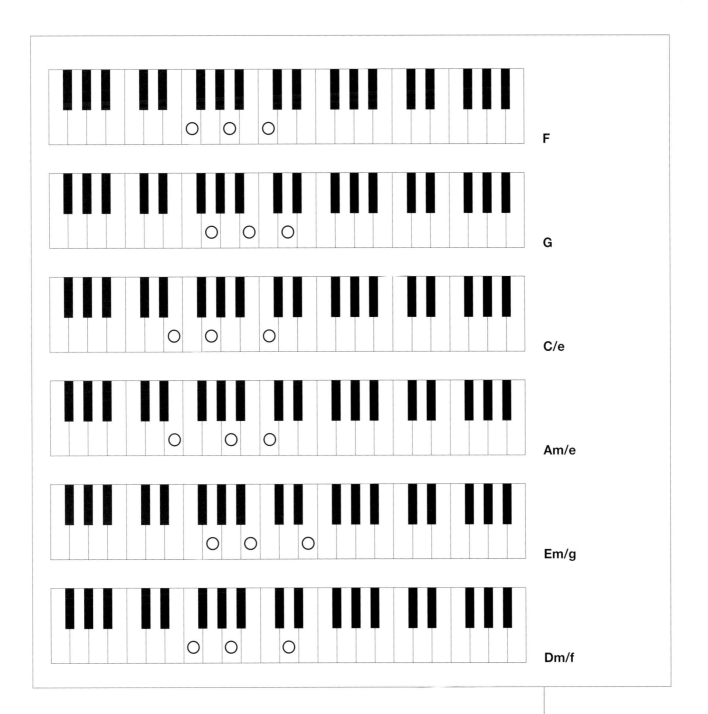

F

G

C/e

Am/e

Em/g

Dm/f

TECHNIQUE 46   # THE ♭VII MUSCLES IN

So far our song examples have confined themselves to chords I to VI, plus their inversions, making a total of 18 chords – or to use a painting metaphor, six colours with three shades of each. But you can get even more chords with which to paint your music.

Chords I to VI are derived from the major scale. But if some of the notes of the scale were to be reduced by a semitone, as often happens in blues and blues-influenced music, then there is a way of making new chords. Three in particular are part of every songwriter's palette and are crucial to rock and soul music. To find out about the first of these means solving the mystery of why VII, one of the original seven chords, was put aside. Here are the seven chords of C:

I	II	III	IV	V	VI	VII
C	D	Em	F	G	Am	Bdim

If a scale has seven notes and a chord may be constructed on each, why have we only worked with six chords? Chord VII has been omitted in all the musical keys in which the CD tracks are written. This is because it is neither major nor minor, but falls into a third category – the diminished chord. The theoretical reason for this is not important for our purposes. Suffice to say that the straight diminished chord is almost never used in modern pop or rock songs. It is rather unsettling, discordant, and hard to sing over.

There is another approach to the problem of chord VII, which is more useful for songwriting. It's this simple formula: take the 7th degree of a major scale, lower (flat) it by a semitone, and treat that note as the root of a major chord. This makes a chord numbered ♭VII, the '♭' indicating that it is built on a lowered (flatted) degree of the scale. If done in the keys above, this is the result:

	I	VII	=	♭VII
Key of C		Bdim	=	B♭
Key of G		F♯dim	=	F
Key of D		C♯dim	=	C
Key of A		G♯dim	=	G

The ♭VII chord is everywhere in the harmony of popular music, regardless of genre. It has a particular relation to blues music, which shaped rock'n'roll and then rock, as well as soul, and also European folk-music.

The ♭VII has the following attributes:
• It brings a sense of the unexpected.
• It can 'toughen' up a chord sequence.
• Can be used in a three-chord trick or a three-chord turnaround.
• Can be used in a four-chord turnaround.

118

• Its first inversion shares the same bass note as chord II, so ♭VII's first inversion could replace II.
• Its second inversion shares the same bass note as chord IV.

The ♭VII chord can be approached comfortably from chord I, II, IV, or VI; less so from III and V.

CD Track 46 has an example with ♭VII in G major. Bars 7-8 is one of the classic 1960s' uses of the ♭VII chord as an approach chord to V when V goes to I. The V-I change at the end of a section or phrase is called a 'perfect cadence'. Listen for the touch of surprise that ♭VII brings, and an equal (and sometimes touching) surprise when it finds its way to chord V. To bring out the emotional potential of the ♭VII-V change, save it for the end of a section and don't repeat it very much. Repetition will undo this particular magic:

CD TRACK 46

CD TRACK 46 **The ♭VII chord in G major**

I				V				bVII				I				
G	\	\	\	|D/f♯	\	\	\	|F	\	\	\	|G	\	\	\	:||

I				IV				bVII				V				
G	\	\	\	|C/e	\	\	\	|F	\	\	\	|D/f♯	\	\	\	|

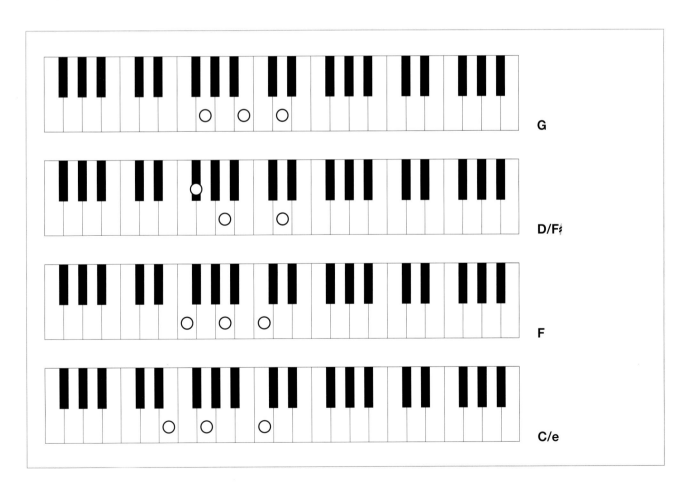

G

D/F♯

F

C/e

119

TECHNIQUE 47

SO THIS ♭VII WENT INTO A 12-BAR...

The ♭VII is naturally at home in any blues or blues-influenced context. Track 47 shows a way of using it to give extra muscle and movement to a 12-bar blues sequence:

CD TRACK 47 bVII 12-bar in G

I				I		♭VII		I				I		♭VII	
G	\	\	\	G	\	F	\	G	\	\	\	G	\	F	\

IV				IV				I				I		♭VII	
C/e	\	\	\	C/e	\	\	\	G	\	\	\	G	\	F	\

V				V		♭VII		I				I		V	
D/f♯	\	\	\	D/f♯	\	F	\	G	\	\	\	G	\	D	\

The ♭VII chord can be used in three and four-chord turnarounds as laid out earlier. There is no problem with I-♭VII-V replacing I-IV-V, but there is a risk of key ambiguity with I-IV-♭VII.

♭VII AND A CAUTION

When a song only has chords drawn from I to VI, there is little doubt about its key. As the range of harmonic colour increases because of new chords there is a chance of harmonic ambiguity. The ♭VII chord is the first we have dealt with that brings that risk. There are two reasons for this:

- the omission of chord V makes I-IV-♭VII sound like it could be in a different key. The progression C-B♭-F (I-♭VII-IV) in C major could be heard as V-IV-I in F major.
- ♭VII itself is constructed on a scale degree which is not supposed to be in the proper major scale.

Why does this matter? A songwriter needs to have a grip on what key a song is supposed to be in, in order to be able to create certain pleasing effects. Ambiguity is fine if it suits your musical and lyrical purpose, but otherwise it may cause a song to feel as though it doesn't hang together.

CD TRACK
47

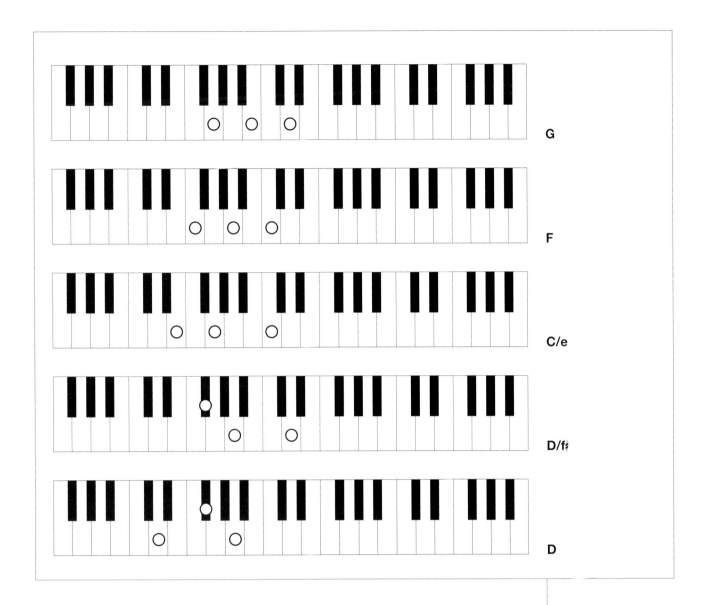

G

F

C/e

D/f♯

D

CD TRACK
47

TECHNIQUE 49   # BETWEEN FIVE CHORDS AND A HARD PLACE

There is a well-established formula for writing hard rock songs with a Stones/Bad Company/Black Crowes feel which involves the ♭III and ♭VI chords.

Step 1. Choose a key – let's take A major. Here are the seven chords:

I	II	III	IV	V	VI	VII
A	Bm	C♯m	D	E	F♯m	G♯dim.

Step 2. Bring in the ♭VII to replace the diminished VII:

I	II	III	IV	V	VI	♭VII
A	Bm	C♯m	D	E	F♯m	G

Step 3. Replace the three minor chords – II, III and VI – with ♭III and ♭VI:

I	♭III	IV	V	♭VI	♭VII
A	C	D	E	F	G

We now have six chords, all major. These can be put together in the usual ways to get a rock progression. The normal rules apply about not using them all at once, creating turnarounds from them, etc. The emphasis will still fall on chords I, IV and V, so think of ♭III, ♭VI and ♭VII as secondary to them. These chords are effective if played as fifths: A5, C5, D5, E5, F5 and G5 (see Section 8 for information about chord types).

CD TRACK 49 **Hard rock song in A major**

Intro

I				I		♭VII		I				I		♭VII	
A/e	\	\	\	A/e	\	G/d	\	A/e	\	\	\	A/e	\	G/d	\

Verse

I		♭III		♭VII		♭III		I		♭III		♭VII		I	
‖: A/e	\	C/e	\	G/d	\	C/e	\	A/e	\	C/e	\	G/d	\	A/e	\ :‖

♭VI				♭VI				IV				IV			
F	\	\	\	F	\	\	\	D/f♯	\	\	\	D/f♯	\	\	\

♭VI				♭VI				V				V		♭VII	
F	\	\	\	F	\	\	\	E/g♯	\	\	\	E/g♯	\	G	\

Note:
- The varying rate of chord change.
- The intro uses only two chords.
- The verse divides into two: the first half is a riff-type figure where bar 2 and 4 are alternate endings. The second half of the verse brings in the ♭VI chord. Notice how the ♭VII in bar 16 makes a tougher approach to the presumed chord I that would come in bar 1 of the chorus (not given) than going from chord V.

CD TRACK
49

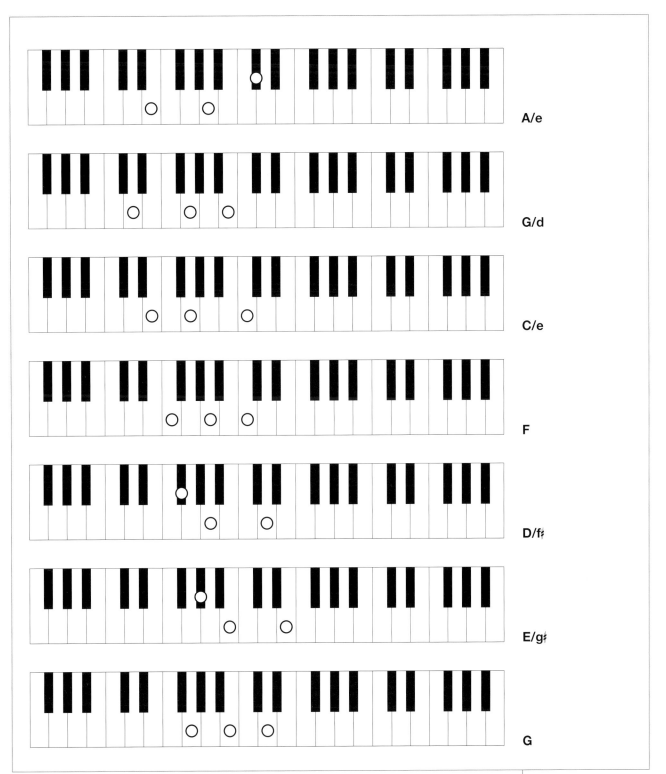

A/e

G/d

C/e

F

D/f♯

E/g♯

G

CD TRACK
49

| TECHNIQUE 50 | # REVERSE POLARITY – PLAYING WITH MAJORS AND MINORS |

Through Sections 3-6 the range of chords available for your songs has gradually increased. You started with the three major chords of a key I, IV and V. To these you've added the three minors of the key – II, III and VI – making six. A flatted chord VII was created, and then two further lowered-degree chords, the ♭III and ♭VI. This gives you a resource of nine chords in a single major key. If the first and second inversions of all these chords are added, you have a total of 27 chords to use in whatever major key you choose.

Are you ready for more? We can further increase the available root chords from 9 to 13 with a technique I call 'reverse polarity'. 'Polarity' in this context means whether a chord is major or minor. 'Reverse polarity' means changing a chord from major to minor, or minor to major. It describes what happens when a chord is reversed from what it would *normally* be in the key. Reverse polarity can apply to chords II, III, IV and VI. Chords II, III and VI turn from minor to major; chord IV turns from major to minor.

Here are the changes in two of the musical keys already used for our musical examples:

C major

I	II	III	IV	V	VI	VII
C	Dm	Em	F	G	Am	Bdim
	D	E	Fm		A	

G major

I	II	III	IV	V	VI	VII
G	Am	Bm	C	D	Em	F♯dim
	A	B	Cm		E	

The musical effect of putting one of these 'reverse-polarity' chords into a song is one of surprise. A reverse-polarity chord creates the impression that the music is about to change musical key, followed by a second surprise when it doesn't. They are like doors opened halfway, so you glance into the room, but closed before you can enter.

We are so accustomed to hearing music in major keys that unconsciously our ear expects chords II, III and VI to be minor, and IV to be major. When this is altered we register the fact even if we know no music theory. Songwriters experimenting intuitively with chords feel this surprise for themselves when they put one of these chords into a progression. They like the effect, and so write a song with it.

CAUTION ABOUT 'REVERSE-POLARITY' CHORDS

Even more than the ♭III and the ♭VI, these four chords must not be thought of as being of the same level of importance as chords I through to VI. Use them sparingly, usually no more than two in a single section of a song, because they can disrupt the sense of key, create exotic changes in the melody line, and trip up soloists in an instrumental passage. This is because they always contain at least one note foreign to the scale of the key.

Reverse-polarity chords are handy for contrasting one section of a song with another. A common weakness of songs is that the bridge is often less interesting than either the verse or chorus. A reverse-polarity chord can really give the bridge a lift.

Reverse polarity can't really be applied to chords I, V, and VII without pushing the music out of the home key. Chords VII, V and I severely disrupt the stability of the home key if they are changed in this manner. Reversing chord I is tantamount to a key change from the tonic major to tonic minor. If chord V is subjected to reverse polarity it will tend to imply a key change down a 5th. Chord VII cannot be subjected to 'reverse polarity' because it is diminished.

CD TRACK
50

127

CD TRACK

50

THE REVERSE-POLARITY TURNAROUND

The quickest way to get a feeling for what reverse polarity can do is to take the primary turnarounds described in Section 5 and subject them to reverse polarity, creating the sequences I-II^-IV-V, I-III^-IV-V, and I-VI^-IV-V. (In this book the sign ^ after a Roman numeral indicates a reverse-polarity chord). Notice that these sequences are entirely major. They have a breezy freedom reminiscent of classic 1960s pop.

To be proper turnarounds, each of these four-bar ideas ought to be repeated; to save time and space, CD Track 50 features each once only.

CD TRACK 50 Reverse-polarity turnarounds in C major

I				II^				IV				V			
C/e	\	\	\	D/f♯	\	\	\	F	\	\	\	G	\	\	\

I				III^				IV				V			
C/e	\	\	\	E	\	\	\	F	\	\	\	G	\	\	\

I				VI^				IV				V			
C/e	\	\	\	A/e	\	\	\	F	\	\	\	G	\	\	\

128

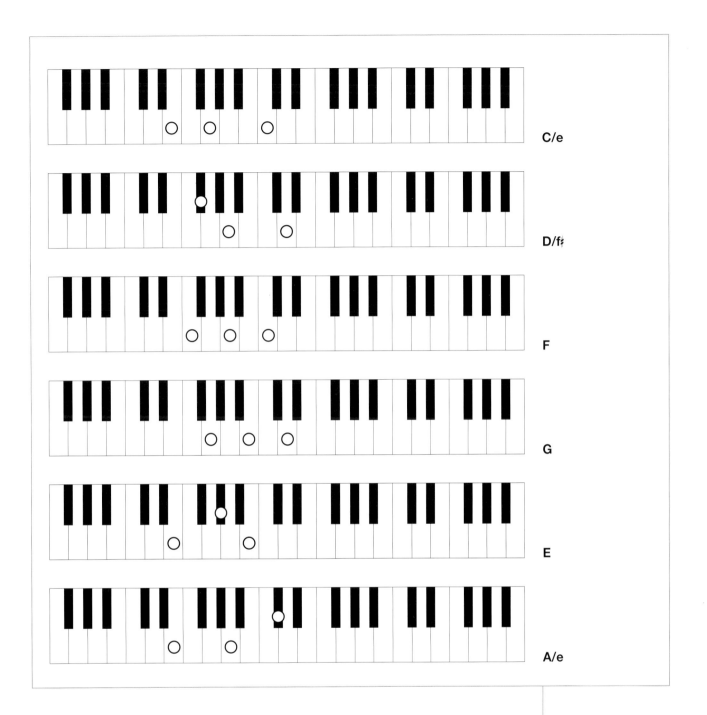

C/e

D/f♯

F

G

E

A/e

CD TRACK
50

| TECHNIQUE 51 | THE 'SLUSH-MAKER' |

The turnarounds in Track 50 omit one reverse polarity chord, IV as a minor. I call this chord the 'slush-maker'. Play a I-IV (C-F) change, then the sequence in CD Track 51, and you'll hear why.

The IVm chord has an instantly recognisable tragic-but-sweet gloom about it that has made it popular in romantic ballads and MOR songwriting. If you wish to darken the emotion of a song in an appealing way, reach for IVm. It is pure melodrama. In the right context – such as a James Bond theme song – (think of 'You Only Live Twice') it can be simultaneously erotic, grandiose and forlorn. Think of the darkest hour just before dawn. Think of a prisoner's last meal turning out to be a huge slice of cheesecake. Think of Bryan Adams singing "I'd die for you" in 'Everything I Do'. That's the IVm for you. The art of using IVm often lies in the choice of approach chord. A common note is helpful, so, for example, the Dm in bar 7 here has an F in it, which makes a good preparation for the Fm chord.

CD TRACK 51 IVm verse in C

I				IVm				I				IVm			
C	\	\	\	Fm/c	\	\	\	C	\	\	\	Fm/c	\	\	\

I				IV				II				IVm		V		I
‖: C	\	\	\	F	\	\	\	Dm	\	\	\	Fm/c	\	G/b	\	:‖ C ‖

CD TRACK

51

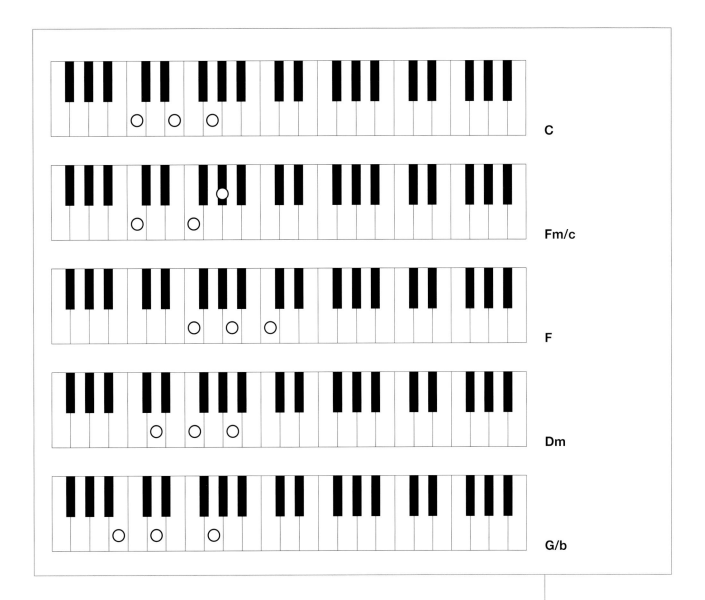

C

Fm/c

F

Dm

G/b

CD TRACK
51

TECHNIQUE 52	# LOWERED-DEGREE CHORDS WITH SLUSH

A IVm chord can combine with the three flat-degree chords ♭III, ♭VI and ♭VII – though there is a risk of harmonic instability. In practical terms (as opposed to theory), harmonic instability means that an audience may not be able to relate to the emotion of the song. These are also unusual-sounding progressions. Note that in CD Track 52, the Cm7 in bar 7 is created by leaving the E♭ RH triad from the previous bar, so there is no separate chord diagram for Cm7. It's the C in the bass guitar that turns it into Cm7 (E♭ = E♭-G-B♭, and Cm7 = C-E♭-G-B♭).

CD TRACK 52 IVm and ♭III in G

I				♭III				IVm				V			
G/d	\	\	\	B♭/d	\	\	\	Cm/e♭	\	\	\	D	\	\	\

I				♭VI				IVm				V			
G/d	\	\	\	E♭	\	\	\	Cm7	\	\	\	D	\	\	\

I				♭VII				IVm				V			
G/d	\	\	\	F/c	\	\	\	Cm	\	\	\	D	\	\	\

Normally, it wouldn't be a good idea to use three different lowered-degree chords in a single song section. It would be better to use one and repeat the line in which it occurs, so the listener can appreciate its unusual flavour. In CD Track 52 the three 'flat' degree chords (B♭/d, E♭, and F/c) sound acceptable because they happen in the second bar of each four-bar phrase, and the rest of the phrases are very similar to each other. They all start with I, end on V, and have IVm in the third bar. The I and V chords stop the sense of key from getting blurred too much. Any one of these four-bar phrases could be repeated and thus turned into a turnaround.

CD TRACK
52

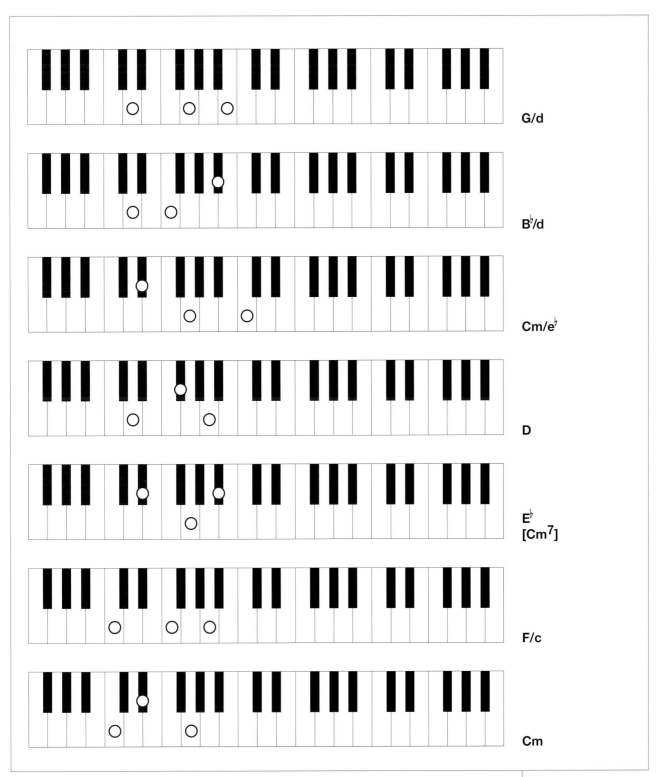

G/d

B♭/d

Cm/e♭

D

E♭
[Cm⁷]

F/c

Cm

CD TRACK
52

SECTION 7
Songs of rain– writing in a minor key

"I was in this really dark room in Liverpool, and there was a piano so old and out of tune... I really wanted to try and work out the George Harrison song 'Isn't It A Pity', but I couldn't. Then this song came out at once. I said, 'Can you turn on the recorder?' The first time I sung it is what's out there."

Chris Martin, Coldplay (about writing 'The Scientist')

So far we've restricted ourselves to writing sequences in a major key. But of course there is such a thing as a minor key, built on a different scale, and in which chord I is a minor chord. You might decide to compose in a minor key if a song's lyric is about loss or sadness, or perhaps just to strike a more contemplative, or even bitter mood. So what is the difference between a major key and a minor one?

MINOR KEY OPTION 1: MODAL MINOR

There is only one sequence of intervals that makes a major scale pattern (2-2-1-2-2-2-1), but there are several variations of minor scale, and each variation results in alternative sets of chords. We don't need to delve into the scales themselves, but instead let's go straight to a list of songwriting chords for the minor key. As with major and minor *chords*, so every major *key* has a relative minor that shares the same chords. Compare the chords for C major with that of its relative minor, A minor:

C major

I	II	III	IV	V	VI	VII
C	Dm	Em	F	G	Am	Bdim

A minor

I	II	III	IV	V	VI	VII
Am	Bdim	C	Dm	Em	F	G

We have the same set of chords, but they're in a different order. For convenience we can call this version of A minor, 'modal' A minor. There are seven scales called modes which historically pre-date the modern system of keys. One of them became the major scale. Another, the aeolian mode, is also known as the 'natural minor' scale.

That old diminished problem

Another consequence of A minor and C major sharing the same chords is that we still have that problematic diminished chord on B. Instead of being chord VII, it's now chord II – which in some ways is more awkward. So, just as with VII in the major key, the diminished chord II of the minor key tends not to be used. If the awkward diminished chord is discarded, the six chords a songwriter uses in a 'modal' minor are I, III, IV, Vm, VI and VII. These are the 'modal' minor key equivalents to the six covered for the major key.

MINOR KEY OPTION 2: THE 'CLASSICAL' MINOR KEY

There is a variation of the minor scale which does make the minor key immediately distinguishable from its relative major. This second type of minor key was used in baroque, classical and romantic music. It requires one simple change: chord V is turned into a major chord, so in the key of Am the note G♯ is available to the singer or soloist, especially over this chord. (Note that the III and the VII remain C and G, because they're more useable here.) Here is the full list of chords for the classical minor in A:

I	III	IV	V	VI	VII
Am	C	Dm	E	F	G

Throughout this book, V in a minor key is assumed to be a major chord, in keeping with the classical minor key. The 'modal' minor chord V has an 'm' after it to indicate reverse polarity, like IVm in the major key. VII is always assumed to be a major chord *a tone* below the key-note, and so is not written as ♭VII.

Every time a chord sequence uses the change V-I (E-Am) the 'classical' minor key's identity is underlined. There is no confusion with the relative major, as there can be with the chord change Em-Am (or Bm-Em in E minor), where Vm-I in the minor can be confused with III-VI in the relative major. It is possible to use both forms of chord V in the same minor key song, but better if they are kept in separate sections (it has a kind of muddying effect, as well as causing potential problems for a vocalist or lead guitarist).

TECHNIQUE 53

THREE-CHORD RAIN

Remember that a primary three-chord trick uses I, IV and V. The minor-key equivalent of a three-chord trick in A minor would have the chords for Am, Dm and Em. In Track 53 you can hear both the modal and classical minor forms:

CD TRACK 53 Modal and classical minor three-chord trick

I	IV	Vm	IV
Am \ \ \	Dm/a \ \ \	Em/b \ \ \	Dm/a \ \ \ :‖

I	IV	V	IV
‖: Am \ \ \	Dm/a \ \ \	E/g♯ \ \ \	Dm/f \ \ \ :‖

CD TRACK
53

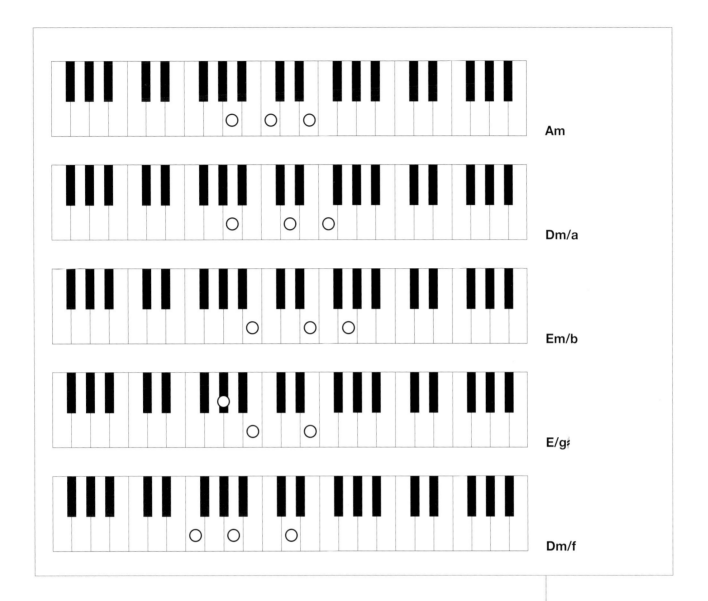

Am

Dm/a

Em/b

E/g♯

Dm/f

TECHNIQUE 54

RAIN IN A LATIN QUARTER

MINOR KEY OPTION 3: THE DORIAN MINOR

There is one further harmonic option for the songwriter and that's to reverse the polarity of chord IV from minor to major:

I	III	IV^	Vm	VI	VII
Am	C	D	Em	F	G

This harmony is derived from a scale called the dorian mode. The chord change Am to D (rather than Dm) is often heard in Latin-American songs. It's the quintessential Santana groove, and is also often heard in Pink Floyd's music, for instance on songs like 'The Great Gig In The Sky'. There is no risk of confusion with the relative major key, as there is with the 'modal' minor, because this chord change will not occur in that key (in C major chord II is Dm, not D), but possible harmonic ambiguity with the major key one tone below the minor you're composing in. Song sections might still sound OK in isolation, but songwriters can come unstuck when joining different sections together. Compare these:

A minor (Dorian)

I	III	IV^	Vm	VI	VII
Am	C	D	Em	F	G

G major

I	II	III	IV	V	VI	♭VII
G	Am	Bm	C	D	Em	F

In this version of A minor, I-IV^ happens to be the same chords as II-V in G major. This effect can be offset if the major form of chord V (here E) is used in the minor key, since it doesn't occur in this major key. Track 54 has IV^ with the modal minor Vm and the classical minor V.

CD TRACK 54 IV^ in a minor key

I		IV^		V		IV^		I		IV		V		IV^	
Am	\	D/f♯	\	‖Em/g	\	D/f♯	\	‖Am	\	D/f♯	\	‖E/g♯	\	D/f♯	\ :‖

The Moody Blues' classic 'Nights In White Satin' is a good example of a minor key song which brings in the IV^ chord (A in E minor) to devastating effect on the first use of the word 'love' in the phrase "'cause I love you". The song also uses the less common ♭II chord (F in E minor) in its verse at the end of each of the two main phrases.

CD TRACK

54

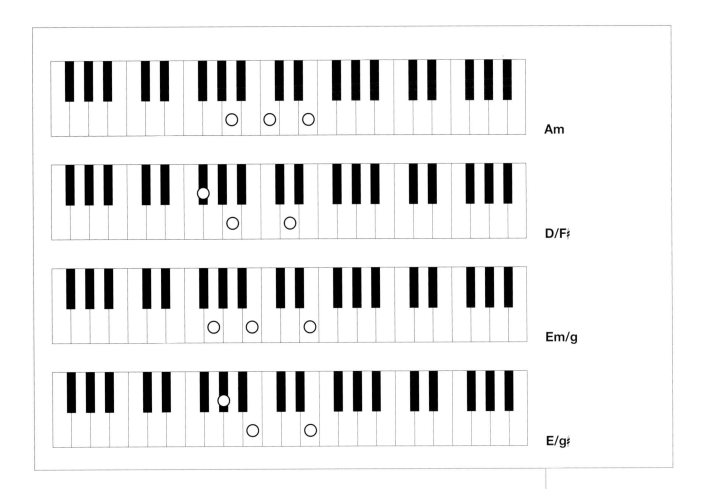

Am

D/F♯

Em/g

E/g♯

TECHNIQUE 55

THE FOUR-CHORD MINOR SONG

I took the options already mentioned for the modal, classical and dorian versions of the minor key and combined them into this 'composite minor' that provides eight chords to choose from:

MINOR KEY OPTION 4: A SONGWRITER'S COMPOSITE MINOR KEY

I	III	IV	(IV^)	V	(Vm)	VI	VII
Am	C	Dm	(D)	E	(Em)	F	G

To write a four-chord minor song, add one of chords III, VI and VII to I, IV (or IV^) and V (or Vm). A four-chord song in a minor key can omit chord V, but this can weaken the impression of the minor key.

The principle of 'keeping your powder dry' now applies in reverse: it's the major chords that are held in reserve. For the strongest minor feel use minor forms of IV and V – Am, Dm, Em – and then choose one of III, VI or VII (C, F or G) but hold it back until a point in the song where you want the music to lift away from the sad effect of the minor chords. That way the major chord can act like a ray of sun lighting up the gloom. The usual rules of chord substitution apply – the chords remained paired as before. Each minor chord has its relative major. Notice in CD Track 55 that the bridge section is entirely made up of true inversions.

CD TRACK 55 **Eight-bar verse in A minor**

I				IV				I				IV			
Am	\	\	\	Dm/a	\	\	\	Am	\	\	\	Dm/a	\	\	\

I				IV				Vm				V		IV	
Am	\	\	\	Dm/a	\	\	\	Em/g	\	\	\	Em/g	\	Dm/a	\

Chorus

I		IV		Vm		iV		I		IV		Vm		iV	
Am	\	F/a	\	Em/b	\	E/G♯	\	Am	\	F/a	\	Em/b	\	E/G♯	\

Bridge

iVI				iiVII				iiVI				iiVII			
‖: F/A	\	\	\	G/D	\	\	\	F/C	\	\	\	G/D	\	\	:‖

CD TRACK
55

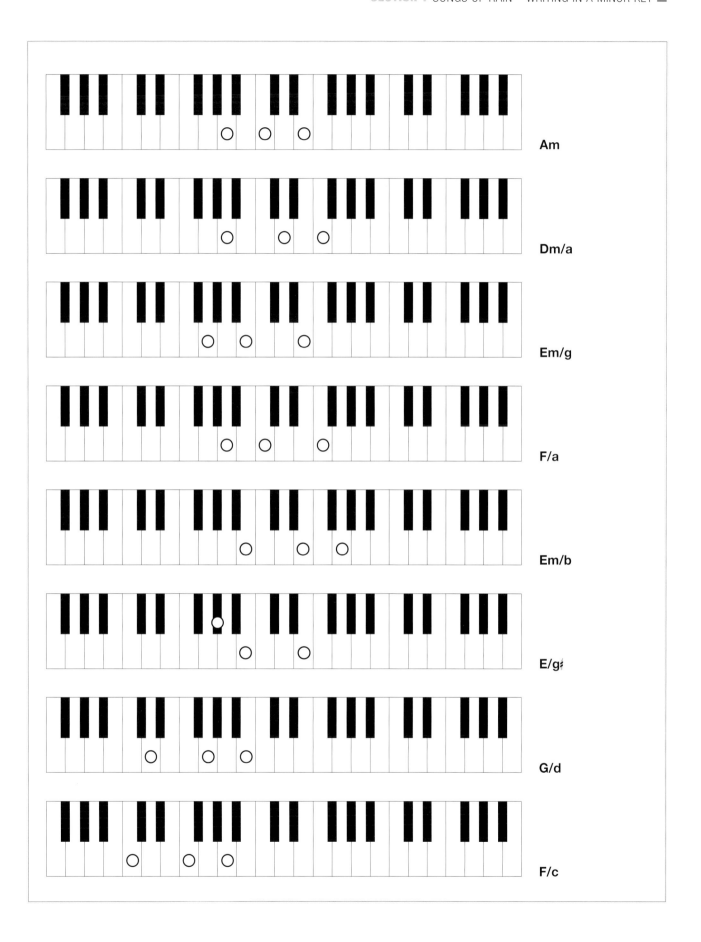

Am

Dm/a

Em/g

F/a

Em/b

E/g♯

G/d

F/c

TECHNIQUE 56

WHEN THE RAIN HIT THE BLUES

The 12-bar structure can generate a minor-key blues. In CD Track 56 the change from Vm to V is introduced in bar 10, not only to achieve harmonic variety but also to change the rate of chord movement. To make things more interesting, this 12-bar has bars 11-12 repeated, so it's actually 14 bars in total, and in those two bars the rate of chord change increases to a chord every two beats, giving more urgency. The Am/C has no chord diagram because the bass guitar supplies the C note – the piano RH just carries on with the root Am shape.

CD TRACK 56 **12-bar variation in E minor**

I				IV				I				iI			
Em	\	\	\	Am/e	\	\	\	Em	\	\	\	Em/G	\	\	\

IV				IV		iIV		I				I			
Am	\	\	\	Am	\	Am/C	\	Em/g	\	\	\	Em	\	\	\

Vm				Vm		V		I		III		IV		iiV	
Bm/d	\	\	\	Bm/d	\	B/d♯	\	:Em	\	G/d	\	Am/e	\	B/F♯	\ :‖

Notice the 'swing' rhythm of CD Track 56. This is a product of the 12/8 time signature. There are still four beats in a bar but each divides into three rather than two as in 4/4. As a result the track has the distinctive *One…two…three…, One…two…three…* of 12/8. This is a popular rhythm for slow blues songs and instrumentals.

As for the variation to the 12-bar structure, if you are ever stuck for an idea for a verse sequence, try playing a 12-bar and then changing a chord or lengthening part of it.

CD TRACK

56

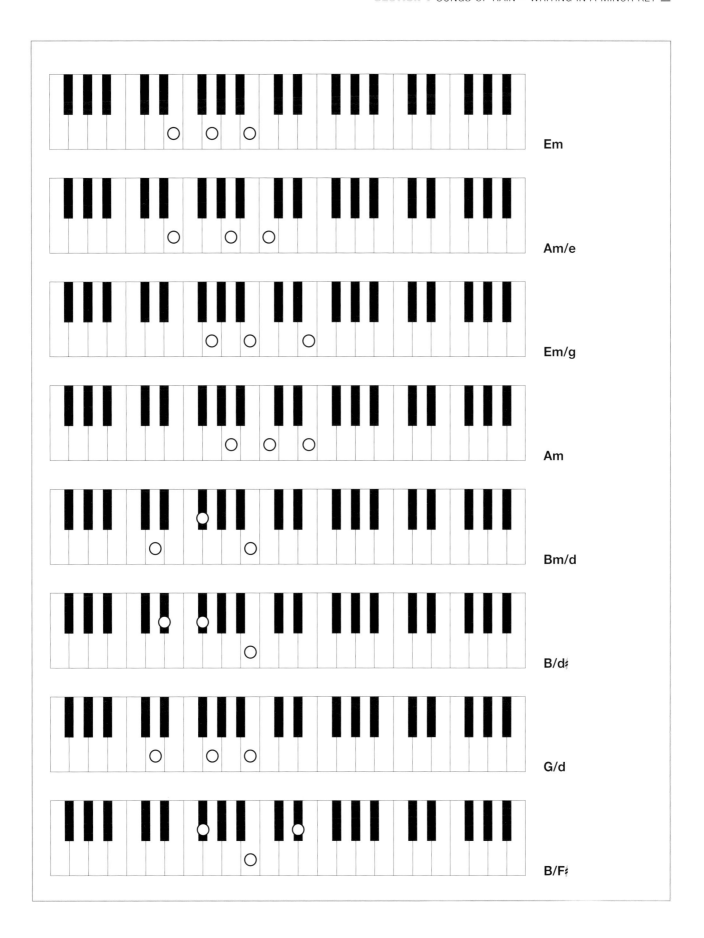

Em

Am/e

Em/g

Am

Bm/d

B/d♯

G/d

B/F♯

TECHNIQUE 58 COMMON MINOR-KEY PROGRESSIONS (2)

The bassline can move down stepwise (in tones or semitones) by the use of inversions. These colour the sequence, making it happy or sad depending on whether a major or minor inversion is replacing a root major, or a root minor.

CD TRACK 58 Inversions on an A-G-F-E bassline

I				iiIII				VI				V			
Am	\	\	\	C/G	\	\	\	F	\	\	\	E/g♯	\	\	\

I				iVm				VI				Vm			
Am	\	\	\	Em/G	\	\	\	F	\	\	\	Em	\	\	\

I				iVm				iIV				iIII			
Am	\	\	\	Em/G	\	\	\	Dm/F	\	\	\	C/E	\	\	\

Whether you use one of these four-bar phrases in a song or alternate two of them for contrast is a matter of taste. They are popular on the guitar in this key of A minor, and have been frequently used by folk-influenced singer-songwriters. The advantage of the keyboard over the guitar is that you can play the same sequences in a variety of keys. This opens up the possibility of creating an unexpected musical contrast by dropping out of the minor key into a major one for another section – perhaps with keys that would be hard to play on the guitar.

CD TRACK

58

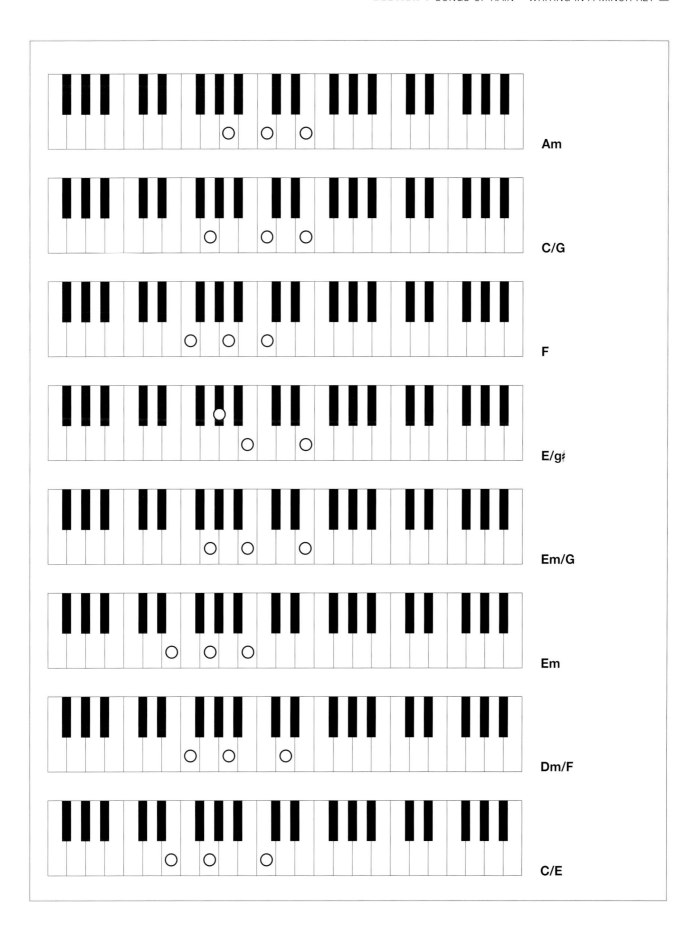

TECHNIQUE 59 | COMMON MINOR PROGRESSIONS (3)

Now the descending bassline starts to include more movement in semitones. This example has the basslines A-G-F♯-E and A-G-F♯-F-E. The F♯ bass note has to be harmonised as a first inversion because a root F♯ chord would be wildly out of key and unsettling (so if you want unsettling try an F♯m or F♯ chord). Added interest is given to bars 8 and 12 because there are two chords to finish each descent instead of one.

Minor progressions on a bassline with more semitones

I				VII				iIV^				V			
Am	\	\	\	G	\	\	\	D/F♯	\	\	\	E	\	\	\

I				iiIII				iIV^				VI		Vm	
Am	\	\	\	C/G	\	\	\	D/F♯	\	\	\	F		Em	\

I				iVm				iIV^				iIV		V	
Am	\	\	\	Em/G	\	\	\	D/F♯	\	\	\	Dm/F	\	E	\

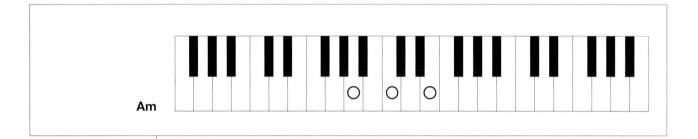

Am

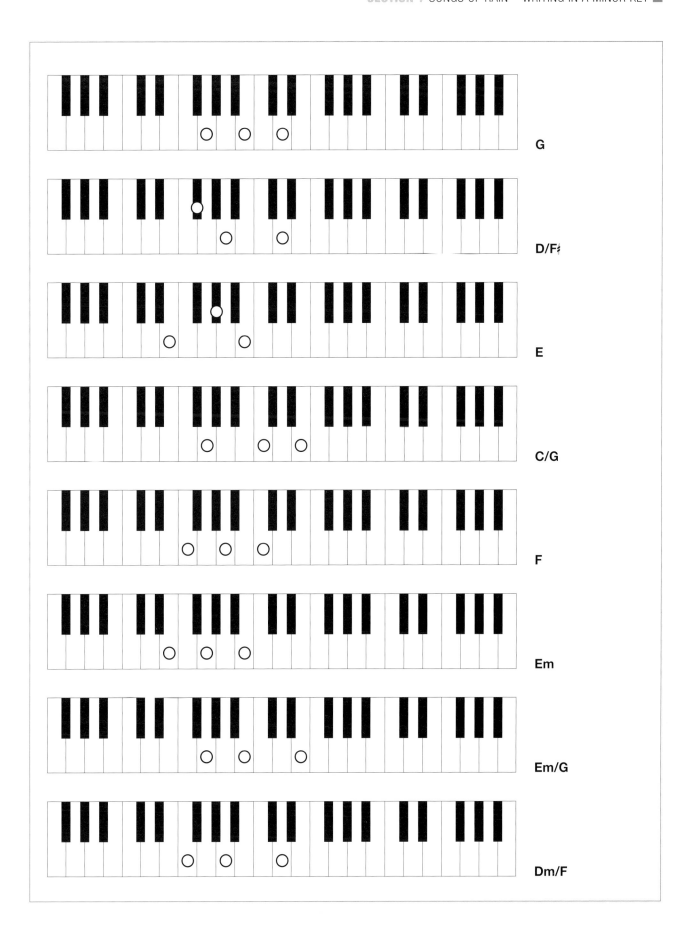

G

D/F#

E

C/G

F

Em

Em/G

Dm/F

| TECHNIQUE 60 | COMMON MINOR PROGRESSIONS (4) |

The last stage in developing these ideas is to introduce a semitone bass note between A and G, namely G♯. This means that the bassline is now moving in semitones all the way from A down to E, and we have chords to harmonise every note. The rate of chord change is now every two beats. Going down this bassline one chord to a bar would make for a long sequence, so the chords are now changing at the rate of every two beats.

CD TRACK 60 A complete semitone descending bassline, A-D

I		iV		VII		iIV ^		VI		V		IV		iiVII	
Am	\	E/G♯	\	G	\	D/F♯	\	F	\	E	\	Dm	\	G/d	\

I		iV		iiIII		iIV ^		iIV		V		IV		I	
Am	\	E/G♯	\	C/G	\	D/F♯	\	Dm/F	\	E	\	Dm	\	Am/c	\

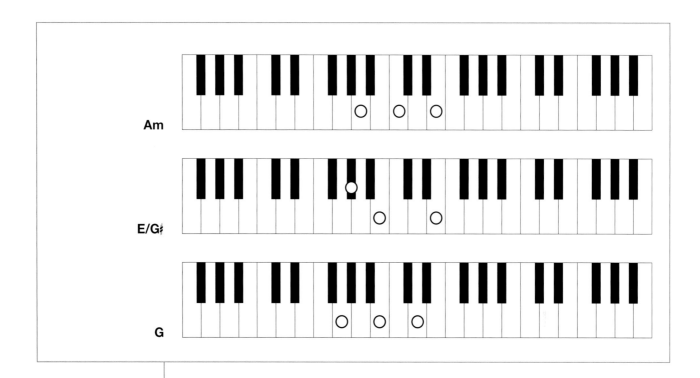

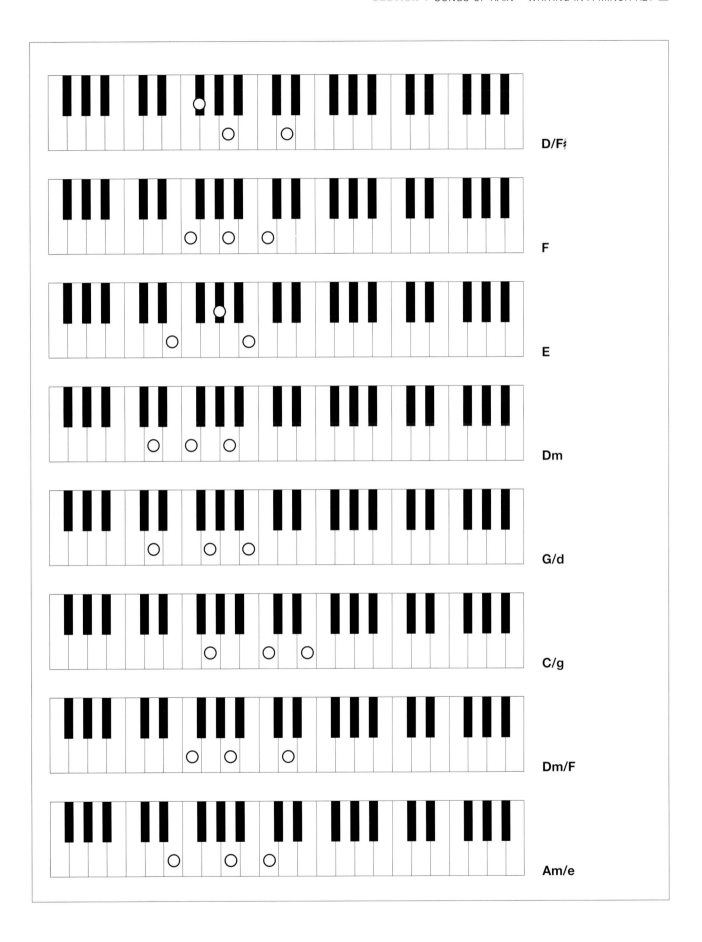

D/F♯

F

E

Dm

G/d

C/g

Dm/F

Am/e

TECHNIQUE 61 'BIG THREE' TURNAROUNDS IN THE WET

Many of the progressions given in this section could be adapted and edited into minor key turnarounds. The 'big three' turnarounds in a minor key are I-III-IV-V, I-VI-IV-V, and I-VII-IV-V, along with their 'modal' equivalents in which IV is a major or V is a minor.

The final example in this section has the primary turnarounds in the key of E minor:

Primary turnarounds in E minor

I				III				IV				V			
Em	\	\	\	G	\	\	\	Am	\	\	\	B/f♯	\	\	\

I				VI				IV				V			
Em	\	\	\	C/e	\	\	\	Am/e	\	\	\	B/f♯	\	\	\

I				VII				IV				Vm			
Em	\	\	\	D/f♯	\	\	\	Am	\	\	\	Bm/f♯	\	\	\

Minor chord turnarounds are not as common as major key turnarounds. One famous song you may know which has two minor chord turnarounds to make its verse is 'The Passenger' by Iggy Pop. Minor turnarounds can be made more poignant if their chord order is displaced so that they rise towards the key minor chord, as in the sequence F, G, Am, Em/G. The use of the first-inversion Em to harmonise the G bass note makes it contrast with the earlier G chord. You can hear this effect in a song like Kate Bush's 'Running Up That Hill' or Siouxsie & The Banshees' 'Overground' (a song also worth investigating for putting a minor key turnaround into 5/4).

CD TRACK

61

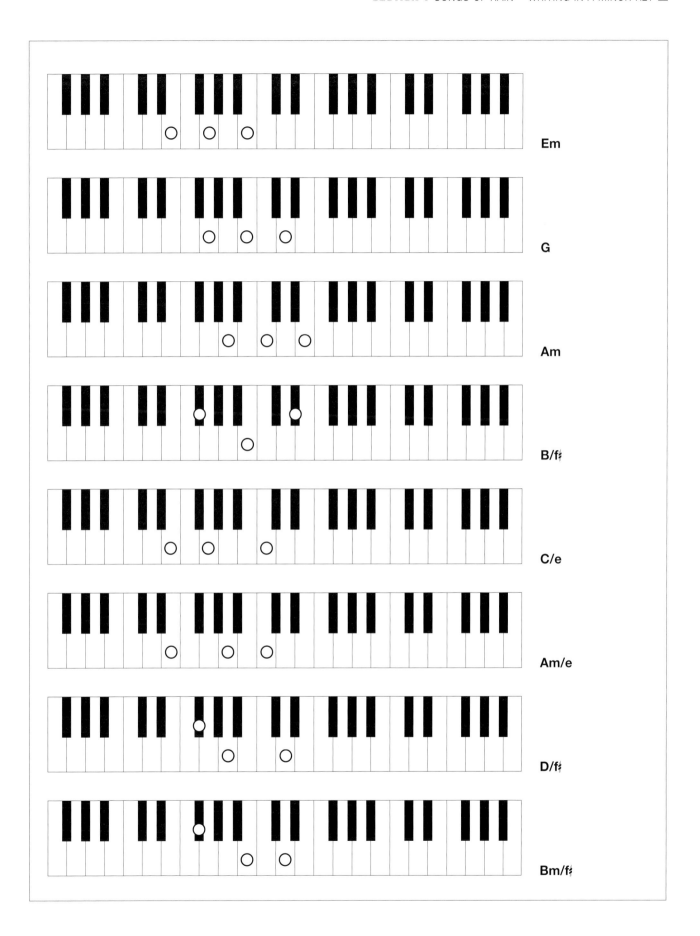

Em

G

Am

B/f♯

C/e

Am/e

D/f♯

Bm/f♯

Get that emotion – the chord colourbox

"On piano, keys have a personality and an atmosphere of their own ... Something does feel very romantic to me, and introspective in a way, about keys that have a lot of black notes. There's something tremendously exotic about G-flat or F-sharp. It's not bright. I get a visual impression of those keys. I think everybody does, whether they know it or not."

Van Dyke Parks

Up to now, *How To Write Songs On Keyboards* has deliberately confined itself basically to major and minor triads. But any major or minor chord can, by the addition of extra notes, turn into a sus2, sus4, 6th, 7th, 9th, 11th, 13th, or one of many other chord types. These do not have any direct relevance to the rules that govern the basic chords on which a songwriter draws, as set out in Sections 3-7, but let's survey some of the more popular chord types to see what use a songwriter can make of them.

HOW TO PLAY THE SHAPES IN SECTION 8

Some of these chords have four different notes in them. If you are not already a keyboard player, holding these chords using the right hand alone, as you did with the triads, is difficult. The way around the problem is to use both hands, with the root note of the chord transferred to your left hand, and the remaining notes held by the right. Alternatively, re-arrange the order of the notes so that the 1st and 5th of the chord are in your left hand and the remaining two notes in your right. The scale numbers are marked on the chord diagrams. If a chord has four different notes, the lowest note in the diagram will be played by your left hand.

In Section 8 you will see chord types described like this:

'Dominant 7th (C7) – formula 4+3+3'.

This gives you the correct name (eg 'dominant 7th'), the way the chord is usually written when C is the root (eg 'C7'), and, most importantly, the measurement of the three intervals that make it up, counted in semitones (each representing a white or black key) – in this case 4+3+3. If you memorise these numbers you will be able to construct the same category of chord on any note.

TECHNIQUE 62

HOW TO MAKE A CHORD PROGRESSION TOUGHER

THE DOMINANT 7TH (C7) – FORMULA 4+3+3

Other than straight majors and minors, the most common chord type is the dominant 7, written C7, G7, etc. This 7th is a major chord with a note added which is a tone *below* the root note. In traditional harmony only one of these can occur in a major key, and that's on the 5th note (the dominant) of the major scale – so in the key of C, the dominant 7 would be G7. If the notes of the scale are used to build a 7th chord, a dominant 7 chord will only occur on the 5th note. But as some popular music is based on blues harmony, the 'dominant' 7 chord can also be used on chord I and chord IV in their own rights. So for instance in the key of C major, you can play not just G7, but C7 and F7.

To play a dominant 7th on keyboards, hold the root note with your left hand, and let your right hand hold the piano key four semitones away, then three, then three again (4+3+3).

As with all the chords in this section, the dominant 7 adds interest if the music stays on a single chord for a number of bars. Adding the 7th to the chord for the final bar (or bars) suggests activity. This works particularly well if the next chord is IV or II (F or Dm in C) as the 7th will fall a semitone to a note in the next chord.

A progression of dominant 7s make for a tougher-sounding sequence than if these chords were straightforward root chords.

CD TRACK 62 Dominant 7 in G major

I				I				IV				I			
G	\	\	\	G7	\	\	\	C	\	\	\	G7	\	\	\

VII				♭VI				IV				V			
F	\	\	\	E♭7	\	\	\	C7	\	\	\	D7	\	\	\

The first six albums by The Beatles are full of songs which use the dominant 7 to toughen the chord progressions. One excellent example is 'You Can't Do That'.

CD TRACK
62

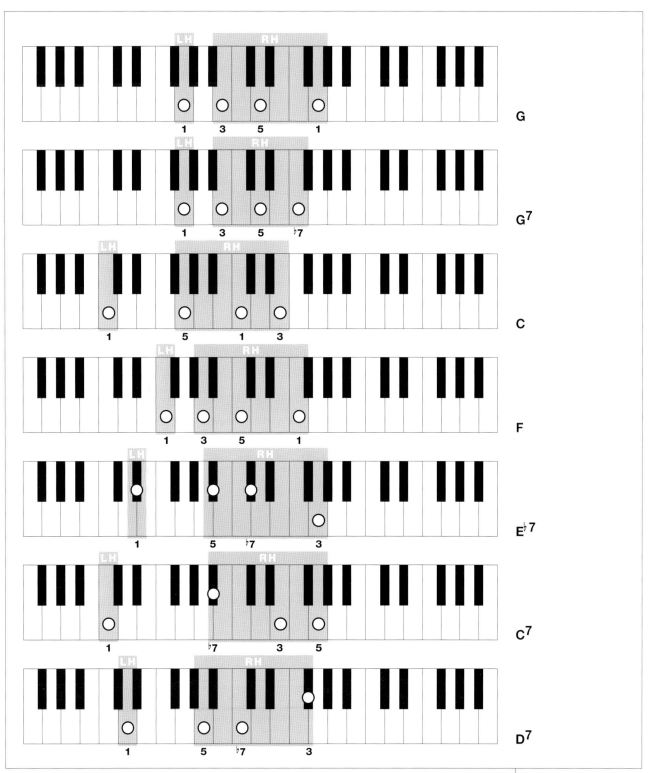

| TECHNIQUE 63 | # HOW TO MAKE A BLUES BLUESIER |

The classic use of the dominant 7 in rock is in a 12-bar blues, as the verse in CD Track 63 shows. This is in the key of E major, the most popular key for blues music, and shows how the dominant 7th is characteristically used in a 12-bar, especially where the same chord occupies more than one bar.

CD TRACK 63 *12-bar in E with dominant 7ths*

I				IV				I				I			
E	\	\	\	A	\	\	\	E	\	\	\	E7	\	\	\

IV				IV				I				I			
A	\	\	\	A7	\	\	\	E	\	\	\	E7	\	\	\

V				IV				I				I			
B7	\	\	\	A7	\	\	\	E	\	E7	\	B7	\	\	\

If you want a greater sense of movement within the chord progression you can add the dominant 7 to more of the bars so that they all resemble bar 11.

CD TRACK

63

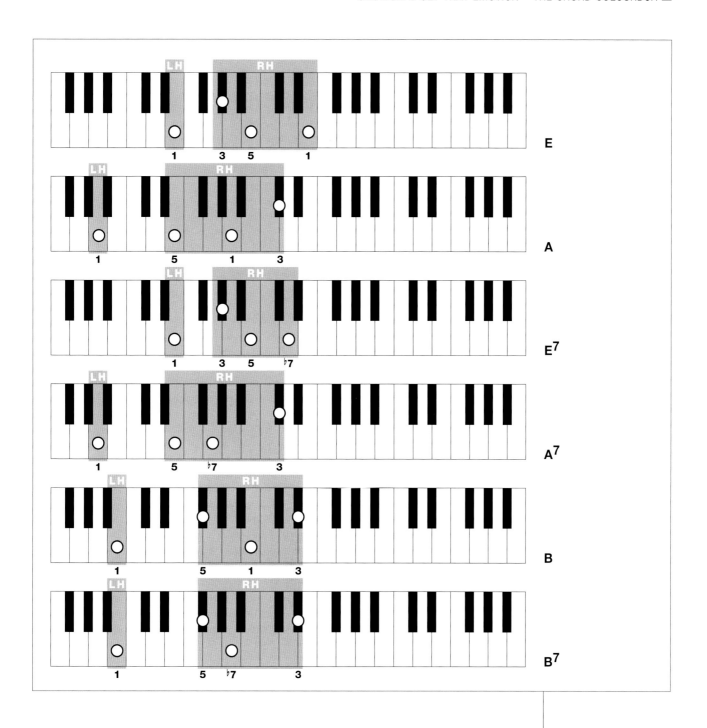

CD TRACK
63

TECHNIQUE 64

HOW TO MAKE CHORDS MORE ROMANTIC

THE MAJOR 7TH (Cmaj7) – FORMULA 4+3+4

There is a second type of 7th made from a major chord. In this one the extra note is only a *semitone* below the root note. It's written Cmaj7, Gmaj7, etc. In traditional harmony the major 7th occurs on chords I and IV in the major key.

The emotive nature of the major 7th lends itself to medium-to-slow tempi and more reflective songs. The major 7th will soften a chord sequence, and make a progression sound dreamier and romantic. Many a gentle ballad has sailed tearfully into the sunset or lazed in the sunshine with this famous change (as heard/seen in Track 64) between chord I and IV in their major 7th forms, and it makes a natural transition to its relative minor. This is a time-honoured method of using a major 7th to colour a basic change. The underlying movement is chord I-IV. By using the 7ths like this it's as if two chords have been made to sound like four.

CD TRACK 64 Major 7th verse for a song in G

I				IV				I				IV			
Gmaj7 \	\	\		Cmaj7 \	\	\		Gmaj7 \	\	\		Cmaj7 \	\	\	

I				VI				IV				II			
‖: G \		Gmaj7 \		Em \	\	\		C \		Cmaj7 \		Am \	\	\	:‖

CD TRACK
64

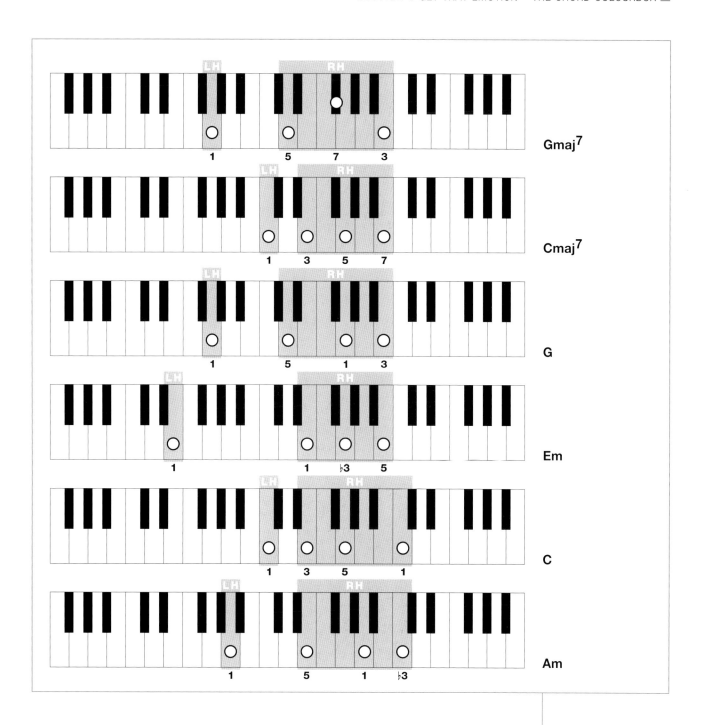

CD TRACK

64

161

TECHNIQUE 65   HOW TO MAKE CHORDS BLEND

By using the major 7th and the dominant 7th one after the other, a sense of movement is created within the same chord. This technique has great potential if you are writing a song with only three or four chords. In the key of G, the change of G to G7 to Gmaj7 has the basic chord staying the same but a single note (G-F♯-F) changes within it, descending in semitone steps. If this is done from chord I, the likeliest chord to follow is chord IV (the note F drops to E), but either chord II or VI would work too, because they both have the note E, which is next in the semitone descent. If the same descending idea is applied to chord IV, we get the progression found in Track 65:

CD TRACK 65 Combined major 7/dominant 7 verse

I		I		IV		IV	
G \ \ \		Gmaj7 \ \ \		G7 \ \ \		C \ \ \	

IV		IV		IV		II	
C \ \ \		Cmaj7 \ \ \		C7 \ \ \		Am \ D7 \	

Probably one of the most famous songs to use this maj7-dominant7 link effect is Burt Bacharach's 'Raindrops Keep Fallin' On My Head'. Sometimes the emotional impression is that the maj7 expresses a touch of sadness and then the dominant 7 shrugs its shoulders, as if to say, "Well, that's life, can't be helped", and this resignation brings the music to the next major chord.

CD TRACK
65

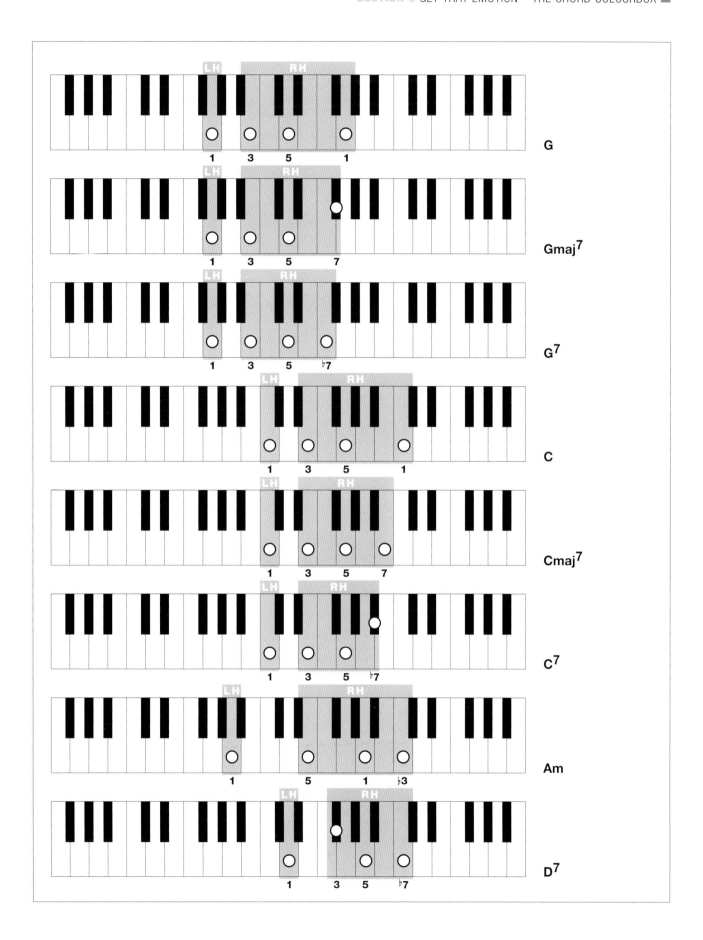

TECHNIQUE 66

HOW TO MAKE SAD CHORDS LESS SAD

THE MINOR 7TH (Cm7) – FORMULA 3+4+3

The minor chord can also be turned into a 7th by adding the note a tone below the root. In a major key, the three minor chords (II, III and VI) all take this form. It's written Am7, Bm7, Em7, etc. The main uses of the minor 7th are to lighten the emotion of chords II, III and VI by diluting their minor quality, and to make a progression sound mildly 'jazzy'.

CD Track 66 is an example of a bridge in G with the minor chords as minor 7ths. The minor 7ths give it a 'lighter' feel than pure minors would have done. The minor 7th can link chords through a common tone, or even two, as in this case. The common tones are given under the second line of chords:

CD TRACK 66 Minor 7th bridge in G

I				VI				IV				II			
G	\	\	\	Em7	\	\	\	C	\	\	\	Am7	\	\	\

I				II				III		V		VI			
G	\	\	\	Am7	\	\	\	Bm7	\	D	\	Em7	\	\	\
g				g				a+d		a+ d		d			

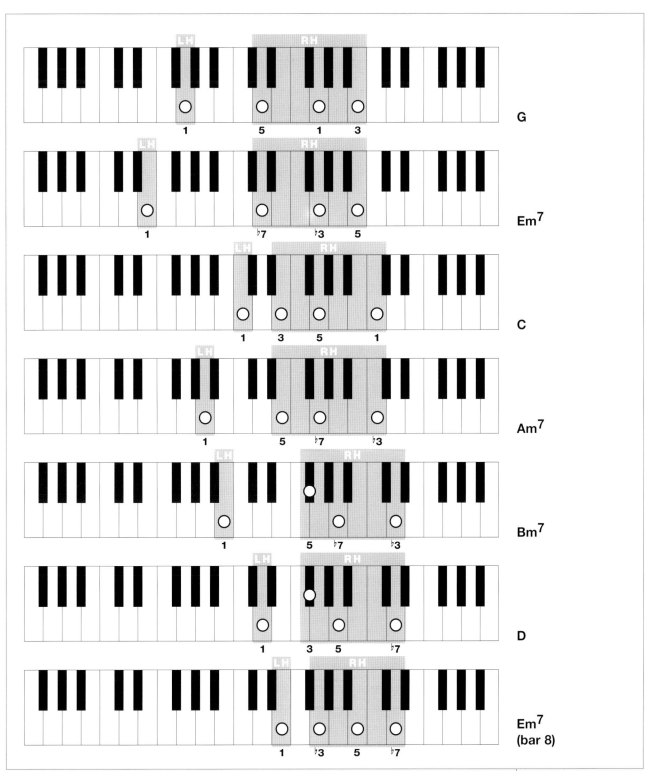

G

Em⁷

C

Am⁷

Bm⁷

D

Em⁷
(bar 8)

CD TRACK
66

TECHNIQUE 67

HOW TO MAKE MINOR CHORDS THREATENING

THE MINOR/MAJOR 7TH (written Cm/maj7) – FORMULA 3+4+4

This other form of the minor 7th chord involves a 7th which is only a semitone below the root note. This chord has an unmistakeable slinky and threatening sound. It rarely occurs on its own but nearly always as a passing chord between a minor and a minor 7th. The chord progression in Track 67 is like a minor version of the major 7th–dominant 7th change of Track 65. If the moving note were to descend after bar 3 it could resolve to chord VI (F) or IV (Dm) or a first inversion (dorian minor) IV ⌢ (D/F♯).

CD TRACK 67 Minor/major 7th verse in A minor

I				I				I				I			
Am	\	\	\	Am/maj7	\	\	\	Am7	\	\	\	Am\maj7	\	\	\

IV				IV				IV				IV			
Dm	\	\	\	Dm/maj7	\	\	\	Dm7	\	\	\	Dm/maj7	\	\	\

CD Track 67 has a startling effect because at bar 5 we don't expect to hear another sequence with a second min/maj7 chord straight after the first. See if you can find other chords than the minor 7 for the min/maj7 chord to resolve to. That way you will have an original chord sequence that takes an unexpected turn.

CD TRACK

67

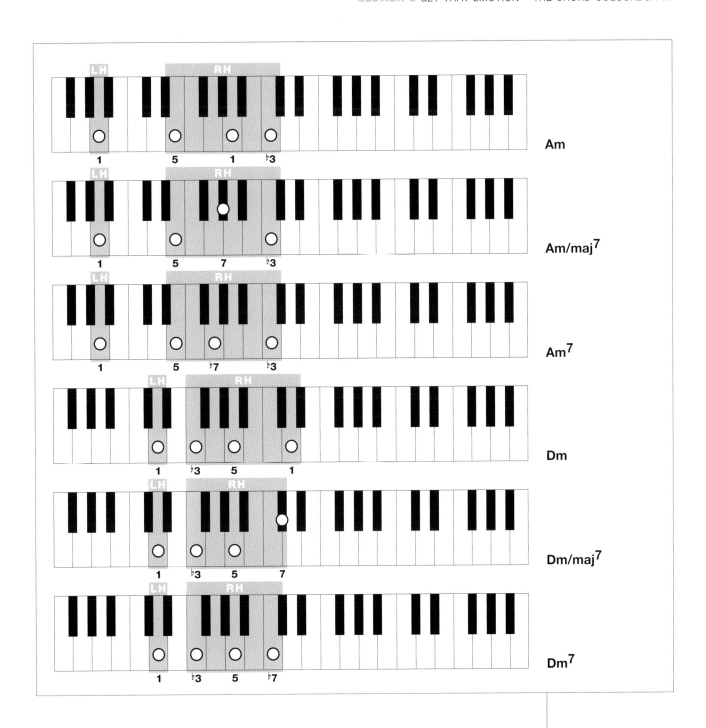

Am

Am/maj⁷

Am⁷

Dm

Dm/maj⁷

Dm⁷

CD TRACK
67

TECHNIQUE 68   HOW TO MAKE MAJOR CHORDS SOUND EXOTIC

THE MAJOR 6TH (C6) – FORMULA 4+3+2

The major chord becomes a 6th by the addition of the 6th note of the scale. Major 6ths (known simply as 6ths) can be created on chords I, IV, and V, and also on chord II^ and ♭VII, without including a note which is not on the key's scale. Playing 6ths is much easier on a keyboard than on a guitar, where they create fingering problems – it can be hard on guitar to find a comfortable shape for the 6th you want. The main uses of the major 6th are to add colour and mild tension to major chords, and make a progression sound jazzy, exotic, or Latin. They mix well with minor 7ths.

CD Track 68 is a song section that uses 6ths. Usually there would not be so many in a song. The effectiveness of 6ths, as with most exotic chords, declines the more of them there are.

CD TRACK 68 6ths, verse idea in C

I	VI	IV	III	V
C6 \	Am7 \	|F6 \ \ \	|Em7 \ \ \	|G6 \ \ :||

CD TRACK

68

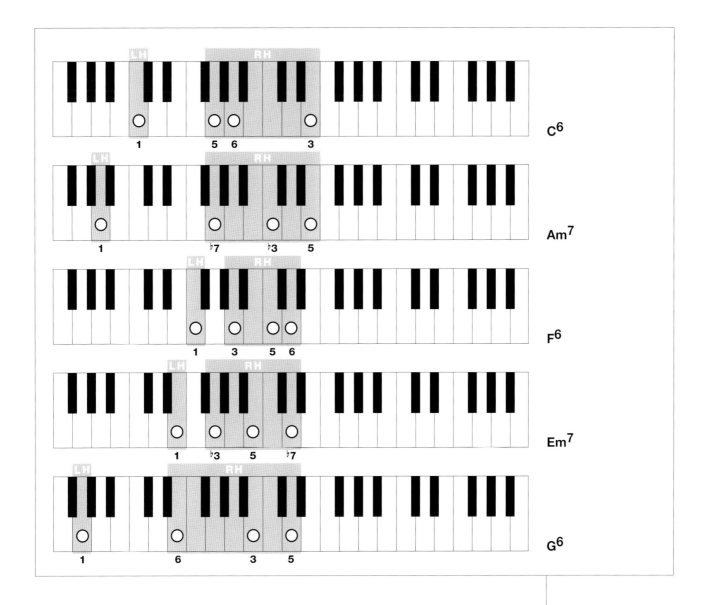

C⁶

Am⁷

F⁶

Em⁷

G⁶

CD TRACK
68

169

TECHNIQUE 69

HOW TO MAKE CHORDS MORE DRAMATIC

THE SUS4 (Csus4) – FORMULA 5+2

This is a type of chord that's neither major nor minor, but neutral. The note that would have indicated this has been removed ('suspended') and replaced with the 4th note above the root. The sus4 is focused and tense. The main use of suspended chords is to add tension to a progression, especially at approaches to a new section.

In CD Track 69 an eight-bar I-IV change is made more interesting by the sus4s. The Dsus4 note G provides a common tone as an opportunity to insert a ♭VII G chord. Sus4 chords are great for dramatic intros, especially in rock songs. Simply alternating with a straight chord I can work. *Remember that the same sus4 can resolve onto a major or a minor chord.* This happens in bar 7 of the verse.

CD TRACK 69 Sus4 intro in E

I				I				I				I			
E	\	\	\	Esus4 \	\	\		E	\	\	\	Esus4 \	\	E	\

Verse in A

I				I				♭VII				I			
A	\	\	Asus4	A	\	\	Asus4	G	\	\	\	Asus4 \	A	\	

IV				IV				IVm				IV			
D	\	\	\	Dsus4 \	\	\		Dm	\	\	\	Esus4 \	E	\	

The fact that a suspended chord can resolve onto a major or a minor chord offers other opportunities for the songwriter. If you put one at the end of a song section and stay on it for a bar or two without resolving it, you can then resolve it onto an unexpected minor chord (if you're in a major key) which could function as chord I of a minor key. For example, CD Track 69 is in the key of E. If the last bar was entirely Esus4 it could resolve not to E but Em. This could have the effect of changing the key to E minor and the next section could have a sequence like Em, D, C, Bm.

CD TRACK

69

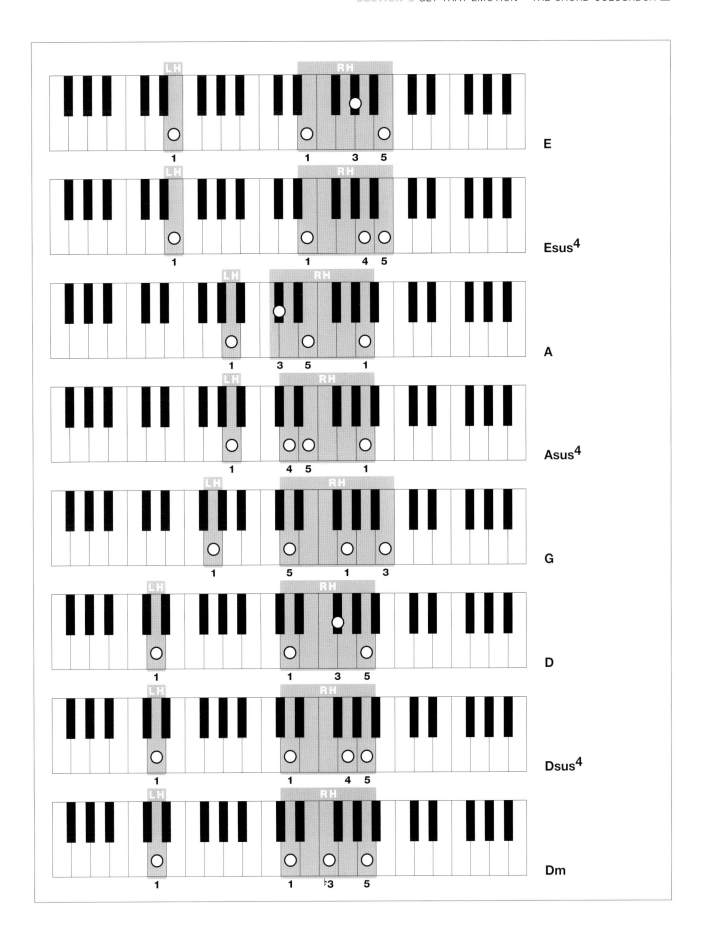

<table>
<tr><td>TECHNIQUE 70</td><td colspan="4"># HOW TO MAKE CHORDS ENIGMATIC</td></tr>
</table>

THE SUS2 (Csus2) – FORMULA 2+5

The sus2 is not as tense as the sus4, but is also neutral, poised between major and minor. The note that would have indicated major or minor has been removed (suspended) and replaced with the second note above the root. CD Track 70 is an example of the sus2 adding colour and mystery to a sequence:

CD TRACK 70 Sus2 verse in A

I				II				IV				V			
Asus2	\	\	\	Bsus2	\	\	\	Dsus2	\	\	\	E	\	\	\

VI				IV				I				V			
F♯m7	\	\	\	Dsus2	\	\	\	Asus2	\	\	\	Esus2	\	\	\

These chords are much easier to play on keyboards than on guitar. You can also use them to side-step your way onto an unexpected minor chord on the same root note. The Esus2 in the last bar could resolve in a new section to Em.

CD TRACK

70

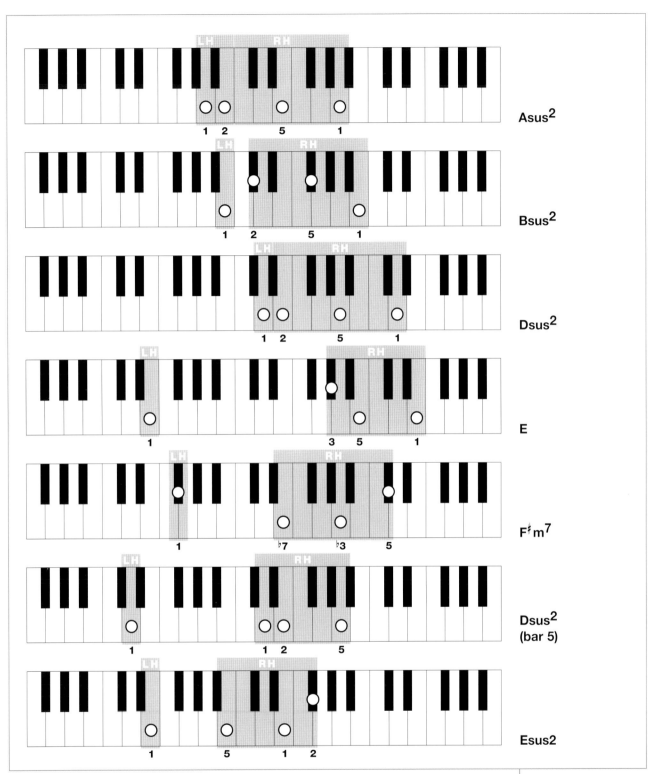

Asus²

Bsus²

Dsus²

E

F♯m⁷

Dsus²
(bar 5)

Esus2

CD TRACK
70

TECHNIQUE 71

HOW TO MAKE CHORDS BREEZIER

THE ADD9 (Cadd9) – FORMULA 4+3+7

This chord is closely related to the sus2 and is an easy way to add strength to a simple sequence. Compare Csus2 (C-D-G) with Cadd9 (C-E-G-D) – the additional note is the E, which makes it clear that the add9 chord is a major chord, not a neutral one like the sus2. This chord is called an add9 to distinguish it from the full major 9th (C-E-G-B-D) which has five notes in it. Add9 chords are more popular than full 9ths because they're easier to play and their sound is more suited to rock music.

CD Track 71 has a standard I-IV change decorated with add9s. Add9s are often used in situations where the 9th itself is a common tone with the preceding or following chord. The change from C major (bars 1-4) to D major (5-8) is facilitated by the A7 in bar 4. This is a reverse polarity VI^ in C, but happens to be V in D major.

CD TRACK 71 Add9 change in C and D

I			IV			I			IV		VI^ [V]	
Cadd9 \	\	\	Fadd9 \	\	\	Cadd9 \	\	\	Fadd9 \	A7	\	

I			♭VII			IV			II			
Dadd9 \	\	\	Cadd9 \	\	\	Gadd9 \	\	\	Em7 \	\	\	

An interesting tip for when you are writing a melody is to try singing the add9 note of whatever chord you are playing, regardless of whether you are playing an add9 note or not. In a melody the note brings an expressive but not disturbing tension. If you find it hard to pitch this note singing over a straight major, play the add9 on the keyboard as part of the chord. It will help your voice find and stay with that note.

CD TRACK
71

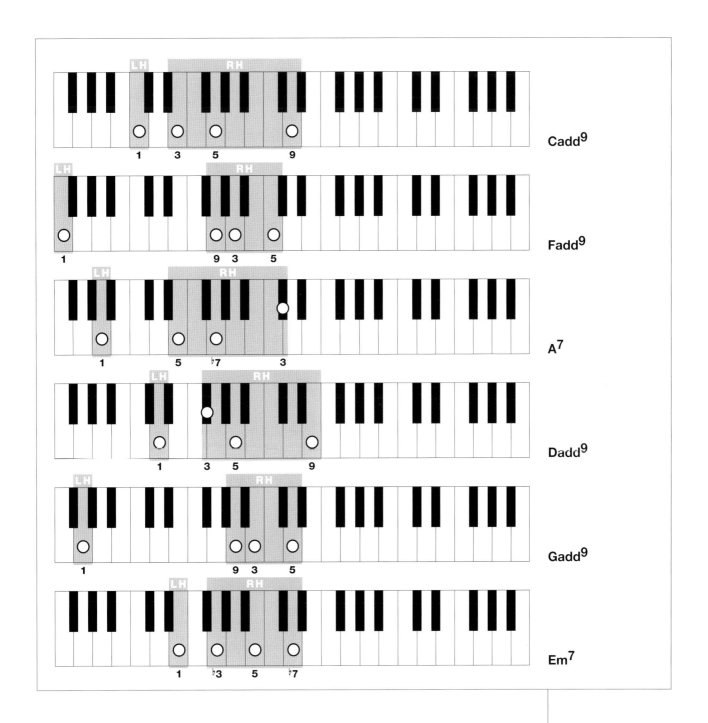

Cadd^9

Fadd^9

A^7

Dadd^9

Gadd^9

Em^7

TECHNIQUE 72

HOW TO MAKE MINOR CHORDS MORE TRAGIC

THE MINOR ADD 9TH (Cm add9) – FORMULA 3+4+7

This chord also resembles the sus2. Compare Asus2 (A-B-E) with Am add9 (A-C-E-B) – the additional note, C, makes it clear that the add9 chord is a minor chord, not a neutral one like the sus2. This chord is called an add9 to distinguish it from the full five-note minor 9th (A-C-E-G-B). The minor add9 chord is an intensifier – it makes the minor chord not just sad but tragic. It links effectively with the major 7th chord, as in CD Track 72.

CD TRACK 72 Minor add^9 in E minor

I				VI			IV				VII			
Emadd9	\	\	\	C	\	Cmaj7	\	Amadd9	\	\	\	Dsus4	\	D	\	:‖

As with the previous track, singing the min9 note in your melody will emphasise the tragic quality of this chord. There are few notes more highly-charged than a well-placed melody 9th over a minor chord as the climax of a suitable lyric phrase.

CD TRACK

72

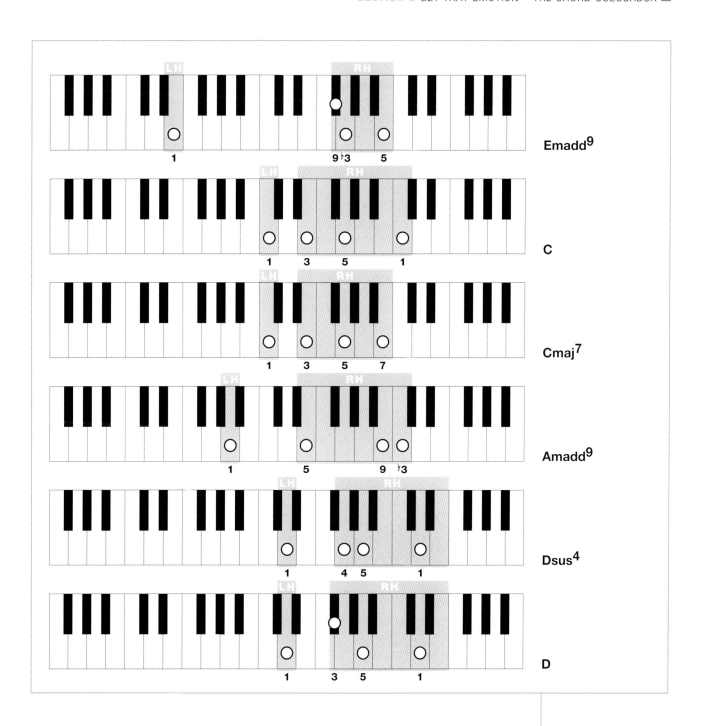

Emadd⁹

C

Cmaj⁷

Amadd⁹

Dsus⁴

D

CD TRACK
72

TECHNIQUE 73

CD TRACK

73

HOW TO MAKE CHORDS SUITABLE FOR ROCK

THE 5TH (C5) – FORMULA 7

When looking at the two suspended chords we saw how both were tonally neutral because they omitted the note that defines a chord as major or minor (the 3rd), replacing it with another note. So what would happen if this note was not replaced with anything? What remains would be two notes making the interval known as a perfect 5th, which is measured as seven semitones. Bare, perfect 5ths played on the lower strings are an integral part of rock guitar, particularly in heavy rock and metal styles. We can call this 'interval' a '5th chord' (written C5, D5, etc). Chords I-VI, as well as ♭VII, ♭III and ♭VI could be turned into 5th chords.

All 5th chords combine effectively with most other chords, especially the suspended chords and the major add9, and they toughen a chord progression. Notice the stark quality they give a simple three-chord trick idea. If you turn a 5th upside down (so the notes are reversed) you get a 4th so, for variety, chords C5 and B♭5 occur as 4ths in the RH in the progression in CD Track 73, and are marked as C4 and B♭4 on the chord diagrams:

CD TRACK 73 5th change in A

♭VII	I	♭VII	I	♭III				♭VII		♭II		IV		♭III	IV	
G5	A5	G5	A5 \	C5 \	\	\	G5 \	B♭5 \	D5 \	C5	D5 \ :‖

TECHNIQUE 74

HOW TO MAKE CHORD PROGRESSIONS SOUND SOPHISTICATED

THE AUGMENTED CHORD (Caug OR C+) – FORMULA 4+4

An augmented chord is formed when the 5th of a major triad is raised one semitone. We first encountered this shape in Technique 11. G major is G-B-D; Gaug is G-B-D♯. An augmented chord is neither major nor minor. Its strange sound means it almost invariably occurs in songs as a passing chord, not a chord to be dwelt on for bars at a time. The augmented note itself usually moves up a further semitone, in this instance from D♯ to E, which releases the tension. Any chord with an E in it could be used to follow Gaug.

An augmented chord cannot be inverted, as any inversion simply activates one of its notes as the root of yet another augmented: G-B-D♯ is Gaug, B-D♯-G is Baug, D♯-G-B is D♯aug. All of these notes maintain the two-tone interval between them that defines the augmented chord. You cannot form an augmented chord from a minor chord – this would create a first-inversion major chord: Am is A-C-E; augmenting Am would give us A-C-E♯; E♯ is the same note as F; A-C-F is a first-inversion F chord.

In CD Track 74 a ♭VI is turned into an augmented chord that shares two common tones with the chord either side of it. The common tones are written underneath the progression. In this context the augmented ♭VI is close in sound to a IVm, only tougher:

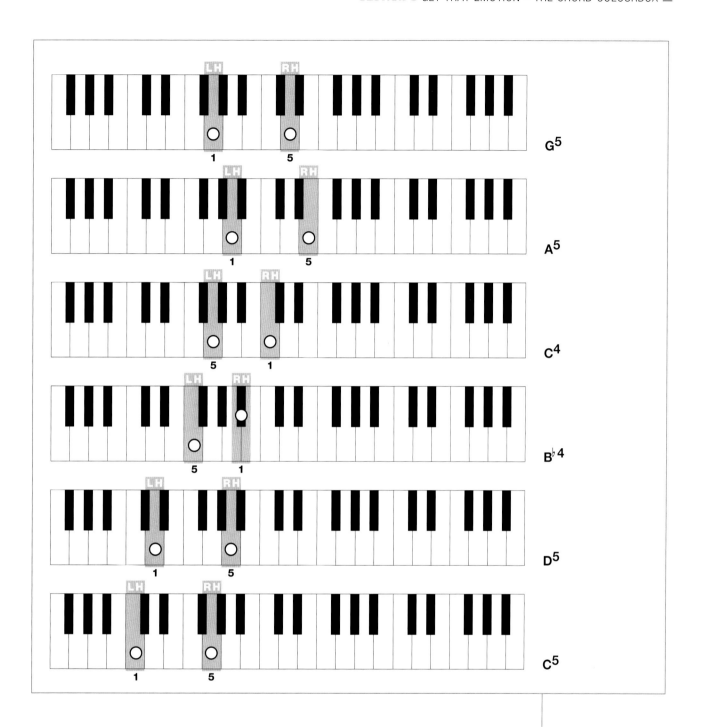

G⁵

A⁵

C⁴

B♭4

D⁵

C⁵

CD TRACK
73

More polish, more inspiration

"I don't like some keys, but other keys are fine.
I never write in B major. Or in C-flat. I'm
comfortable in E-flat, F, G, C. Not so much in D,
but I can write in D. It always helps me in
writing, if I get stuck, to switch keys. Because
maybe then you will hear something else.
Maybe your hands will go somewhere else..."

Burt Bacharach

Keys are an important aspect to the way we hear and interpret music. They're much easier to hear than describe. A key offers a way of organizing what we hear so that everything seems related to everything else. Put in simple terms, the key note and chord function as a center to the experience of the music. Every time the key chord is heard we feel as though we have 'touched base' or visited home. The key-chord sounds like the place where everything in the music begins and ends. This is why songs often end on the key-chord. Nothing else can make the song sound completed in the same way.

Popular songs tend to emphasise this phenomenon of 'key-centredness', partly because the key-chord is frequently heard and also because the overall number of chords is limited and drawn from the key. We never stray very far from the key centre. In technical terms, the sense of key is created from the scale used and the chords made from it.

Changing key is a powerful way to create contrast in music. It is essential for music longer than the three or four-minute song, but even these can benefit from a change of key. It reduces monotony and takes the listener on more of a journey.

The key you choose for a song depends on many factors:

• Sometimes a melody comes to a songwriter and the pitch of the notes suggests a key.

• Sometimes a chord sequence suggests the key.

• Sometimes the songwriter chooses chords that are easy to play, and they determine the key. If you write on keyboards, different musical keys may appeal than if you're writing on guitar. On the keyboard, composing in C major or G major reduces the number of black keys you have to finger.

• With experienced songwriters, some keys acquire personal associations because of past songs they have written. If you've composed two atmospheric ballads in C minor, for instance, that key may quickly evoke the same emotion for you. If a songwriter's happiest song is in E major, that key will have an optimistic aura for that writer.

• Certain keys are sometimes chosen because they suit a singer's voice.

• Some keys, like E♭ and B♭, are popular in music where a brass section is used, such as soul. Brass instruments are comfortable in these flat keys. E and A are popular keys for the guitar (at concert pitch) because they allow the use of the two lowest open strings. E♭ and A♭ are popular keys in heavy rock, for the same reason, where the guitar is detuned by a semitone.

REASONS FOR CHANGING KEY INCLUDE:

• Refreshing a section already heard more than once before, by presenting it again at a different pitch. Traditionally the chorus is most likely to move into a new key near the end of a song. After the last verse, bridge or solo, the chorus happens first in the home key and might then be repeated in a new key.

• Another technique is to bring the chorus in immediately after the last verse in the new key. In pop tradition this key change is also either up one semitone or a tone.

• If a song has a repeating section, key-changing enables it to be repeated without monotony. This is handy with turnarounds.

• Key-changing can contrast parts of a song. The verses could be in different keys but the choruses remain in the same one, or the bridge could be in a new key.

• Key-changing gives the listener the subjective feeling of travelling somewhere new in the music. If something in the lyric suggests a new perspective (literal or metaphorical – new love, new job, new town, new emotion) a key-change can make the listener *feel* it rather than the song just telling them it is so. If your new lover makes you feel like you've never felt before (to use a lyric cliché) why not say so with a key that has not been heard before in the song?

• The simpler the chord progression and the more limited the number of chords, the more potentially inspiring a key-change could be. This is particularly true of a three-chord trick.

• There is often a relationship between musical sophistication and more adventurous key-changing. For a start, some musical genres are more liable to have a key-change than others – as a rule you're less likely to hear one in a slow reggae tune, a modern Top 40 pop song, most dance music, R&B, punk, 12-bar blues, 1950s rock'n'roll songs etc. The exception of course is the simple tone or semitone shift towards the end of a song (the final chorus perhaps), which was so popular as a trick in 'easy-listening' pop songs (and *Eurovision Song Contest* entries) in the 1960s/70s that it became something of a cliché to be avoided. Genres at the 'artier' end of popular music – like progressive rock – were, on the other hand, inclined to feature more complex, and often unexpected, key changes throughout their compositions.

DOES A SONG HAVE TO CHANGE KEY?

No – but the simpler the chord progression and the more limited the number of chords the more potentially inspiring a key-change could be. This is particularly true in the case of a three-chord trick.

HOW MANY KEYS ARE THERE?

There is a major key and a minor key on each of the 12 notes, giving 24 in total. So, if a song starts in any major or minor key there are 23 other keys to which it could change – remembering that three majors and three minors can be written as both a sharp key *and* a flat key, as 'enharmonic equivalents': these are B major (C♭ major), F♯ major (G♭ major), C♯ major (D♭ major) and their relative minors G♯ minor (A♭ minor), D♯ minor (E♭ minor), and A♯ minor (B♭ minor).

Some keys are related to the home key because they have notes and chords in common. Some are not related because they have few notes and chords in common.

'NEAR' AND 'DISTANT' KEYS

A 'near' key is one that can be reached relatively easily from the home key. It requires a minimal adjustment of accidentals in the melody, and the change will not perturb the listener. It requires only one chord to reach an important chord in a near key, like a stepping stone. It's easy to return from this key to the home key.

A 'distant' key is one that can be reached from the home key only with some ingenuity. It requires considerable adjustment of accidentals in the melody; the change will sound unusual to the listener, even unsettling if not adequately prepared. It requires several chords to reach an important chord in the new key, and to get back again.

Songwriters develop a variety of personal responses and associations with keys. On the guitar this is sometimes caused by the typical chord shapes for a given key and the changing combinations of open to fretted strings in the chords. On keyboards it is sometimes based on the proportion of black to white keys. Some songwriters end up thinking of a key as having an attribute or character – like 'bold and electric' for E major, 'plain and strong' for C major, or 'darkly melancholic' for G minor. E-flat major has been called 'noble and sad or gloomy', whereas B major has been 'brilliant and playful'. There is a long-standing tradition of associating sharps with brightness and flats with darkness, which is confusing on a keyboard, since the same black key can carry both meanings. Keys have also been assigned colour, though nobody's lists match. The Russian composers Rimsky-Korsakov and Scriabin agreed that D major was yellow, but that was all. The former thought C major was white and the latter thought it red.

What chords can be used in the new key?

Once you are in the new key all 8 or 13 chords (depending on whether it is minor or major) are potentially available, the equivalents to the 'pool' drawn from in the home key. To make this clear, imagine a song that starts in C major and changes key to A major for its bridge. The available chords are (in C major) C, Dm, Em, F, G, Am, with B♭, E♭ and A♭ as 'flat degree' extras and D, E, Fm and A as reverse-polarity extras. The available chords in A major would be primarily A, Bm, C♯m, D, E, F♯m and G (the ♭VII). You wouldn't want to bring in too many 'flat degree' or reverse-polarity chords because you are trying to establish A major as a new key for this section, and they would undermine or confuse it. So stick with chords I-VI and ♭VII until you get more experience.

TECHNIQUE 75

A SIMPLE METHOD FOR CHANGING KEY

There are so many ways of changing key that the subject is too big to be covered fully here. So we need a couple of methods that are simple and effective. A new key is established most securely by the use of a V-I (preferably V7-I) chord change in the new key. This is technically known as a 'perfect cadence'. You've already heard one of these in bar 4 of CD Track 71.

Think of the other keys as clubs which will only let you in if you're dressed in appropriate clothes. 'Appropriate' means looking as though you are one of the members in the club – which means being one of chords I-VI of the key you want to go to. Imagine we belong to the club known as C major and we want to infiltrate the club called A major. There isn't a common 'cloak' – no chord is found in both keys, although G, chord V in C major, is the ♭VII of A. Unfortunately, that won't really establish the new key on its own. But chord II (Dm) is the IVm of A, so we could make the change in a single step. If this is done it can be backed up by a perfect cadence in the new key soon after, just to confirm membership of the new club… CD Track 75 shows this change.

CD TRACK 75 V-I key change C major to A major

I				II [IVm]		I		IV		V		V		I	
C	\	\	\	Dm	\	A	\	D	\	E	\	E7	\	A	\

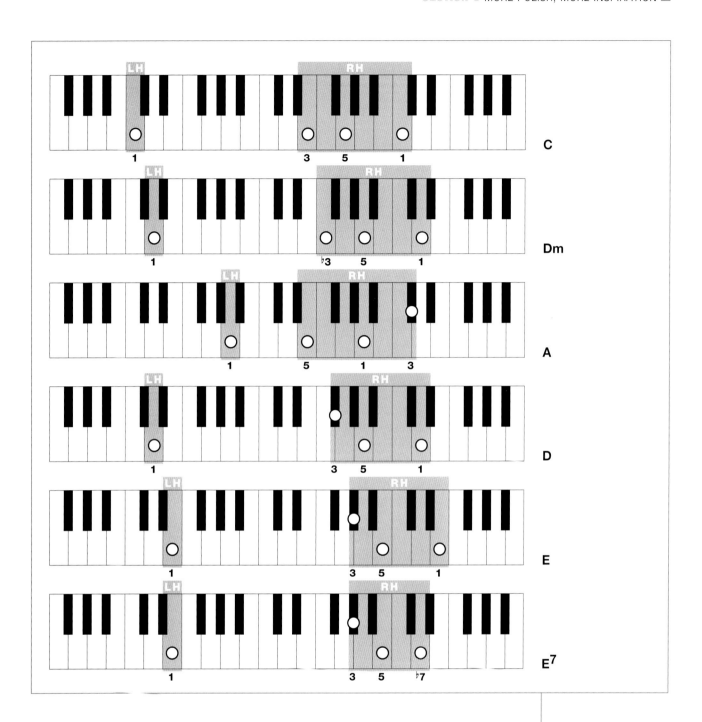

C

Dm

A

D

E

E⁷

CD TRACK
75

187

TECHNIQUE 76 THE REVERSE-POLARITY 'GATE'

It is possible to treat a reverse-polarity chord as chord V of the new key. This is an abrupt but effective way to change key. Here are the chords in D major, with the three reverse-polarity chords and the keys they would take you to if they were interpreted as chord V of a new key:

Scale degree	I	II	[II^]	III	[III^]	IV	V	VI	[VI]	VII
Chord	D	Em	[E]	F♯m	[F♯]	G	A	Bm	[B]	C♯dim
New key I			A major		B major				E major	

In the first four bars of CD Track 76, F♯, which is a reverse polarity III^, doubles as chord V in the key of Bm, and, in bar 8, B major.

CD TRACK 76 III^ as a reverse-polarity gate (D major to B major or B minor)

IV		I		III^ [V]		I		
G \	Gmaj7 \	D \	Dmaj7 \	F♯ \	F♯7 \	Bm \	\	\

IV		IV		III^ [V]		I		
G \	Gmaj7 \	D \	Dmaj7 \	F♯ \	F♯7 \	B \	\	\

Notice the way Gmaj7 is linked to D by the common tone of F♯, and how Dmaj7 flows into the reverse-polarity F♯ (III^) by the common tone of C♯. In the latter case, the common tone helps to link a chord which is in musical key with one (III^) which is not, so that the change is more acceptable on the ear. Usually a common note between chords will mean you don't have to move the finger that is holding down that particular key on the piano when you do the change.

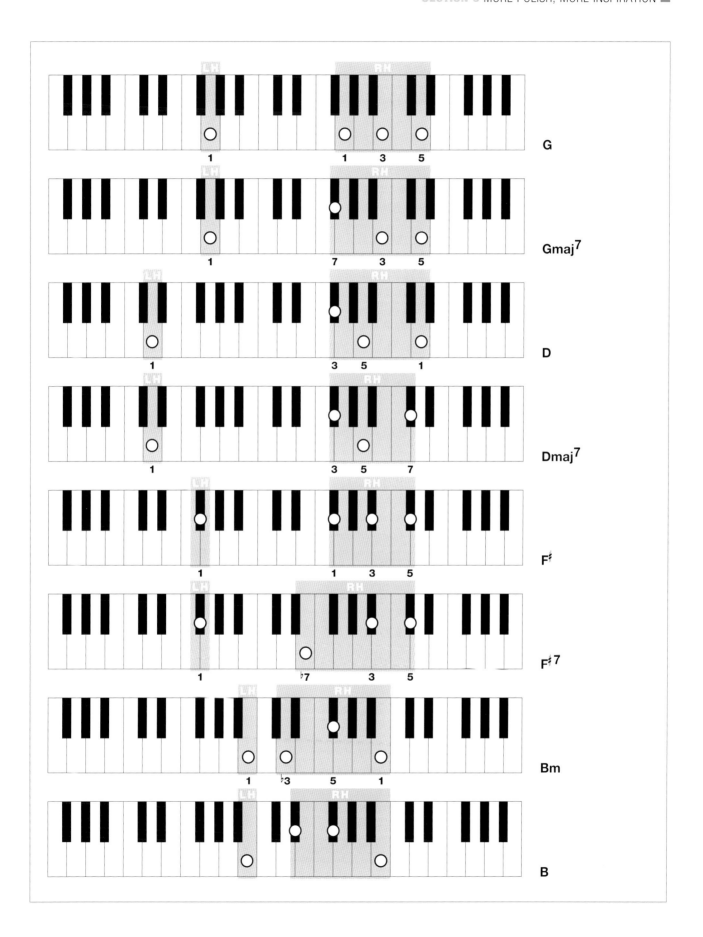

G

Gmaj⁷

D

Dmaj⁷

F♯

F♯⁷

Bm

B

TECHNIQUE 77 | # THE GATEWAY OF SLUSH – USING IVm TO CHANGE KEY

Of the four reverse-polarity chords, IVm is unique because it can't function as chord V of another key as it isn't a major chord. But there are two ways of approaching it that enable it to be a stepping stone to a new key. The first is to treat it as one of the normal minor chords of a major key – II, III or VI – and from there move to chord IV and V (or even just V) of the new key, and then to the new chord I. The second method with the IVm chord is to take the three minor chords of the key you're in – II, III and VI – and work out in which keys they can play the harmonic role of IVm.

In bars 1-4 of Track 77, the progression starts in F major. In bar 3 we reach chord II, Gm, which also happens to be IVm in the key of D. After two beats it goes to chord V in D, A and then to D. In bar 5 the music drops into C major. Chord VI (Am) is also chord IVm in E major, which is where the music lands in bar 8.

CD TRACK 77 Using IVm to change key from F to D and C to E

I				IV				II [IVm]		V		I			
F	\	\	\	B♭	\	\	\	Gm	\	A	\	D	\	\	\

I				IV				VI [IVm]				I			
C	\	\	\	F	\	\	\	Am	\	\	\	E	\	\	\

The emotional effect of changing key by IVm is quite distinctive. The IVm chord arouses a tragic emotion, as though something awful has happened or is about to happen. But it then resolves onto an unexpected major and establishes a new major key. The contrast is considerable. The expected tragedy is immediately put right by the major key into which we have stumbled. The sense of being pulled back from the brink at the last moment is thus stronger than in some other key changes. The exact impression will, of course, depend on the lyric at this moment of key change.

CD TRACK
77

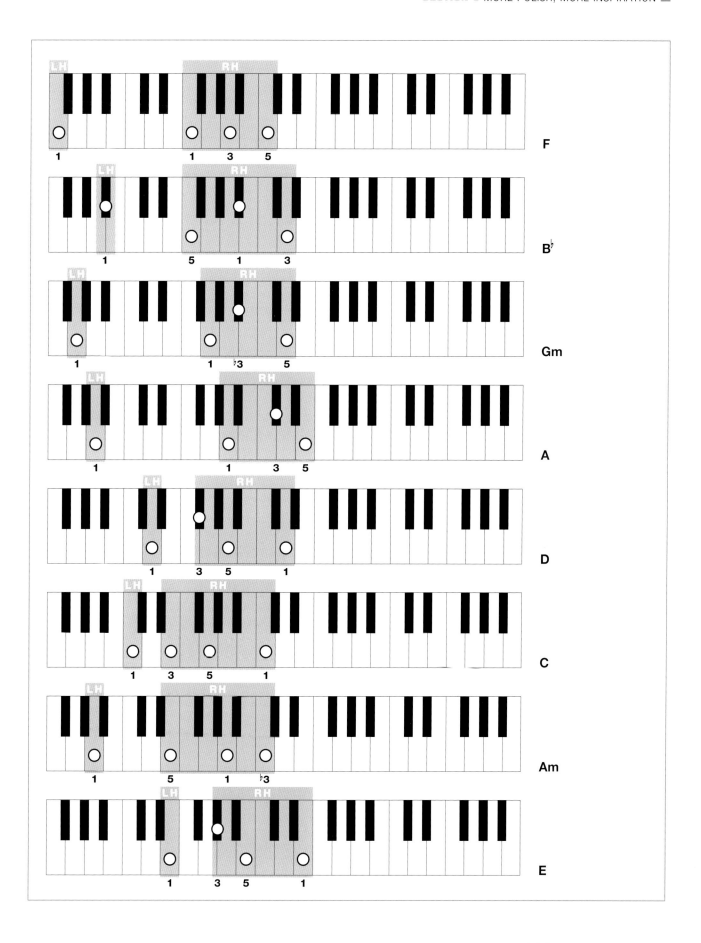

F

B♭

Gm

A

D

C

Am

E

TECHNIQUE 78 | # THE BRIDGE USING MINORS AND AVOIDING I

A useful variation to attempt is to try composing a song that has a 12-bar verse with dominant 7 chords but no minor chords, and then move to a bridge section which does have minors, as in Track 78, and avoids chord I altogether.

CD TRACK 78 Bridge with minors in D

VI				IV				III				i bVII			
Bm	\	\	\	G	\	\	\	F♯m	\	\	\	C/E	\	\	\

VI				IV				II ^				II		[V]	
Bm	\	\	\	G	\	\	\	E7	\	\	\	Em	\	A7	\

The contrast of a 12-bar verse with a middle-eight in which there are minor chords was exploited by The Beatles on early songs such as 'Can't Buy Me Love'. Such songs offer the listener two contrasted moods – the tough assertion of the verse and the softer, regretful middle-eight. It's a bit like splicing an out-and-out rocker onto a ballad, and having the best of both worlds.

CD TRACK

78

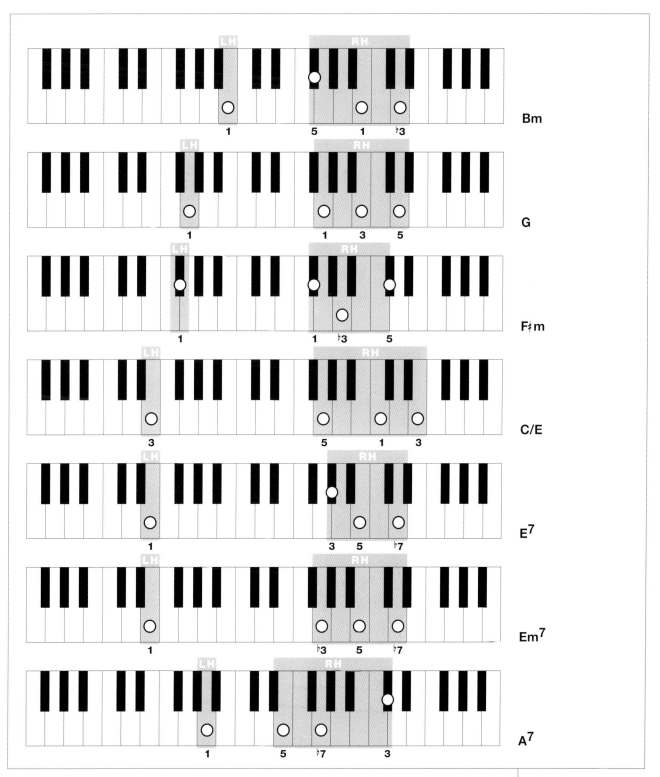

CD TRACK
78

193

TECHNIQUE 79 | THE CODA

The section of a song that comes after the last chorus is known as a coda (literally meaning 'tail'). A song does not need to have a coda – it could end on the chorus's last chord or, if it's a studio recording, fade on a repeat of the chorus. Some codas use an instrumental version of the chorus over which the singer (and/or soloist) can ad lib. A coda might also use any links in the song, or the intro – which would give the song a neat circularity. CD Track 79 features two possible endings: the first is a typical use of a 'down escalator' sequence as an ending; the second (which follows after a sustained C chord) is a more rousing ascending sequence with a classic sus4 on chord V. The chords are played only in the right hand.

CD TRACK 79 Two codas for a song in C

V				IV				II				I		
G/d	\	\	\	F	\	\	\	Dm/f	\	\	\	C/g		‖

II			iI	IV				V				I		
Dm	\	\	C/E	F	\	\	\	Gsus4	\	G	\	C/g		‖

In both these instances the music ends on chord I. If you want a less secure ending try finishing on chord IV or V of the key you're in. Avoiding chord I as the last chord and ending with something else can be a good method for segueing straight into the next song. For example, imagine the first song of your set is in C major and the second is in A major. Make your listener think you are going to end on a C chord (I) in the last bar but instead land on a Dm (II) and hold it. Dm happens to be IVm in the key of A major. You can then hit A major and start the second song, having joined the two by the 'gateway of slush'.

CD TRACK
79

194

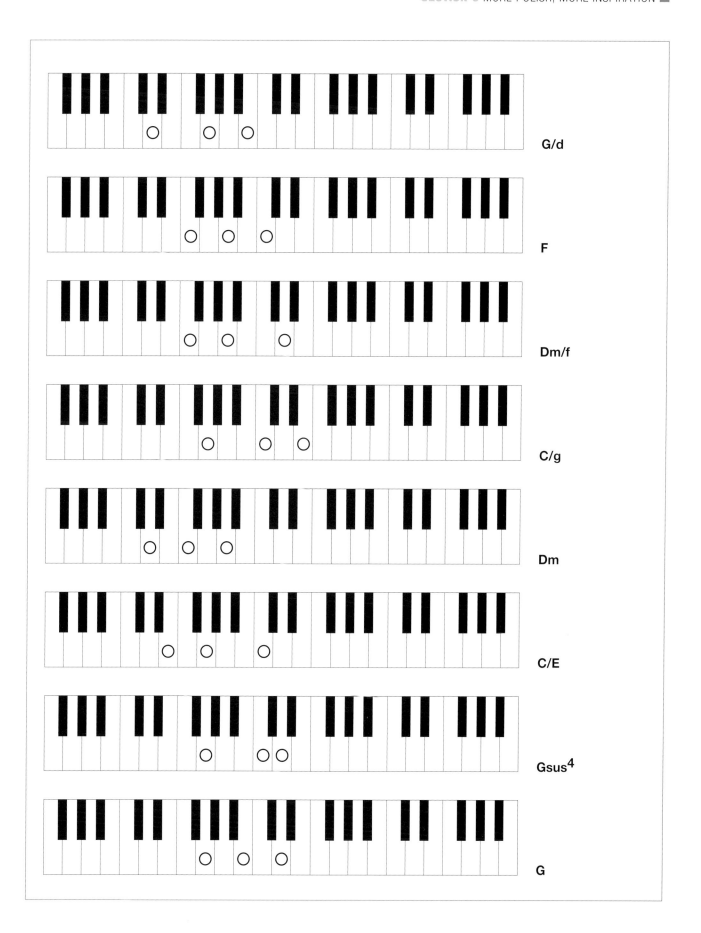

G/d

F

Dm/f

C/g

Dm

C/E

Gsus^4

G

| TECHNIQUE 80 | # THE IMPLIED TURNAROUND INTRO |

This technique makes an interesting start to a song. You play the bassline of a turnaround that will feature in the song but hold one of the chords static above it. Only if the bass note coincides with either of the chord's upper notes will a simple first or second inversion result. Take the turnaround I-II-IV-V in D major: the chords D, Em, G, A. The bassline is D-E-G-A under a held D chord. Only the last chord, D/A, is an inversion (second inversion in this case). Such a technique generates more harmonic tension than if the turnaround were to be turned into first and second inversions. The relationship between the bass note and the chord in bar 2 is more complex.

CD Track 80 might only have four chords, but more mileage will be had from them by changing the bass notes. Try it with the bass note in your left hand, chord in your right.

CD TRACK 80 Song in D major, turnaround I-II-IV-V

Intro

I				I				I				iiI			
D	\	\	\	D/E	\	\	\	D/G	\	\	\	D/A	\	\	\ :‖

Verse

I				I				II				V			
‖: D	\	\	\	Em	\	\	\	G	\	\	\	A	\	\	\ :‖

You could re-use this intro later in the song as a middle-eight, as an instrumental passage, as a link to the last verse, or even as a coda.

CD TRACK
80

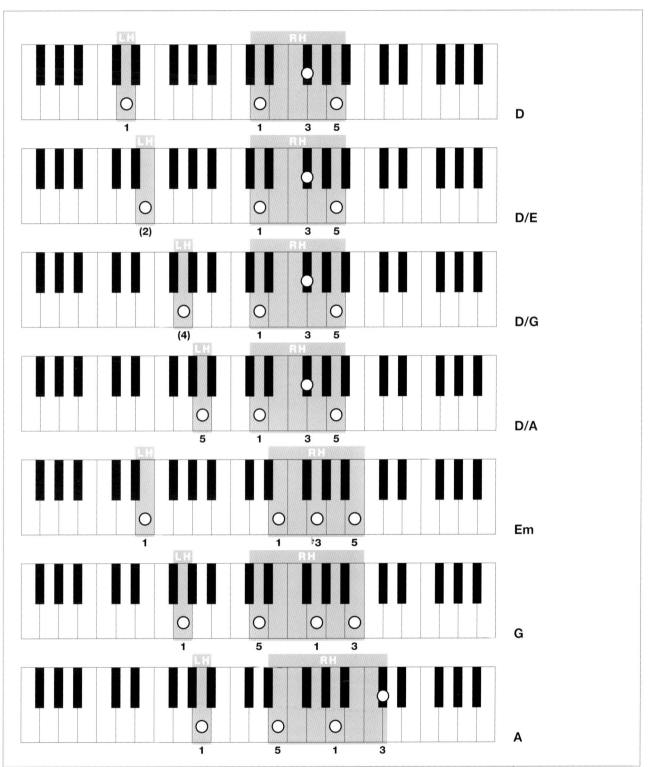

D

D/E

D/G

D/A

Em

G

A

CD TRACK
80

TECHNIQUE 81

CD TRACK
81

DESCENDING BASSLINE WITH STATIC CHORD INTRO

Another idea for an intro is to keep chord V static and let the bassline move down the scale from the 5th note to the 5th note an octave lower. This creates tension and anticipation – which can be increased if you double the rate of change to one chord per bar. The addition of a dominant 7th will help differentiate it from the chord V at the start and lead powerfully to the much anticipated and delayed chord I.

The same approach could be applied to any of the other chords in the key. After chord V, chord IV is probably the next favourite. In CD Track 81, bars 1-4 have a descending bassline under chord IV, with the bassline moving from the 4th of the scale down an octave, and then bars 5-8 do the same thing but under chord V (only two chord diagrams are given, for the basic G and A triads).

CD TRACK 81 Descending bass intro

IV	IV	IV	iiIV	IV	iIV	IV	
G \	G/F♯ \	G/E \	G/D \	G/C \	G/B \	G/A \	G \

V	iiiV7	V	iiV	V	iV	V	
A \	A/G \	A/F♯ \	A/E \	A/D \	A/C♯ \	A/B \	A7 \

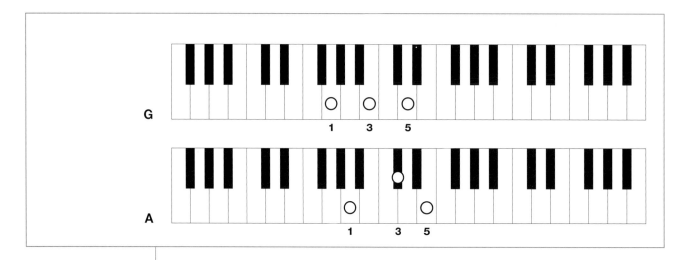

TECHNIQUE 82

CD TRACK
82

A DESCENDING BASS FROM I TO V

The descending bassline is a very appealing musical idea, whether played in an intro or elsewhere in a song. This is partly because it has a compelling melodic force – it grabs our attention because we want to know just how far it will descend. There are many ways of harmonising such a bassline, but to begin with we'll work with notes that lie between the key note and the 5th of the scale in D major, namely the notes D-C♯-B and A. CD Track 82 is a major-key version of the descending bassline heard back in Section 7 under Technique 57.

In CD Track 82 these notes are harmonised only with major chords – second time through with first and second inversions.

CD TRACK 82 Descending bassline in D major

I				I				I				V			
D	\	\	\	D/C♯	\	\	\	D/B	\	\	\	A	\	\	\

I				iV				iIV				V			
D	\	\	\	A/C♯	\	\	\	G/B	\	\	\	A	\	\	\

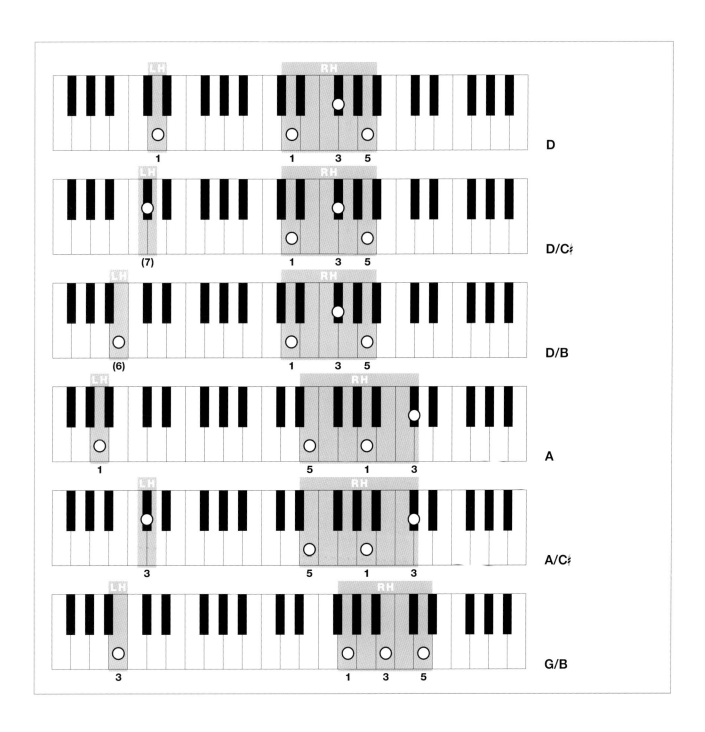

199

TECHNIQUE 83 | A DESCENDING BASS FROM I TO V (2)

This time the same bassline is harmonised by minor chords and inversions of minor chords like III and II. Listen for the subtle difference in sound compared to the previous track. You can exploit this difference to shade different meanings in your lyric. Notice the effect of the first chord in bar 8. The G/A here could also be described as A11.

CD TRACK 83 Descending bassline in D major

I				iV				VI				iIII			
D	\	\	\	A/C♯	\	\	\	Bm	\	\	\	F♯m	\	A	\

I				iiIII				iiII				IV		V	
D	\	\	\	F♯m/C♯	\	\		Em/B	\	\	\	G/A	\	A	\

Remember that a descending bassline like this one, taken from the major scale, can at one extreme be harmonised entirely with major chords, and at the other entirely with minor chords, and anything in-between. The chords you use will depend on what proportion of sad minor chords suits your lyric, and which chords you want to put to one side to use in other parts of the song. Consider the next technique in this regard.

CD TRACK

83

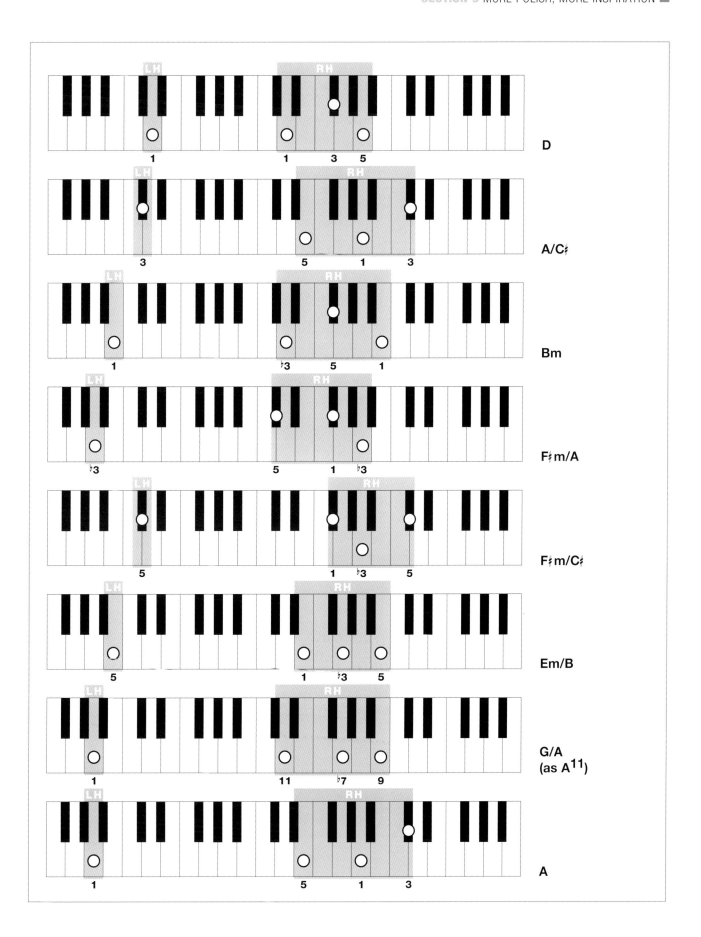

D

A/C♯

Bm

F♯m/A

F♯m/C♯

Em/B

G/A
(as A^{11})

A

TECHNIQUE 84

A DESCENDING BASS WITH MAJOR CHORDS

In CD Track 84 the bass moves down one note at a time on the scale of C major. This descending bassline can be entirely harmonised by a white-note three-chord trick – chords I, IV and V, and their inversions. It's important to grasp that it is possible to harmonise any note on the major scale with one of the three major chords. It means that if you want those notes in the bass you don't have to harmonise them with minor chords. It might be the case that minor chords would be too sad for the mood of the song, or perhaps you want to keep them for another section so they have more impact when they do appear. The chord diagrams show how the bassline is a single note in the left hand, and the chords are in the right hand.

CD TRACK 84 Descending bass under I, IV and V

I		iV		iIV		V		IV		iI		iiV		V	
C	\	G/B	\	F/A	\	G	\	F	\	C/E	\	G/D	\	Gsus2 G	:‖

This approach of just using majors and their inversions on a descending line is less frequently heard than a line with a mixture of majors and minors. It tends to carry an element of surprise. We half expect to hear Am on the A bass note in bar 2 and get F/A instead. Such a harmony also has the advantage of keeping the minor chords back for another song section where they will certainly make themselves felt as minor.

CD TRACK
84

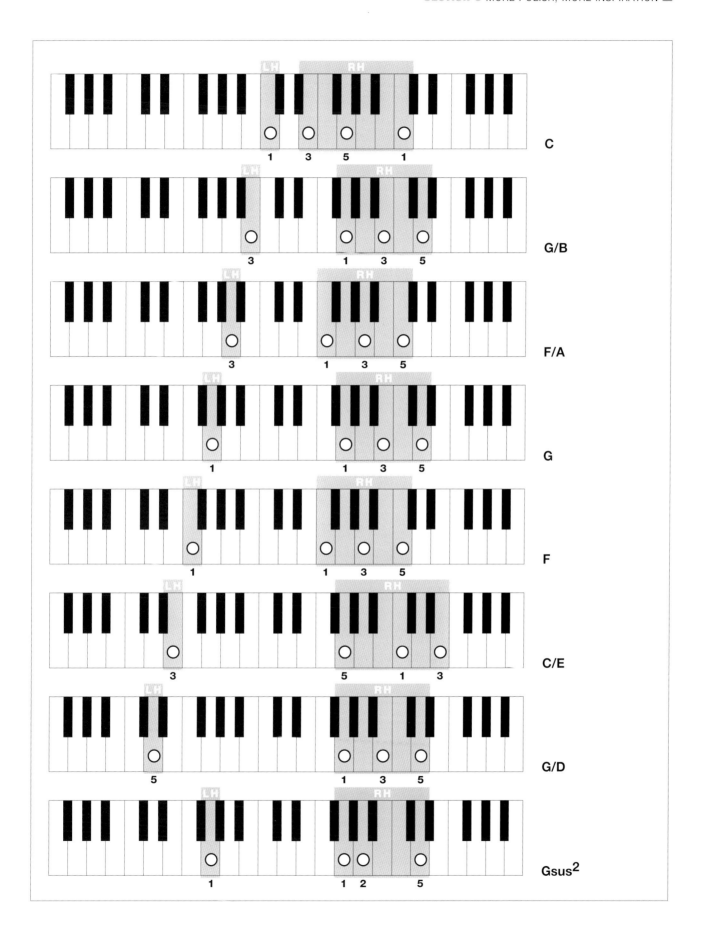

TECHNIQUE 85 A DESCENDING BASS WITH MINOR CHORDS

This example takes the basic idea of Track 84 but shows how a descending bassline can be harmonised with entirely minor chords (II, III and VI). The left hand plays down the white keys from D to E and each bass note supports either a Dm, Em or Am. This line is presented as though in the key of C major, starting from chord II. You can, of course, use any mixture of major and minor chords from the key to harmonise such basslines.

CD TRACK 85 Descending bass under II, III and VI in C major

II		iVI		iiIII		VI		iIII		iII		III		V		
Dm	\	Am/C	\	Em/B	\	Am	\	Em/G	\	Dm/F	\	Em	\	G	\	:‖

This all-minor harmonising of a descending bassline is the rarest of all the types we have examined. The inversions help to put a fresh slant on the minor chords. It sets up the possibility of major chords having more impact in a later song section.

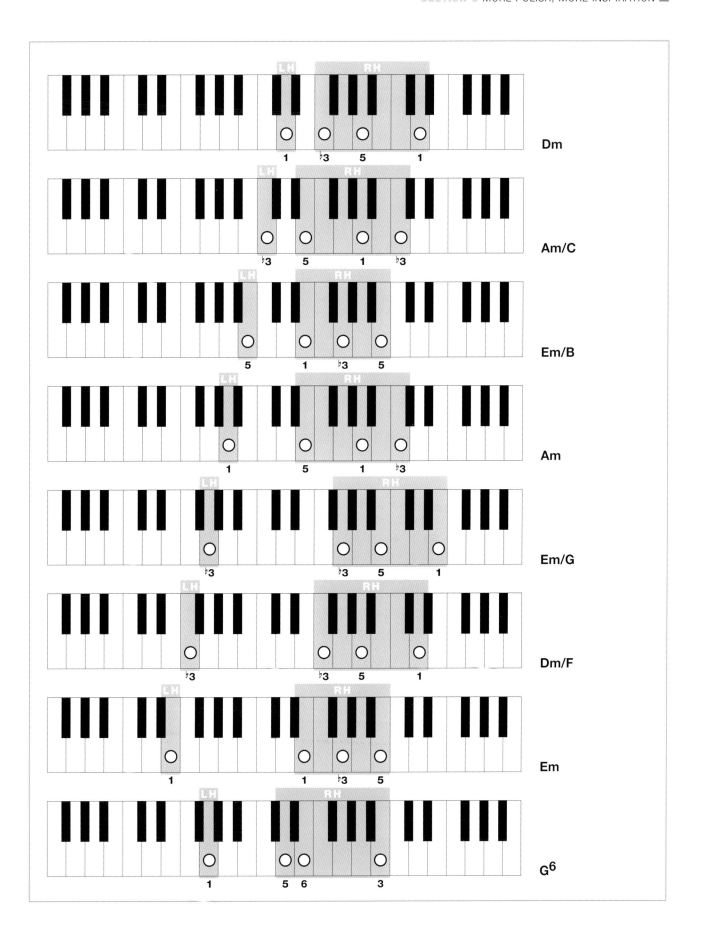

TECHNIQUE 86   CHROMATIC DESCENDING BASS

The previous two basslines sound quite smooth and musical because they keep strictly to the notes of C major. On CD Track 86, the descending bassline wanders off the scale onto black keys that don't belong to C major, adding what are known as 'chromatic' bass notes ('chromatic' literally means 'coloured'). These increase the feeling of tension in the chord sequence and suggest a more troubled and complex emotion. In bars 1-4 the right hand holds the same C major triad steady, only the left-hand bass note changes. In bars 5-8 the right hand holds a Dm triad steady. The C/A chord would usually be heard as Am7 and the Dm/B♭ as B♭maj7, but alternative names have been given to highlight the interaction between the bass and the triad.

CD TRACK 86 Descending chromatic bassline in C major

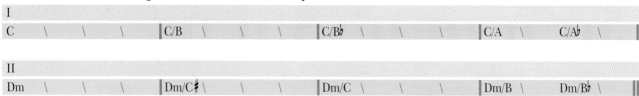

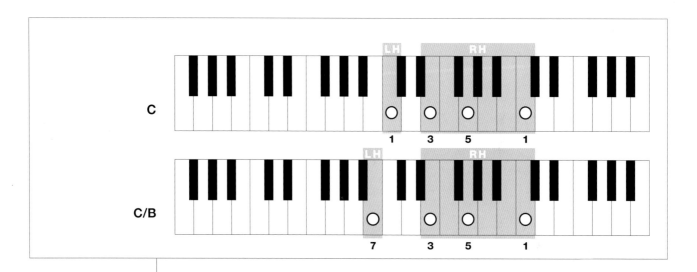

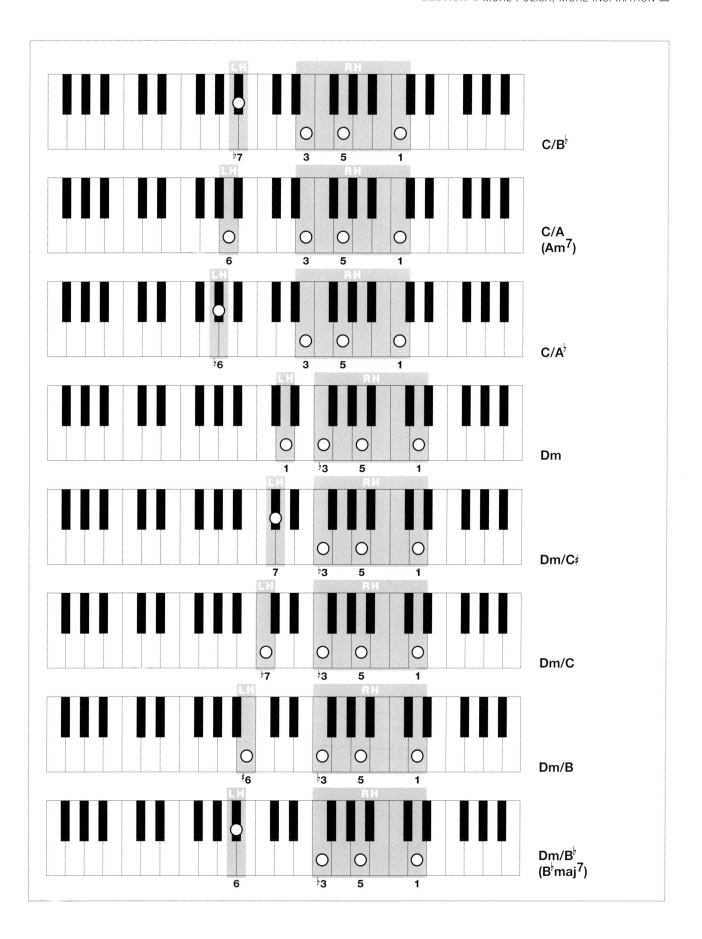

C/B♭

C/A
(Am⁷)

C/A♭

Dm

Dm/C♯

Dm/C

Dm/B

Dm/B♭
(B♭maj⁷)

TECHNIQUE 87

THE 11TH TRICK

Here's a neat trick for giving your harmony a certain sophistication, commonly replacing or accompanying chord V where it appears in the run-up to a chorus. With six different notes in them, 11th chords are hard to play, but they are more manageable if abbreviated. To create an abbreviated (four-note) 11th, start by holding a major chord in your right hand and its root note in your left (in any octave); to make this into an 11th, move your right hand chord down to the major chord that's *one tone lower* (two semitones to the left) but keep the LH bass note the same. At one time this chord was associated by session players with singer-songwriter Carole King, and its classic deployment is in a prechorus.

In the key of C major, a G dominant 11 (to give it its correct name) is G-D-B-F-A-C. If you knock off the top two notes you can see it is related to the dominant 7th (G-B-D-F). The top three notes are F-A-C, which on its own is an F major triad. If you then play a G in your left hand you will have an F/G chord, which is the same notes as the 1st, 7th, 9th and 11th of G dominant 11th. The easiest way to arrive at this chord is the method described in the previous paragraph. The F/G can resolve to the straight chord V (G) if you have enough room in the bar(s). On CD Track 87, bars 1-4 demonstrate the effect of the G11.

Bars 5-8 offer an alternative way of creating a similar sophisticated sound (though not an 11th), where in bar 8 the F bass note stays still, creating a third inversion G7 on the last two beats of the final bar. To get this effect, the right-hand chord stays still and the left-hand bass note goes up a tone (the physical reverse of the first example).

A similar idea can be played by going from chord I to a reverse polarity II set over the root note of chord I, as in bars 4-5. The chord in bar 5 can be thought of as either a third-inversion D7 or a C13♯11 (ouch). In this example it's considered as the former.

CD TRACK 87 Prechorus in C major with 11th

I				iV				IV				IV			
C	\	\	\	G/B	\	\	\	F	\	\	\	F/G	\	\	\

I				II^				iiIII		i IV		IV		V	
C	\	\	\	D/C	\	\	\	G/B	\	F/A	\	F	\	G/F	\

CD TRACK
87

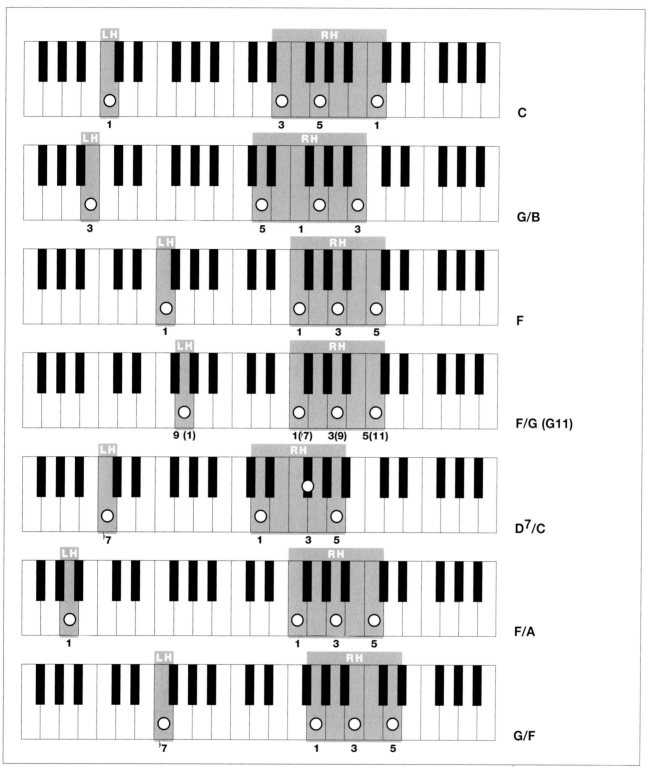

| TECHNIQUE 88 | # ADDING MOVEMENT WITH INVERSIONS |

Inversions can make a chord sequence sound less secure and more mobile, as in the example on CD Track 88. Notice how strongly the C/E rises to the F chord in root position. Linking first inversions to root chords, where the bass rises by a step, creates powerful forward motion. If one inversion leads to another, as in bars 3-4, there is an increasing sense of restlessness, as the music goes hunting for a root chord.

CD TRACK 88 *Four-bar inversion sequence in C*

iI				IV				iiV		iIV		iV		iVI		
C/E	\	\	\	F	\	\	\	C/G	\	F/A	\	G/B	\	Am/C	\	‖

This is a useful technique for keeping your music flowing and not allowing it to get a firm base. Sequences of rising inversions can be set up to make the music sound as though it is continually climbing. Technique 88's last bar just needs a bass note D on the final beat to join up with the bass note E on which the sequence started and the whole thing becomes a circle. This results in the 'rootedness' of an ordinary root position chord becoming transformed into something exotic and much-anticipated. When a series of root chords do finally appear they will sound more grounded than usual.

CD TRACK
88

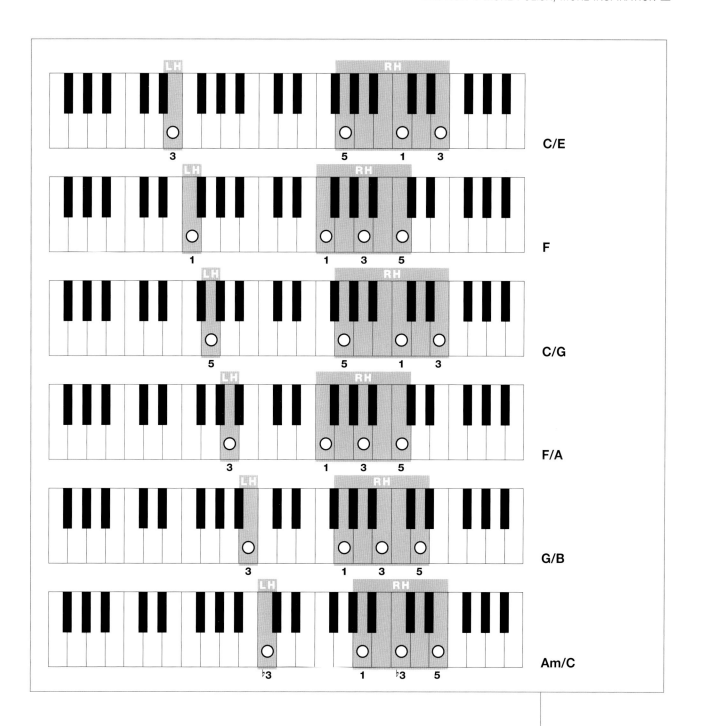

C/E

F

C/G

F/A

G/B

Am/C

CD TRACK

88

TECHNIQUE 89

THE PEDAL NOTE

A pedal is a note in the bass that stays still while chords move above it. A 'tonic' pedal uses the key-note and a 'dominant' pedal uses the 5th of the scale. These are the commonest pedal notes. On the guitar, pedal notes tend to be E, A and D, the lowest open strings, because they leave the fingers free to move around the neck. On a keyboard you can just as easily use any note of the 12. If it's in the left hand it leaves the right hand free to change. Pedals are an excellent means of presenting a chord sequence in more than one way. A sequence might be heard over a pedal through an intro or a verse, then the same sequence might make a chorus with normal root notes in the bass.

If Track 89 sounds like a Brian Wilson/Beach Boys intro, that's because their songs are often characterised by bass notes that have a less-than-predictable relation to their chord.

CD TRACK 89 Four-bar idea in C, over dominant bass pedal

I				VI				IV				♭VII		II		
C/G	\	\	\	Am/G	\	\	\	F/G	\	\	\	B♭/G	\	Dm/G	\	:‖

The relative sophistication of many of The Beach Boys' mid-1960s songs, as heard on albums like *Pet Sounds* and the recently-completed *Smile*, compared with their earlier surfing songs, has a lot to do with the number of inverted chords, chords whose bass notes are not simple roots, and pedal notes. There are some magical things that happen when you take simple chords in the right hand but mess around with the bass note in the left.

Even if your keyboard technique is limited, there's no problem in holding a steady octave in the left hand on the same notes while the right hand moves around.

CD TRACK
89

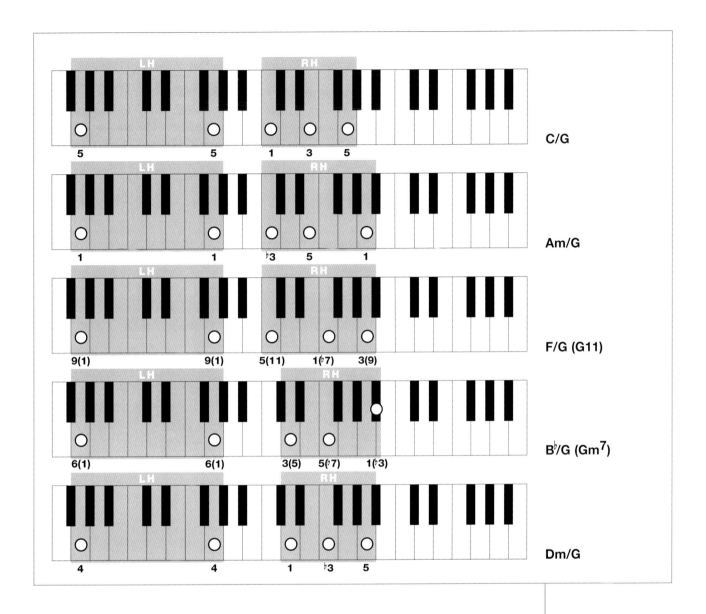

C/G

Am/G

F/G (G11)

B♭/G (Gm⁷)

Dm/G

SECTION 10
Structure, melody, lyrics

"There's a lot of hard work involved in songwriting. The inspiration part is where it comes through you, but once it comes through you, the shaping of it, the craft of it, is something that I pride myself in knowing how to do."

Carole King

This section briefly surveys the additional steps needed to get you from chord ideas to a finished song. When you have several chord sequences that excite you, they need to be placed into a song structure, and then you compose a melody and write some lyrics. We'll look at the structure first.

Most songs have three main sections: the verse, the chorus, and the bridge. These are topped and tailed with an intro and an outro/coda.

THE CHORUS

This is usually the most memorable element in the song. It's the part that an audience remembers the longest and enjoys singing the most. It's often the section where the emotion central to the song is strongest. If the song makes a statement of some kind, this is where you will most likely find it. The commercial success of a song usually rests on its chorus – and this is also true, to a lesser degree, of how songs go over in live performance. If you have ideas for two sequences, put the stronger one in the chorus, provided it isn't too long or complicated. There is a tendency for choruses to simplify musically to achieve greater focus.

THE VERSE

This is the section that alternates with the chorus. The verse often maps out the broad emotional territory of the song. If the chorus is the house, the verse is the plot of land on which it's built. A good verse not only holds interest in its own right but prepares for the chorus, both lyrically and musically. It may describe a situation so the chorus can comment on it. For instance, in a love song, a verse may state that X is in love with Y but Y is in love with Z. In the chorus X will declare his/her position: ie whether he/she will pursue Y or walk away.

THE BRIDGE/MIDDLE-EIGHT

As James Brown once cried in 'Sex Machine', "Can I take it to the bridge?". Once you've had two verses and two choruses it's time for something new. The bridge should contrast with the verse and the chorus, a chance to introduce new musical content and new lyric ideas, so it can briefly take the song somewhere else. For the lyric, this is a chance to imagine an alternative to the events and emotions previously described. Musical devices, such as different chords, a key-change, or a change of instruments, can enhance this feeling of contrast. The bridge might lead straight to the final chorus, or another verse. The bridge is also sometimes known as the 'middle-eight' – for the plain reason that it comes in the middle of the song and is often eight bars long. A bridge can be complemented or replaced by an instrumental solo of some kind; the solo could be the bridge itself, or it could come before or after the bridge.

Verse, chorus and bridge are the three *primary* sections of a song. If a songwriter gets these right the rest of the song will usually fall in place. Often the first ideas a songwriter has are going to be a verse or a chorus. But songs also have *secondary* sections. These include the intro, the outro (coda), the prechorus, short link passages, and solos.

THE INTRO

Although a song could begin at bar 1 of a verse or chorus, most have some kind of introduction. The intro's job is to set the scene. It signals to the listener what type of a song to expect. It establishes the dynamics (loud, soft, medium volume), the tempo (from fast to slow), the beat (4/4, waltz, shuffle, etc), the instrumentation, the key, and most important of

217

all, the atmosphere and mood – much of which depends on the initial harmony. Major chords provide an upbeat intro; minor chords evoke unhappiness or loss.

THE LINK

If a song went straight from verse to chorus and back to verse it could sound too hurried. There might be a lack of pauses in the melody and lyric, which would make a song seem gabbled. A link creates breathing space for both singer and listener. Links are often short – four bars is an average – and are usually instrumental. They can recycle a chord sequence from another part of the song, like the verse or intro. They can be given extra interest if instrumental hooks are placed in them – like a keyboard or guitar riff, or other melodic figure.

THE PRECHORUS

Sometimes a verse has effectively two distinct sections. The first part is lyrically different (and possibly musically altered) each time a verse comes round, but the second remains the same. This is a prechorus. A prechorus is a powerful signal that the song is heading for the chorus, because the same words heard before chorus 1 are the ones heard before chorus 2. It is like sending the message: hold on, the chorus is coming. So a good prechorus can be something of a hook in itself.

THE OUTRO (CODA)

This covers everything after the last chorus, assuming that the track doesn't just repeat the last chorus and fade. A variation on this is to repeat the basic structure of the chorus but simplify it in some way – for example, have a solo over the chorus's chord sequence while the singer ad libs. A coda may also have a new sequence, which might suggest that the situation described in the song has now been changed in some way. If the intro is recycled as the coda, the song will possess a strong circularity, which can be satisfying if this is suitable for the lyric. Always remember to consider if the theme of your lyric might itself imply one structure more than others.

These are the basic elements of song structure, the moulds into which harmony is poured. You will find your song easier to visualise if you write your chord sequences down in bars (like the examples in this book) as you compose and label them verse, chorus, bridge, etc.

WRITING A MELODY

Imagine you have constructed several pleasing chord sequences arranged in a verse/chorus/bridge structure. You are still two vital things short of a song. To achieve a finished song you need to write a melody and some words to sing. Obviously the subject of melody writing is big enough to need a book to itself (see *Melody: How To Write Great Tunes*, Backbeat 2004). But here is a brief summary of some of the main points about writing tunes:

HOW DO I KNOW WHICH NOTES TO SING?

The vast majority of people who try writing songs probably never worry about this question. The reason? People who want to write songs are generally into music. Years of consciously and unconsciously absorbing music conditions our hearing and sense of pitch, so that when faced with a chord sequence in a given musical key we naturally sing the right notes for that key. We might not know what those notes are or why they fit, but they will.

We may even have enough aural grasp of a musical idiom such as soul or blues to be able to bend those melody notes in ways that are common to those styles, say, by introducing certain 'blue' notes. But if you want to know the notes of the scale for the key in which you're writing, there are some simple formulas to apply to the keyboard. Here we've given three of the most common scales used by songwriters:

The major scale:

2-2-1-2-2-2-1 (C-D-E-F-G-A-B)

To find the notes of the major scale for any given song sequence, start from its key note, and advance by the number of keys, black or white – whatever comes next – according to this pattern of tones (two keys) and semitones (one key): 2-2-1-2-2-2-1. That will give you the most common scale for melodies. You can play a major scale from any of the 12 piano keys by this method.

The mixolydian scale:

2-2-1-2-2-1-2 (C-D-E-F-G-A-B♭)

This scale is also popular in melody writing, especially in sequences where you use the ♭VII chord. It's the same as the major scale until the last two notes, where the 7th is lowered by a semitone. This is a 'blue note' when heard in the melody over a I-IV-V three-chord trick or 12-bar. The other important 'blue note' for a melody is the lowered 3rd – in the case of C major this is an E♭. Blue notes give a tougher feel to a melody but are tricky to use over the major scale's three minor chords, II, III and VI. To hear the effect of blue notes, hold down a C triad and sing the notes E♭ and B♭ against it.

The natural minor scale:

2-1-2-2-1-2-2 (C-D-E♭-F-G-A♭-B♭)

This scale will fit many minor-key chord progressions. If you want more of a 18th/19th-century classical sound to your melody, raise the last note by a semitone (here, from B♭ to B). Minor scales lend themselves to sad, mournful songs.

HOW DO I WRITE A MELODY?

If they don't yet have any words, most people hum or sing nonsense syllables while playing their chord progression at the keyboard. Listen for notes that sound good over the chords. Some, like a note that's in the chord you are holding, will blend perfectly. A note outside the chord sounds more tense, even if it belongs to the correct scale for the musical key. Every melody is a mixture of notes that blend and notes that are tense in varying degrees. The length of time you hold each note will decrease or magnify the effect.

CHROMATIC NOTES

If you want to write a tune that has a jazz feel, you will probably need to link melody notes from the scale by using 'chromatic' notes. A chromatic note is one that doesn't belong in that musical key and scale. If a scale has seven notes, and there are 12 notes altogether, then it must logically follow that there are always five chromatic notes to use for this purpose. Your broader musical sense will tell you that some 'wrong' notes are 'right' in a certain context. Some of the most expressive melodies ever written make passing use of tense, dissonant notes. These may be technically 'wrong', in so far as they are outside the musical key or scale, but they could be just what the words require.

WRITING A MELODY ON THE KEYBOARD

Working at the keyboard you have the option of writing melodies by playing rather than singing them. If you want to do this, try putting simple major and minor triads into your left hand so that your right hand is free to play single melody notes. Don't worry about trying to do anything interesting with the chords in the left hand. Just sound each one and hold it down so it sustains.

The advantage of writing a melody on the keyboard is that you can see its pitch contours. If you hang onto one note a lot it will be more noticeable than if you were singing it. If you put leaps into your melody, that will be obvious too, because you can see your right hand jumping around. Just be careful not to get carried away by all those piano keys and octaves and write a tune which goes too low, too high, or too low *and* too high for you to sing. To test if the key you're working in suits your voice, try playing its scale and singing that scale as you go. Find the lowest note you can comfortably sing and the highest. That will give you a clue as to which keys and chords suit your singing voice.

MELODY BEFORE CHORDS

You might already have a tune in mind and want to try fitting chords to it. This is called harmonising. If it seems there's too much choice in terms of chords, you need to figure out the scale of the music key you want to write in – play the notes on a piano and see if they fit an existing scale. Turn the first six notes of the scale into chords in keeping with the pattern major (I) minor (II) minor (III) major (IV) major (V) and minor (VI). That gives your six primary chords. Then take the 7th note of the scale, lower it by a semitone and turn it into a major chord.

Imagine you want to write a song in E major and you have a tune on that scale. Here are the steps:

1	**Start-note of scale:**	**E**
2	**Major scale (2-2-1-2-2-2-1):**	**E-F♯-G♯-A-B-C♯-D♯**
3	**Turn into chords:**	**E, F♯m, G♯m, A, B, C♯**
4	**Lower (flat) the 7th note:**	**D♯ = D**
5	**Turn into a major chord:**	**D major**
6	**Seven songwriting chords:**	**E, F♯m, G♯m, A, B, C♯m, D**

The advantage of coming up with a melody first is that it will dictate the chords, rather than the other way around, as can happen – if the chords are already set down, it can constrict the melody, because it's often harder to change the chords than it is to alter the melody.

MELODY HAS RHYTHM TOO...

Remember to give your melody an interesting rhythm as well as making sure the notes fit with the chords. Beware of always starting phrases in the same place in the bar and stopping in the same place in another bar – is it always before the bar-line and before a chord-change, or on the beat of a new bar and a new chord?

Think about short, medium and long notes in relation to the beat that underpins your tune. Are you using lots of short notes because you have a lot of syllables to fit into each bar? Or do you have a few words that are sung with long, held notes?

MELODIES ARE MADE OF PHRASES

The melody of a song is created from shorter individual phrases. You might have one basic phrase that dominates the verse and is sung four times. If so, try putting subtle small variations so you don't sing exactly the same thing each time. That will give it more interest. Sometimes this has to be done anyway because the lyric lines are not exactly the same length. Also, try singing the same phrase over four different chords and notice adjustments you might have to make to the tune so it fits each chord. Think about how separated you want your phrases to be, like having one or two instrumental bars between the end of one phrase and the start of the next.

MELODY RANGE

Are you writing a melody which is encompassed in a narrow pitch range – say, of a 6th (C to A) – or does your melody have big jumps and stretch beyond an octave? Are you writing a melody that is substantially horizontal in pitch, or vertical, or a mixture? It's good to be aware of these variables.

CONTRAST THE MELODY STYLE OF SECTIONS

It can be an effective technique to consciously contrast the melody style of a verse with that used for the chorus or the bridge. The contrast might arise from the dominant rhythm values of the melody, or its pitch, or how the notes fit with the chords.

TO MAKE MELODIES MORE COLOURFUL

It's easy to start phrases on the 1st, 3rd or 5th of a chord. Instead of holding down a straight major or minor, choose one of the extended chords described in Section 8 and start your melody on the extra note, whether it's a 2nd, 4th, 6th, 7th or 9th.

THE ARPEGGIO: EVERY CHORD IS A MELODY IN WAITING

Remember that many great melodies develop from arpeggios – meaning the notes of a chord played one after the other instead of all at once. In this sense any chord can be turned into the raw material of a tune by playing its notes one after the other, ascending or descending, or in any order you like. This means every chord type in Section 8 is a potential melodic phrase…

PITCH AND CLIMAX

Be sensitive to where the highest note of your melody is going to come. Everything after it may sound like an anti-climax. You may want to save your higher notes for your chorus. Some melodies have been written so that the very last few notes of the entire song are the ones where the singer gets to belt out the phrase for a dramatic finish – the 'My Way' style of ending.

TRANSPOSITION IS A TUNESMITH'S BEST FRIEND

When a chord change occurs you may be able to move an entire phrase up the same distance as you just did with the chord. This results in a new version of the phrase higher or lower than before. The technique is called transposition. There are a number of ways this can be done, depending on whether each note of the melody is moved up or down by the same amount or whether there are small adjustments to make it fit the new chord better. The classic instance of this is when a melody phrase moves up in bars 5-6 of a 12-bar blues with the words staying the same.

Another tip is to try re-writing a melody from major to the minor scale of the same note, or vice versa. The basic contour stays the same but there are significant little differences. Adjust the chords from major to minor to match.

RATE OF CHORD CHANGE

A melodic phrase could be harmonised with a single chord or many chords. You have to choose. How you approach this depends on how many chords you want in the song. Fewer chord changes will throw the emphasis more on the tune and words, but could be dull. Too many chord changes could be exciting or could be restless and distracting. You will certainly want to vary the rate of chord change in different sections.

CONTRARY MOTION

This is a simple but elegant principle that can be exploited to good effect. A rising melody makes a pleasing contrast to a descending chord progression, and vice versa. If you have a bassline going down in steps, try writing a melody that ascends.

WRITING A LYRIC

At some point in the songwriting process you need to write a lyric (or find someone to write lyrics to your music). Lyrics can arrive, complete or half-formed, at any point during the writing of the music for a song. Some songwriters start with a lyric and then look to find music and melody for it. Some find odd lyrical phrases come while they are putting the chord sequence together, or one lyric line will arrive with melody attached. I often get inspired by a title, which serves to focus the mood and theme. Or you can write a lyric at the end. Songwriters also find that songs arrive by many different routes.

A lyric is the place where the emotional suggestions that arise from pure music get defined as concrete human concerns, situations, events and themes. Like melody, lyric-writing is a subject that deserves a whole book. But here are some tips to get you going:

LYRICS AND POETRY

Lyrics are not poetry. They may have poetic qualities, but that's a different thing. Poems are intended to be standalone and to signify alone. Lyrics need music to bring out their full force. Music has the power to rescue phrases that are just too dull or clichéd to be used in a poem. For this reason, many song lyrics use language in sloppy, uninteresting ways and no-one notices (or if they do, they're not bothered) because of the music's saving grace.

LYRICS AND RHYME

Lyrics do not have to rhyme, or do not have to rhyme every line, and do not have to rhyme exactly. Often the last syllable of a word sung on a popular song is hardly audible. So rhyming 'mind' with 'time' in a lyric is perfectly OK, because the vowel sound 'i' counts more than the words' terminations.

THE MAGIC OF TITLES

Never underestimate the power of a good title. Consider one like 'Baby I Want Your Love' – how many times has that, or something similar, been used? If you're writing a group of songs for an album, imagine yourself picking up the CD and glancing at the titles on the back. Do they entice you into wanting to hear the songs? Or do they read like a million others? Do they have character? Do they immediately stir your imagination and your curiosity. Conversely, how many songs are there called 'Alone Again Or' or 'Positively Fourth Street' or 'Novocaine For The Soul'? All great titles. So be clever and/or memorable.

Think about where in the lyric you want to put the title, or even if it's going to be there at all. 'Desperado', 'Eight Miles High', and 'Everybody's Talkin' At Me', are three songs where the title is the first phrase of the lyric. Traditionally it crops up in the chorus. If it isn't anywhere in the song, listeners would have to hope the DJ says something like, "That was 'Amber Sunlight Blues' by The Fire Department" afterwards. Word-play in a title is good: did the Moody Blues sing about nights or knights in white satin? Meatloaf famously declaimed he would do anything for love but he wouldn't do *that* – much head-scratching followed, as listeners amused themselves wondering what 'that' referred to.

NOTES AND DRAFTING

Don't try to write perfect stanzas out of thin air and then find you've been staring at a blank sheet of paper for three hours because your rampant perfectionism has rejected every single first line you've come up with. When you sit down to write a lyric, just write. Don't worry if it comes out clichéd and horrible at first. You can cut that stuff later. Think of the process as being like panning for gold. Few prospectors ever waded into shallow water and immediately picked up gold with their fingers. You have to sift a certain amount of mud to get the couple of gold nuggets that will be the basis of a good lyric which knows where it's going.

To get ideas, keep a notebook with you. Jot down odd lines and phrases, even when you're not actually at a musical instrument. Listen and make a note of what people say around you. Sometimes fragments of conversation can be turned into lyric ideas. Odd turns of phrase, sometimes accidental (think of Ringo's "hard day's night" expression), can stimulate a lyric.

GET A GOOD FIRST LINE

Many lyrics have evocative first lines that grab the listener's attention. Often, thinking of a good first line can make the rest of the lyric flow (but, as I've said, don't sit waiting for it forever – move on and go back to it if needs be). You can try writing provocative first lines for their own sake and see if you can develop a lyric from the situation they imply. Good first line tactics include posing a question or making a conditional statement, ie one that includes words like 'if', 'why', 'because', 'how', 'only', etc.

Here are the opening lines of some famous songs. Consider how much they achieve in so short a space:

"Do you know the way to San Jose?" *(the question and the title).*

'Wake up Maggie, I think I've got something to say to you" *(overheard conversation)*

"I am a line-man for the county" *(a character and his work)*

"Ain't no sunshine when she's gone" *(a proposition to be explored)*

"Woke up one morning, half asleep" *(a blues variation)*

"I looked out this morning and the sun was gone" *(verb – I did something and something followed)*

"She's a maid in heaven/he's a knight on the tiles" *(word-play)*

"It's over now – you've had your fun" *(conversational, and what is over?)*

"Pushing through the market square" *(setting a scene)*

"Here comes Johnny Yen again" *(introducing us to a character)*

POINT OF VIEW

Remember that a song doesn't have to be written in the 'first person': "I looked out this morning..." could be "He/she/they looked out this morning". So who is speaking your lyric? If you feel exposed by writing in the first person, you can get a new perspective on personal themes by addressing yourself as 'you'. Most listeners will think you are talking to someone else instead.

THE PATTERNED LYRIC

A lyric can be constructed from a single type of phrase, where a simple grammatical formula is repeated over and over in a parallel form. Take the lines:

> "Never ask me why I need you
> Never ask how long I'll be
> Never know what's false or true
> Never ask the blind to see."

This is a sequence of phrases using 'never' followed by a verb. Roy Orbison's 'Pretty Woman' does this to some degree with phrases that start with the title. The Police's 'King Of Pain' does it enigmatically by using only descriptive images in the verse, each of which stands for the speaker. The images include a flag, a dead salmon, a black spot on the sun, a hunted fox, and in each case the backing vocals deliver the explanatory phrase, "That's my soul up there".

IMAGERY

When Bruce Springsteen wrote "I'm On Fire" he was using a metaphor – he didn't mean it literally. He was on fire with passion, and was not the first singer (or the last) in the annals of popular music to feel that way. A powerful metaphor, simile or image can generate a whole lyric as you work through the meaning of it. Sometimes this image will become the title. In some of Elvis Costello's early songs (say the first five albums) the lyric is spun out of a nucleus of associated images and puns. Even if the meaning sometimes got derailed, it was still a lot of fun and the lyrics had a certain linguistic energy of their own, separate from the music.

LYRIC THEMES

Love is the most popular topic for song lyrics. There are innumerable angles and situations from which you can write, as people go through all the various stages of falling in, out, and back in love. Here, the need is to strike a balance between the general and the specific, the personal and the universal. The most universal of experiences comes across more powerfully when the lyric evokes a specific time and place, as Dylan did to bittersweet effect with the polaroid snapshot imagery in 'Sara', and as Al Stewart did in 'Year Of The Cat' (another great title).

EVERY STORY TELLS A PICTURE

Love songs often express an emotion or set of emotions around a situation, especially a conflict or crisis. The lyric may not tell us much of the 'backstory'. One way to move away from always writing about feelings is to consciously tell a story with a beginning, middle and end. This can grab the listener's attention through narrative interest – they want to know what's going to happen next.

GEOGRAPHY AND TRAVEL

Thinking geographically is a good way to evoke pictures and suggest a story which can turn into a lyric. As soon as you try to describe a journey you are committed to describing where it started, why it started, where it's going, and how long it might take. In popular song lyrics people have walked, cruised the freeways on bikes or in cars, hitch-hiked, jumped on trains and taken jet-planes – they've even been through deserts on horses without names.

LIVING IN THE CITY

Millions of people live and work in cities. Maybe they would like to get away, but they can't. Maybe they dream of another town, another city, another coast, another continent. Or maybe they like it where they are. Are they born to run, or are they the only living boy in New York? You could write about the dramas of life in a modern city, the excitement, the danger, the surprises – write about wanting to be there or wanting to get away.

TIME AND TIDE

Time, memory, days, months, seasons, years – these are rich subject areas for song lyrics because they speak to universal concerns about being the age we are, being young, being old, maturing, about change, looking forward and looking back. How many songs do you know that either have a month or a day of the week in the title…?

FAMOUS PEOPLE AND HISTORICAL EVENTS

Many songwriters have periods where they either don't want to write about themselves or they get bored with doing so. One way out of this is to write about famous and infamous characters from history. Think of a character who made an impression on their time and place that interests you. Do a bit of research by reading a book or article about them. The biographical entries in any good encyclopedia can be a useful starting point. Make a list of short phrases that refer to their life. Out of these phrases could come the title and the beginning of a lyric.

EVERY PICTURE TELLS A STORY

Your main interest in the arts may lie in music, but a great source of inspiration can be found when you engage with the other arts – novels, poems, plays, paintings, sculpture, movies. Many songwriters have taken film or book titles as the inspiration for songs, or focused on a character or a scene that inspires them. Don McLean, who wrote 'American Pie' as a phantasmagoric history of the years from the death of Buddy Holly in 1959 through the 1960s, also had a hit with 'Vincent', a song about the painter Vincent Van Gogh.

To sum up, in songwriting it's not just about the raw materials – the musical key or chords or the lyrical subject – it's about what you do with them. Songwriting is all about how you combine those different elements, using a mix of personal experience, style, talent, and of course learned craft.

Famous songwriters on songwriting

"I was lying on the sofa in our house, listening to Yoko play Beethoven's 'Moonlight Sonata' on the piano. Suddenly I said, 'Can you play those chords backwards?' She did, and I wrote 'Because' around them."

John Lennon

Here is a selection of famous songwriters talking about their experiences of creating words and music – over and above the ones that have already introduced each section of the book. Many of these people are chosen here because they compose on keyboards, but I've included some other quotes of broader interest. Note that songwriters don't always agree on some central aspects of the creative process – but that's to be expected with an activity that remains (underneath the craft) a rather mysterious and magical thing.

Burt Bacharach

"Music breeds its own inspiration. You can only do it by doing it. You just sit down and you may not feel like it, but you push yourself. It's a work process. Or just improvise. Something will come. Or turn on the drum machine. Or turn on another stop on the keyboard. Or get away from the piano. But don't sit around and wait for something magical to happen in your head or heart."

"The bottom line is, whatever chord I choose, it's still governed by what I hear in my head and what that melody is dictating. Sometimes you add a major 2nd to a chord, and it doesn't work. Maybe it doesn't work because the melody is crying out to be in a pure chord or triad."

Hal David

"Songs come from a million different places. Somebody says something, and suddenly it rings a bell. You're watching a movie or a show or a television program and you hear a line. You're in the audience and you hear a phrase and suddenly there's an idea for a song."

Lamont Dozier (of Motown's Holland-Dozier-Holland)

"The nature of people is to walk down the street and whistle a tune … But the melody isn't the only important part of a song. There's a marriage between the melody and the harmony – the chords you use that melody has to stand on – that must be strong. And you have to have the lyrics that work with that melody … It's trial and error. You sit and play chords…"

Brian Wilson

"What I'll do is I'll first get a key. Then after that I try to find a chord pattern, some kind of chord pattern that I can write a melody to. Then I play the chord pattern and I play a rhythm in a certain key, and I start thinking of these great, outrageous melodies … [Favourite keys are] E and B … I hardly write anything in a minor key. I just don't. I write major songs."

Gerry Goffin

"I'd write a lyric first, or else she [Carole King] would play a chord progression on the piano and I'd write a melody over it. I can't do that now because melodies are more sophisticated and not as symmetrical. And I don't sing on key that well, but Carole was always able to change a melody enough to make it interesting … I think there are still love songs to be written. It's kind of harder in a high-tech society. People are not as vulnerable to sentiment."

Carole King

"If you are sitting down and you feel that you want to write and nothing is coming, you get up and do something else. Then you come back again and try it again. But you do it in a relaxed manner. *Trust* that it will be there. If it ever was once, and you've ever done it once, it will be back. It always comes back, and the only thing that is a problem is … worrying about it."

Aimee Mann

"Every time I learn a new chord I write about 50 songs with it."

Joan Armatrading

"Songs I've written on the piano tend to be more melodic, and songs on the guitar tend to be more rhythmic."

Bob Dylan

"On the piano, my favourite keys are the black keys … Guitar bands don't usually like to play in those keys, which kind of gives me an idea, actually, of a couple of songs that could actually sound *better* in black keys."

Leonard Cohen

"Usually I'm working on something … I do sit down now and then during the day and grind out a word or two, but it's a word at a time, you know? Some people write great songs in the back of taxi cabs, and it's no guarantee of their excellence that my songs take years to write. I don't know why they take that long – it just comes very slowly, music and lyrics … It generally starts with a line on the synth or a line in my notebook, but I don't really know how it's done. If I knew that, I'd do it more often."

Midge Ure

"The guitar is my original instrument, but if I sit down and write very simplistic things on a guitar, I tend to dismiss them instantly. If I play them on a keyboard, which is definitely not my instrument, they work – I like the sound or the texture."

Paul Simon

"In 'Still Crazy After All These Years,' that [title] came to me first. And it didn't come with melody, either. It just came as a line. And then I had to create a story … I was studying harmony with a bass player and composer named Chuck Israels at the time, so I was doing more interesting changes … It's hard to get an interesting key change. I also like to write a bridge and just jump a whole-tone up. 'Still Crazy' has that."

Jimmy Webb

(On working with chord patterns) "I'm doing substitutions, I'm taking bass notes that are not in the tonic and putting them with another chord. I'm taking the third out of the right hand and playing it in the left hand, and adding a suspended second to the right hand. I'm playing around with voices. I'm moving things – on one chord I have the 7th in the bass. Which sounds strange all by itself. If you went over to the piano and hit that chord you'd say, 'That's not a very nice chord'. But sometimes it depends on the chord that comes before and the chord that comes after … And so a lot of it is not just sitting around and pecking around until you find an interesting chord. But it's sequencing chords. It's stringing them together like pearls on a string."

"Sometimes at the beginning it just seems like an impossible task … until you plant yourself, put your hands on the keys, and actually push one of them down … Sometimes that's really hard for me to do. I sit there and I go, 'I don't want to play a G. And I don't want to play a B-flat.' It *all* looks unpromising. And I just sit there, and I have to make myself play. I say, 'Play. Play one note.' And that way I get myself going, very slowly sometimes. And then momentum builds and I really get into the joy of it."

Van Dyke Parks

"I like to come back to songwriting because it is, relatively speaking, an unobtrusive window into the soul. It's a very nice escape, too."

Janis Ian

"I love strange chords. But sometimes you've got to throw it out. You want to jar people when they need to be jarred. You don't want to jar them for the sake of jarring them."

"Pythagoras felt that specific notes affected people to very minute gradations of feeling. And every songwriter, I think, knows that D is a great key for a love song. It just happens to work. And B-flat is always a great jump key for jazz."

Walter Becker (Steely Dan)

"You have, in the key of C, an E in the bass, a D, a G and a C on top … it's a Cmajor chord with an E in the bass [as well as the major 2nd]. I've been told that in some circles this is known as the 'Steely Dan chord'."

Rickie Lee Jones

"Songwriters have a thing, a basic couple of chords that they are, and they usually gravitate around those. I'd say there're probably harmonies and types of chords and intervals that are of me and I always like to play them."

"On the piano I just play little chords. I don't play the melody, but I hear the melody with the chords. It's always different … I'm not thinking what the chord is at all. I have no idea what the chord is. I just pick them out by sound."

Bruce Hornsby

"Sometimes it helps me if I write the melody on the piano. I tend to play, perhaps, more interesting melodies than what I hear in my head."

Mike Mills (R.E.M.)

"Generally, when people are trying to write hit songs, they have a very simple one or two-chord verse and then a three or four-hook chorus. But we would have five chords in the verse and then three in the chorus. But we would have a whole lot going on before the vocal melody."

"Minors are very powerful keys, and very powerful chords. My favourite chord is a 7th. Whenever there's a chord and I think it's boring, I play a 7th on the bass."

Paul McCartney

'I wrote 'When I'm 64' on the piano, and from there it's really been a mixture of the both. I just do either, now. Sometimes I've got a guitar in my hands, sometimes I'm sitting at a piano. It depends whatever instrument I'm at – I'll compose on it, you know."

John Lennon

(On writing 'Good Morning, Good Morning') "I often sit at the piano, working at songs, with the telly on low in the background. If I'm a bit low and not getting much done, then the words on the telly come through. That's when I heard "Good morning, good morning" … it was a Cornflakes advertisement."

Bruce Springsteen

"The orchestral sound of *Born To Run* came from most of the songs being written on piano. Few of the album's songs were written on guitar. It was on the keyboard that I could find the arrangements needed to accompany the stories I was writing. 'Born To Run', which began on the guitar with the riff that opens the song, was finished on the piano."

Kate Bush

"I feel as though I've built up a real relationship with the piano. It's almost like a person. Like, it's really comforting just to sit down and play it. And the piano almost dictates what my songs will be about. If I haven't got a particular idea I just sit down and play chords and then the chords almost dictate what the song should be about because they have their own moods. Like a minor chord is very likely to tell me something sad. A major chord tells me something a little more up-tempo and, like, on a more positive level of thinking."

(On writing 'Sat In Your Lap') "I already had the piano patterns but they didn't turn into a song until the night after I'd been to see a Stevie Wonder gig. Inspired by the feeling of his music, I set a rhythm on the [drum machine] and worked in the piano riff to the hi-hat and snare. I now had a verse and a tune to go over, but only a few lyrics ... so the rest of the lyrics became 'na-na-na' or words that happened to come into my head."

Andrew Farris (INXS)

"The way I work now is I say, 'I'm going to allot myself this amount of time to work, and whatever comes out is going to be important.' And I'll record a whole song, finish the song, there and then. If I can't, it obviously wasn't good enough. That's the rules I set myself. I just say, 'Forget it, it's not working.' It's not some sort of golden jewel that's been invented by some mad genius – that's all garbage. If it's not good enough to stay in your mind long enough to write a song, forget it. Just write the goddam thing. If you can't finish a song, don't worry about it, try again."

Paul Heaton (The Beautiful South)

"I think the songs I write with Dave [Hemingway] are better than the ones I come up with in my head. There's a sort of clash between melody and chords that's a bit more interesting. The ones that you come up with in your head are immediately catchy, but don't grow on you."

Frank Zappa

"Usually after I finish a song, that's it. It doesn't belong to me any more. When I'm working on a song it takes weeks and weeks to finish, and the orchestra stuff takes even longer than that. It's like working on the construction of an airplane. One week you're a riveter, or you're putting the wiring in, or something like that. It's just a job you do and then you go on to the next step, which is learning how to perform it, or teaching it to somebody else."

A gallery of keyboard songs/albums

"The world don't need any more songs... They've got enough. They've got way too many. As a matter of fact, if nobody wrote any songs from this day on, the world ain't gonna suffer for it. Nobody cares. There's enough songs for people to listen to if they want to listen to songs ... unless someone's gonna come along with a pure heart and has something to say. That's a different story..."

Bob Dylan

As well as writing books about songwriting, guitar-playing and popular music, I also work as a music arranger, transcribing songs from the 1950s to the present day, within the format known as the chord songbook. These economical publications are designed for people who don't read music, as they consist simply of lyrics, chord names and guitar chord boxes. I've had over 1,000 such arrangements published, including the entire output of The Beatles.

Based on my experience as an arranger, I can say it's often a very different experience arranging a song written or performed on keyboards as opposed to guitar and, within the limitations of the chord songbook, often a more difficult a task. It's also made clear to me the traits that songs composed on keyboard exhibit, in contrast to those written on guitar.

From creating many such arrangements I have noticed the following about songs composed on keyboards:

- Songs written on keyboards often have more chords. This is partly because it's easier to be content strumming a single guitar chord than striking it over and over on the keys. It's also because the temptation to colour a chord on keyboards by merely moving a single finger is too much to resist (and why not?). Another reason is that it's easier to create new chords from a given position on keyboards than it is on guitar. This means chords are inserted where they might not have been on guitar.

- Keyboard songs are more likely to feature 'chromatic' chords (outwith the key), because they are easy to include as the hands move from one chord to another.

- Keyboard songs often feature a chord vocabulary in which more complex extended chords occur, with more than four different notes, such as dominant 11ths before choruses.

- Songs written with a piano in mind often have a greater rate of harmonic change. For example, it is arguably easier to play a bar of one-chord-to-a-beat on the piano than it is on guitar.

- Conversely, if a synth is used, chords can be sustained for bars and bars to give a smooth background effect, and this could lead to a very slow rate of chord change.

- Songs written on keyboards have more inversions. This is because they are easier to play: the left hand's independence of the right means that bass notes can be changed without the chord shape being altered. Keyboard players are more likely to use so-called 'pushed' (rhythmically anticipated) inversions, backed up by percussion accents, on the last beat of a bar to move to the next root note.

- Keyboard songs are more likely to feature 'slash' chords, again because they are easy to play.

- Keyboard songs are more likely to feature major-to-minor changes (or the reverse) on the same root note because this only involves a single finger move and is more obvious visually on the keyboard.

- Keyboard songs tend to be written in a greater variety of keys, and favour some flat keys which guitarists tend to avoid. The truth of this observation excludes the use of the capo and assumes the guitar is in its 'natural' uncapo'd state.

- Keyboard songs often have chord motion which is shaped by voice-leading. Voice-leading is the movement of notes to their nearest next step in succeeding chords. This may have quasi-melodic implications for the sound of the accompaniment.

- Keyboard songs can have longer and less compromised descending or ascending basslines.

- Keyboard songs can have freer, more sustained, even more unusual pedal notes under the right-hand harmony.

- Keyboard songs are more likely to include octave runs (in either hand) and decorative fills based on fleeting and tumbling major/minor 2nds.

- Keyboard songs are more likely to feature the vocal melody (or parts of it) in the right hand along with the chords.

All of these features can be heard in various songs on the following albums. I've chosen these 24 albums as samples of songwriting in which the piano/keyboard plays a prominent role. The style of music is varied, but it's all of a high quality.

The Kick Inside (1978) – Kate Bush

For the mature Bush go to *Hounds Of Love* and *The Sensual World*, but this first set of songs, which drew on hundreds of earlier efforts at songwriting, is strongly and more nakedly pianistic. High rates of chord changes, unusual keys and chromatic touches are evident throughout, especially on the two hit singles, 'Wuthering Heights' and 'The Man With The Child In His Eyes'.

Classic Tracks & Rarities (2002) – Procol Harum

Procol Harum were a five-piece with Hammond organ and piano, and at times they sounded like a gothic version of The Band. Their most famous song, 'Whiter Shade Of Pale', has a hypnotic bassline that seems to descend endlessly, but 'A Salty Dog' and 'Homburg' both match its nocturnal chandeliered magnificence. 'A Salty Dog' opens with a classic slow quarter-note set of chords shifting from majors through suspensions to minors. 'Homburg' has a verse of chords often inverted or placed over unusual bass notes.

Smile (1966-67/2004) – Brian Wilson

It's little short of a miracle that a new version of *Smile*, rock's most legendary 'lost' album, should have appeared in 2004. It features 17 tracks, 47 minutes of music, based on a project abandoned 37 earlier ago that helped give Brian Wilson a nervous breakdown and fractured The Beach Boys' career. There are plenty of on-the-beat piano chords (in accented quarter-notes), and Wilson makes heavy use of inversions, including those whose bass notes are not necessarily reached by step, as in the chorus of 'Roll Plymouth Rock' and the verse of 'Cabinessence' and much of 'Surf's Up'. These inversions are crucial to his music. They intensify the emotion, and also give the music a dreamy, other-worldly quality.

Little Earthquakes (1991) – Tori Amos

This debut rebukes those who assume that anyone sat at a piano can't deliver spikey, inventive music which is aggressive and beautiful. Amos's considerable technique shows in the piano embellishments. She probably uses more turnarounds than piano songwriters of an early generation, like Carole King, as is evident in the beautiful ballad 'Winter'. 'Crucify' gives a good idea of the effect of 5ths on its intro verse, and of how Amos can include fragments of the melody with fast fills in-between vocal phrases. On 'Girl' she keeps a figure in 3rds going in her left hand while playing melody fills and broken chords in her right. 'Silent All These Years' starts with an insinuating little chromatic figure that continues in a simpler form in the verse. The verse of 'Precious Things' is carried by another repeating figure – Amos's equivalent of a guitar riff.

Greatest Hits 1970-2002 (2004) – Elton John

For much of the 1970s Elton John was the world's biggest act who solely used piano to create his music. His first clutch of albums demonstrated that he was equally happy writing moody string-laden ballads, medium-paced gospel-tinged rock, and uptempo rock'n'roll, with the ivories pounding in the manner of Jerry Lee Lewis or Little Richard. Listen for pianistic songwriting touches such as the subtle inversions in the chorus of 'Your Song', or the intros of 'Someone Saved My Life Tonight' and 'Candle In The Wind', where a left-hand pedal note plays a critical role.

Wind And Wuthering (1977) – Genesis

Genesis were one of the 1970s leading progressive rock bands, from which lead singer Peter Gabriel and drummer Phil Collins went on to have considerable solo success. Keyboards in Genesis were performed by Tony Banks. The complex progressions of the first two songs, 'Eleventh Earl Of Mar' and 'One For The Vine', are prog-rock at its ambitious and thoughtful best.

Amnesiac (2001) – Radiohead

Radiohead's fifth album continued the experimental electronic and ambient vein of 'Kid A'. Many of the tracks on this record from Oxford's finest feature electronic keyboards, synths, and samples. 'Packt Like Sardines In A Crushd Tin Box' is dominated by a bassy electric piano chord sequence built on two-note intervals. In the odd-timed 'Pyramid Song' with its parallel shifted chords, listen carefully to how the top note of many of these chords stays the same – a typical keyboard technique that's very hard on guitar. It also features a major-minor chord shift which happens more often on the piano than the guitar. Slippage from major to minor and augmented chords features on the piano part in 'Life In A Glasshouse'.

237

For Your Pleasure (1973) – Roxy Music

After their rough-edged debut, Roxy Music hit their stride with the second album's arty take on glam rock. Despite the important contributions of guitarist Phil Manzanera and saxophonist Andy Mackay, the core of the band's sound in those days was Brian Eno's synth and Bryan Ferry's often bleak piano motifs. The dance track 'Do The Strand' is driven by stark piano 5ths played at a fast tempo. 'Beauty Queen' has shuddering chords echoed on an electric piano. The 5ths can also be heard on 'Strictly Confidential'. 'Editions Of You' starts with another primitive electric keyboard sequence and 'In Every Dream Home A Heartache' makes brilliant use of a four-chord turnaround with a clever descriptive lyric and slow-burning tension which explodes in a guitar solo/drum entry and a blizzard of phasing.

The Pretender (1976) – Jackson Browne

Browne exemplified a style of easy-going West coast rock which was exploited to greater commercial advantage by The Eagles (for whom he wrote a couple of songs) and Fleetwood Mac. On Browne's songs there are plenty of pushed inversions at the end of bars moving up a step. 'The Fuse' has some unusual chromatic chord changes and an example of a II^ chord over a tonic pedal. There are quick rates of chord change at 2:07 and 3:49, following the appearance of the title in the lyrics. The first 20 seconds of 'Here Come Those Tears Again' has a typical descending bassline which comes to rest on a second inversion chord I, which then goes to chord V (a standard formula), especially under the singing of the title phrase. 'Sleep's Dark And Silent Gate' has a similar motif. Standout title track 'The Pretender' is marked by frequent I-IV shifts.

A Night At The Opera (1975) – Queen

This album is renowned as the home of Queen's most famous song, the epic 'Bohemian Rhapsody'. Despite the fact that Queen's music was grounded in a hard rock/glam amalgam, and you therefore tend to think of Brian May's guitar riffs, Freddie Mercury's piano playing is crucial to this track, composed in several unguitaristic flat keys. And can you imagine trying to compose the operatic middle bit on anything other than a keyboard?

McCartney (1970) – Paul McCartney

The Beatles' catalogue contains a number of piano-composed songs, by both McCartney and Lennon – 'I Am The Walrus', 'Lady Madonna', 'Penny Lane' and 'Golden Slumbers' all spring to mind. Early in his own solo career, Lennon put his fingers to the white keys and came up with 'Imagine', but it's an injustice of musical history that McCartney's blazing 'Maybe I'm Amazed' isn't as celebrated. Full of inversions, pedal notes and linking scales, the full pianistic effect is best heard on the live version released on *Wings Over America*.

Greatest Hits (1995) – Bruce Springsteen

I've cited this album mainly for the track 'Streets Of Philadelphia', as well as for the fact that, despite his association with guitar, Springsteen has written some great songs on keyboards, notably 'Born To Run', 'Thunder Road' (which he sometimes plays solo in concert on piano) and 'The Promise' (on the *Tracks* album). 'Streets…' shows another approach, which is to have a very slow rate of chord change by using sustained synth 'pads', giving a smooth and moody background.

Who's Next (1971) – The Who

Defined as they were by Pete Townshend's Captain Powerchord guitar assault, The Who nevertheless made a significant contribution to the use of electronic keyboards and synths in rock music, notably with the sequencer figures that distinguish 'Baba O'Reilly' and 'Won't Get Fooled Again'. What's more, the beautiful 'Song Is Over' is built around an inspired chord change and fill that could only have been written on piano.

Murmur (1983) – R.E.M.

During their long career R.E.M. have sometimes diversified from their guitar rock by including songs that feature keyboards. Many readers will immediately think of 'Nightswimming' from 1992's *Automatic For The People*, but the standout track from their 1983 debut is the piano-based song 'Perfect Circle', whose basic idea was composed by drummer Bill Berry – which bears out the spirit of this book: pick up a new instrument, write a different song.

T*he Very Best Of* (1994) – Elvis Costello & the Attractions

The sound of the Attractions was roughly balanced between Elvis's guitar and Steve Naïve's keyboards, which range from 1960s Farfisa organ stabs to elegant piano fills. 'Shipbuilding', one of the classiest songs of the 1980s, has a poise and a musical logic about its progression that suggests it would not have looked out of place in the songbook of one of the great writing teams from the 1930s/40s. Typically for a piano song, there are the subtle shifts of harmony as major chords give way to their respective minors. The graceful progressions lend a poignancy to the lyric's description of the human cost of battle and playing politics with war.

Gold (2004) – Abba

Abba's string of chart hits in the 1970s is now viewed as classic commercial songwriting. They may not be your cup of tea, but Bjorn and Benny certainly had a way with hooks. Many of the Abba hits are dominated by keyboards, with decorative touches like the famous piano octaves in 'Dancing Queen', but also at a deeper compositional level, as in 'Mamma Mia' with its pounding chords and frequent inversions.

The Free Story (1996) – Free

Free are rightly remembered as a guitar rock band who found their own signature approach to heavy blues/rock. But singer Paul Rodgers also supplied them with a number of piano-

239

based ballads, of which 'Be My Friend' and the hit single 'My Brother Jake' are the most touching. The former is in the highly unguitaristic key of B♭ minor, and the latter has plenty of inversions, the like of which you don't hear in their other songs.

The Essential Masters (2000) – Laura Nyro

Nyro's highly individual mix of soul/gospel/pop with poetical lyrics gave her a cult following in the late 1960s before her career drifted into the shadows in the mid 1970s. Her posthumous reputation looks set for a revival. Songs like 'Stoned Soul Picnic' have a very pianistic approach to chord sequence and harmony. If you like her music you should also hear Carole King albums like *Tapestry* (1971).

Court And Spark (1974) – Joni Mitchell

Although famous for her idiosyncratic approach to guitar-playing (often using altered tunings), Joni Mitchell's classic early Seventies albums like this, or the earlier *Blue* and *For The Roses*, also feature many piano-composed songs where she was able to transfer from guitar, and extend, her palette of jazzy chords.

Autobahn (1974) – Kraftwerk

The German synth outfit managed a hit single with an edited version of the 20-minute title track of this groundbreaking album. Harmonically primitive and minimalist in outlook, Kraftwerk forged their sound from a range of early synths. Bouncing octave figures support melodic fragments composed from a handful of notes, and both are subjected to the manipulation of electronic tone.

Parachutes (2000) – Coldplay

While the electric guitar has never entirely shaken off its image of being an unruly, badly behaved dog of an instrument compared to 'proper' instruments like the violin, the piano in popular music never quite escapes its elevated origin in the classical world. Slow ballads on piano bring a touch of class to the sound of a rock band. Popular Coldplay songs like 'Trouble' and the later 'In My Place' and 'The Scientist' show how this is done.

The Best Of (2002) – Randy Newman

Despite writing hits like 'Mama Told Me Not To Come' and 'Simon Smith And His Amazing Dancing Bear', and film scores, Newman has remained a cult figure. From his first eponymous solo album in 1968, where his songs were complemented by orchestra, to 1977's *Little Criminals*, which included the controversial hit single 'Short People', Newman has carved out his own path of oblique and satirical piano-based compositions.

The Berry Vest Of (2004) – Gilbert O'Sullivan

Few performers have been so unfashionable for so long as Gilbert O'Sullivan, and the punning title of this compilation is typical of the cheesey blandness that characterised hit singles like 'Clare' and 'Get Down'. But he can be forgiven anything and everything for the brilliant and melancholic trio of 'Nothing Rhymed', 'Alone Again (Naturally)' and 'We Will'. These songs have superb piano progressions and touching, reticent lyrics that, while being grounded in the everyday, elevate them into higher realms of meaning.

The Look Of Love (2001) – Burt Bacharach

Along with lyricist Hal David, Burt Bacharach is a towering figure in songwriting, whose romantic music was a defining part of the 1960s era. No one evokes the anguished joy of love like Bacharach, and his composing instrument of choice is the piano. It's unlikely any guitar-wielding songwriter would have come up with some of his chord sequences.

Appendix

- Easy page-reference table of techniques

- Chord diagrams for all the majors and minors

- Table of chord formulas

- Glossary of songwriting terms and concepts

EASY PAGE-REFERENCE TABLE OF TECHNIQUES

This is a quick, one-stop solution to finding any of the keyboard-songwriting techniques discussed in the book. Note that each technique number listed also corresponds to a CD track of the same number.

TECHNIQUE 1:   a one-finger change *p15*

TECHNIQUE 2:   three chords from one – inversions *p18*

TECHNIQUE 3:   the minor inversion *p20*

TECHNIQUE 4:   white-key minors *p22*

TECHNIQUE 5:   start from a first-inversion shape *p24*

TECHNIQUE 6:   start from a minor first inversion *p26*

TECHNIQUE 7:   start from a second inversion *p28*

TECHNIQUE 8:   start major, move downward *p30*

TECHNIQUE 9:   start minor, move downward *p32*

TECHNIQUE 10:   beyond three fingers *p36*

TECHNIQUE 11:   little finger rises in half steps *p42*

TECHNIQUE 12:   little finger rises in whole steps *p44*

TECHNIQUE 13:   moving the thumb down *p46*

TECHNIQUE 14:   thumb up and down on a minor *p48*

TECHNIQUE 15:   thumb up and down on a major *p50*

TECHNIQUE 16:   middle finger up and down (suspensions) *p52*

TECHNIQUE 17:   moving two fingers *p54*

TECHNIQUE 18:   the 'crab' move *p56*

TECHNIQUE 19:   a left-hand move *p58*

TECHNIQUE 20:   a left-hand 5th and a bass 'crab' *p60*

TECHNIQUE 21:   the 'three-chord trick' (and the eight-bar) *p64*

TECHNIQUE 22:   the blues and the 12-bar *p66*

TECHNIQUE 23:   the 16-bar section *p68*

TECHNIQUE 24:   classic song form *p70*

TECHNIQUE 25:   the three-chord turnaround *p72*

TECHNIQUE 26:   three chords meet the minor *p75*

TECHNIQUE 27:   an easy chord substitute *p76*

TECHNIQUE 28:   RH inversions and relative minors *p78*

TECHNIQUE 29:   hold back the fourth chord *p82*

TECHNIQUE 30:   four chords in a 12-bar verse *p84*

TECHNIQUE 31:   a verse/bridge four-chord song *p86*

TECHNIQUE 32:   the 'big three' of turnarounds *p90*

TECHNIQUE 33:   a 'big three' turnaround in G *p92*

TECHNIQUE 34:   a 'big three' turnaround in D *p94*

TECHNIQUE 35:   get more from a turnaround *p96*

TECHNIQUE 36:   the 'up escalator' *p98*

TECHNIQUE 37:   the 'down escalator' *p100*

TECHNIQUE 38:   the turnaround meets the inversion *p102*

TECHNIQUE 39:   the turnaround meets the second inversion *p104*

TECHNIQUE 40:   going up and going down *p106*

TECHNIQUE 41:   telescoping a turnaround *p107*

TECHNIQUE 42:   secondary turnarounds *p108*

CHORD DIAGRAMS FOR ALL THE MAJORS AND MINORS

Over the next three pages, chord diagrams are given for the 12 major chords and the 12 minor chords.

You can test whether you can apply the 4+3 and 3+4 formula by choosing any of the 12 notes and trying to figure out the triad shape for it. Then look it up and see if you were right.

There is no need to memorise these 24 shapes at present – most of the chord examples in the book only use a small number of the 24 chords. But they're here for reference anyway.

Chord Diagrams

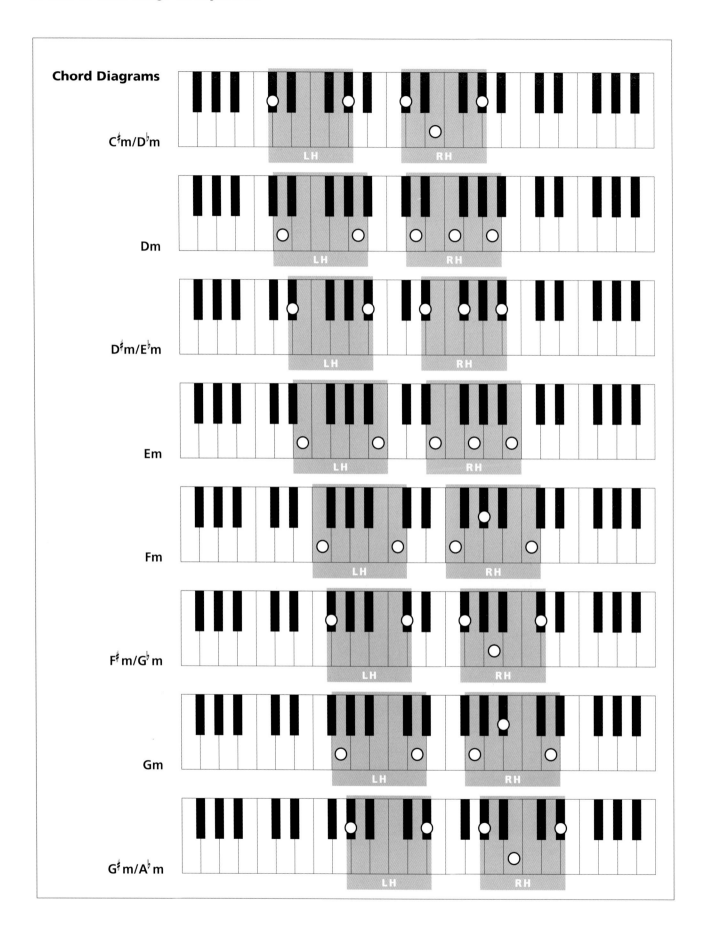

Chord Diagrams

C♯m/D♭m

Dm

D♯m/E♭m

Em

Fm

F♯m/G♭m

Gm

G♯m/A♭m

TABLE OF CHORD FORMULAS

This table gives you a short formula with which to create a certain type of chord on a note of any pitch. The numbers represent the number of keys you have to move up to find the next note in the chord (in semitones). Don't count the key you're on in the first place, and remember not to miss out black keys.

Chord name	scale degree	pitch in C	gap (interval)
Major	1-3-5	C-E-G	4+3
Minor	1-♭3-5	C-E♭-G	3+4
Augmented	1-3-♯5	C-E-G♯	4+4
Diminished	1-♭3-♭5	C-E♭-G♭	3+3
Major 7th	1-3-5-7	C-E-G-B	4+3+4
7th	1-3-5-♭7	C-E-G-B♭	4+3+3
Minor 7th	1-♭3-5-♭7	C-E♭-G-B♭	3+4+3
Diminished 7th	1-♭3-♭5-♭♭7	C-E♭-G♭-B♭♭	3+3+3
5th	1-5	C-G	7
Suspended 2nd	1-2-5	C-D-G	2+5
Suspended 4th	1-4-5	C-F-G	5+2
Major 6th	1-3-5-6	C-E-G-A	4+3+2
Minor 6th	1-♭3-5-♯6	C-E♭-G-A	3+4+2
Add 9th	1-3-5-9	C-E-G-D	4+3+7
Major 9th	1-3-5-7-9	C-E-G-B-D	4+3+4+3
9th	1-3-5-♭7-9	C-E-G-B♭-D	4+3+3+3
Minor add 9th	1-♭3-5-9	C-E♭-G-D	3+4+7
Minor 9th	1-♭3-5-♭7-9	C-E♭-G-B♭-D	3+4+3+4

GLOSSARY OF SONGWRITING TERMS & CONCEPTS

Terms in italics are exclusive to the Backbeat series of books, others are generally-used terminology.

Augmented chord
A triad constructed from two two-tone intervals (4+4, eg C-E-G♯).

Bar-sharing
A bar in which there is more than one chord. This describes a rate of chord change. More specifically, the re-harmonising of half a bar from major to minor, or the reverse.

Blue note
The flatted (lowered) 3rd, 5th or 7th of a major scale, as heard in blues, jazz and rock music.

Blue chord
Another name for chords ♭III and ♭VII in the major key.

bpm
Beats per minute. This figure is a measurement of tempo (speed) and is used by songwriters to calculate how long (as well as how fast) a song will be.

Bridge
Also known as the 'middle-eight', the bridge is the third primary section of a song after the verse and chorus. It is traditionally placed after the second chorus to satisfy the aesthetic need for fresh material at this point. It may open up new territory in the music and/or the lyric.

Cadence
The chord change that marks the end of a phrase, usually involving chord I and/or V. Traditional harmony recognises the perfect cadence (V-I), the imperfect (I-V), the plagal (IV-I), and the interrupted (V-VI). Of these the perfect cadence is the most significant for songwriting, as it's used to change key and to end a song with finality.

Chorus
The part of a song section that's usually the most memorable – the 'hook' – and which often features the singing of the lyric title.

Chromatic
A chromatic note or chord is one that does not usually belong in the key. Since there are 12 notes and a key uses a scale of seven notes, there are always five chromatic notes left over.

Classical minor key
This is the minor key constructed from the harmonic minor scale in which chord V is a major chord. The scale of A harmonic minor is A-B-C-D-E-F-G♯.

Coda

This is the final section of the song, after the last chorus. It can be a repetition of an earlier section such as a link, intro, or chorus, with or without singing or instrumental soloing. In popular recorded songwriting the coda is often a fade.

Common tone

This is a note common to adjacent chords in a progression. F major (F-A-C) and C major (C-E-G) have one common tone, C; F major (F-A-C) and D minor (D-F-A) have two common tones, F and A; Fmaj7 (F-A-C-E) and A minor (A-C-E) have three common tones. An enharmonic note (same pitch, different spelling) can sometimes disguise a common tone. For instance E major is E-G♯-B and F minor is F-A♭-C; G♯ and A♭ are the same pitch, and therefore a common tone. On the keyboard a common tone between chords often means not having to move that finger.

Degree

A way of referring to the notes of a scale.

Descending bass

Popular songwriting device in which a song section's chords are built on a descending sequence of notes in the bass or left hand. The harmony is made subservient to this bassline, or remains static.

Diminished chord

A chord made up of two intervals of a minor 3rd (3+3): C diminished is C-E♭-G♭. It occurs naturally as chord VII in the major key. If another minor 3rd is added, the diminished 7th chord results. C diminished is C-E♭-G♭-B♭♭ (B♭♭ = A).

Dominant

The 5th degree of the scale, and the chord built thereon (chord V).

Dominant suppression

The deliberate avoidance of chord V in a song sequence or turnaround.

Enharmonic note/chord

This is a note or chord that has two names but the same pitch – chiefly the five black keys on the piano: A♯/B♭, C♯/D♭, D♯/E♭, F♯/G♭, G♯/A♭, and the major and minor chords thereof. B, F♯ and C♯ major are the enharmonic equivalents of the keys C♭, G♭, and D♭.

'Escalator' effect

Powerful 'rising' feeling made by chords arranged in numerical sequence. The classic example, often found as a prechorus sequence, is II-III-IV-V.

Hard rock formula

A chord 'recipe' that involves taking chords I, IV and V from the primary six of a major key, and adding ♭II, ♭III, and ♭VI. In C major this would be C-F-G-B♭-E♭-A♭.

Harmonic function/identity

This is the role a chord plays in a major or minor key as designated by a Roman numeral such as I, II, III, etc. The pitch identity of a chord stays the same regardless of what its harmonic function is in any context.

Harmonising
Starting with a melody line made of single notes and finding chords (harmony) to colour and support this melody.

Inversion
Any chord that does not have its root note as the lowest in pitch. A simple triad of C has a first inversion (C/E) and a second inversion (C/G). A Cmaj7 chord could have a third inversion (C/B) because it has four notes. In any simple major (or minor) chord there are three notes. G major consists of the notes G-B-D. The note that gives the chord its name is the 'root' note. The middle note of the three is called the '3rd' (because it is the third degree of the scale of G major) and the last note is known as the '5th' (because it's the fifth degree of the scale). Most of the time the lowest note in the chord (and the one sounded by a bass instrument in the arrangement) will be the root note. But it is possible to make either of the other notes – the '3rd' or the '5th' – the bass note. If the 3rd is the lowest note the chord is a 'first inversion'. If the 5th is lowest the chord is a 'second inversion'. Inverted chords are written with a slash followed by either the 3rd or the 5th. In this book a lower-case i or ii in front of the Roman numeral also indicates first or second inversion, and the lower case letter after the slash (C/e) means the inversion is purely in the right hand.

Leading note
The 7th degree of the scale, one semitone below the key note in both the major and the 'classical' minor scale. Added to a major triad this creates the major 7 chord.

LH
Abbreviation for left hand.

Major chord
Triad formed by an interval of two tones and then one of one-and-a-half (4+3 keys on the keyboard); so C-E-G is C major.

Major scale
Division of the octave into seven intervals (eight notes) on the pattern tone-tone-semitone-tone-tone-tone-semitone (2-2-1-2-2-2-1). It can be heard by playing the white notes from C to C.

Middle-eight
Another name for the bridge, so-called because it's often eight bars long and roughly in the middle of a song.

Minor chord
Triad formed by an interval of one-and-a-half and then two tones (3+4 keys on the keyboard); C-E♭-G is C minor.

Modal minor
Set of chords derived from the natural minor (aeolian mode) scale: A-B-C-D-E-F-G. In popular songwriting this is treated as a version of the key of A minor. It differs from the 'classical' minor in having chord V as a minor.

Modulation

The process of changing key.

Octave

If a scale has seven different notes, the eighth note – the octave – brings you back to the same note that you started on, except higher in pitch (or lower, in a descending scale). For instance, from one C to the next is a complete octave.

Pedal note

A bass note that remains the same while chords change above it, creating differing amounts of harmonic tension. In guitar music the pedal is usually either E, A or D – the lower open strings, but on a keyboard any note is as easy to make a pedal as any other. It should not be confused with a drone note – one that remains unchanging in the middle or at the top of the harmony above a changing bassline.

Perfect cadence

The chord change V-I at the end of a phrase or section.

Pitch identity

A chord considered by reference to its pitch name – C, G, Em etc, – in contrast to its harmonic function as chord I, II, III etc. Pitch identity remains the same regardless of which harmonic role a chord is playing at any moment.

Primary three-chord trick

A song written using chords I, IV and V of a key. In C major this is C, F, G.

Primary turnaround

Any turnaround that uses chords I, IV and V, plus one of the minors, II, III or VI.

Rate of chord change

The frequency with which chords change from bar to bar or within a bar.

Relative chord/key

Every major chord/key has a relative minor to which it is closely related by virtue of having many of the same notes. C major (C-E-G) is the relative major of A minor (A-C-E). The relative minor is always chord VI in a major key, chord III in a minor key.

Reverse polarity

Songwriting technique which changes II, III or VI into major chords, or IV into a minor. These changes are most effective when used selectively.

RH

Abbreviation for right hand.

Root

The note in a chord after which the chord is named. If this note is the lowest in the chord, the chord is in root position.

Scale

Division of the octave into eight notes (seven intervals) from which chords, melody and a sense of key are generated. Blues and rock guitar also uses modes and pentatonic scales, the latter of which have only five notes.

Secondary three-chord trick

Any three-chord song that omits chord V.

Secondary turnaround

Any turnaround that omits chord V or I.

Sub-dominant

The 4th degree of the scale, chord IV, and the key chord IV symbolises.

Suspension

Important harmony effect created when the 3rd of a chord is temporarily replaced by the 2nd or 4th of the scale. The 2nd or 4th rises or falls back to the 3rd. A C triad (C-E-G) becomes Csus2 (C-D-G) or Csus4 (C-F-G). The tension and release thus created is highly significant for songwriting.

Tempo

The speed of music, measured in beats per minute (bpm).

Three-chord trick

A song written with only three chords, usually I, IV and V.

Through-composed

A song section in which there are no repeated sequences that build it up. The entire section must carry a single progression.

Time signature

Two numbers placed at the start of a piece of music which indicate the type of beat used and how many of these beats make a bar. It has nothing to do with tempo. The commonest time signatures in popular music are 4/4 (meaning four quarter-notes in a bar) and 12/8, with examples of 3/4 (waltz time), 6/8 and 2/4 occurring less frequently.

Tonic

The first degree of the scale (also called the root note of the scale).

Tonic minor

The minor chord or key with the same root note as the tonic. C minor is the tonic minor of C major. Counter-intuitively, C minor is actually a more distant key than C's relative minor, A minor, because the scale has fewer notes in common, especially in the natural minor form.

'True' inversion

In this book a true inversion is one in which either the 3rd or 5th of a chord is in the left hand as a bass note, regardless of what form of triad is held in the right. The term is meant to differentiate such an inversion from the exclusively right-hand inversions discussed in Section 1. These right-hand inversions are only intended to show how there are three ways of playing a triad, and that awareness of the three options makes for easier chord-changing. True inversions are notated with a capital letter on the other side of the slash (C/E).

Turnaround

Type of chord sequence with three or four chords which lasts two, four or eight bars. To be a turnaround it has to be repeated.

12-bar

A verse structure central to blues, rock'n'roll, R&B and rock, using chords I, IV and V, and containing its own hook.

Voice-leading

One of the main differences between chord-playing on a keyboard and guitar is what is known as 'voice-leading'. This is based on the principle that, during a sequence of chords, individual notes move to the nearest note in the next chord or stay still if they are also in the next chord. This is reasonably easy to do on a keyboard, and good practise in so far as it reduces the movement of your hands. On the guitar things are quite different: the number of notes in a guitar chord changes quite often between four, five and six strings, because of the number of strings that can be physically held down or the number of open strings that can be included. Of the guitar's eight master-shapes, E, G and Em have six notes, A, C, and Am have five, and D and Dm have four. No keyboard player would differentiate such chords in that way. Changing chords on a guitar (going from D to G, for instance) can sound like a four-part harmony quartet suddenly gaining one or two extra members singing different lines, which appear and disappear in a wholly unpredictable manner. In a piano-version of a chord sequence there would always be four notes, or always five, or more, depending on how full a sound was required. As a result, each voice can move smoothly to the nearest note.

ACKNOWLEDGEMENTS

For their involvement in the preparation of this book I would like to thank Nigel Osborne, Tony Bacon, Phil Richardson, Mark Brend, Paul Quinn and Paul Cooper. Thanks to Tim Turan for mastering the CD. The quotes in Section 11, 'Famous Songwriters On Songwriting' were taken from interviews in *Mojo*, *Making Music*, several volumes in Omnibus' anthologies *In Their Own Words* and *Songtalk*, the journal of the National Academy of Songwriters in Hollywood, collected in *Songwriters On Songwriting* (editor Paul Zollo, Da Capo Press, 1997); there are a couple of quotes from other sources, such as *Rolling Stone* and *Playboy* magazines.

Author Note

Rikky Rooksby is a guitar teacher, songwriter/composer, and writer on popular music. He is author of the Backbeat titles *How To Write Songs On Guitar* (2000), *Inside Classic Rock Tracks* (2001), *Riffs* (2002), *The Songwriting Sourcebook* (2003), *Chord Master* (2004), *Melody* (2004), and *Songwriting Secrets: Bruce Springsteen* (2005). He contributed to *Classic Guitars Of The Fifties*, *The Guitar – Complete Guide For The Player* (2003), *Roadhouse Blues* (Stevie Ray Vaughan biog, 2003*)*, and *Albums – 50 Years Of Great Recordings (2005)*. He has also written *The Guitarist's Guide To The Capo* (Artemis 2003), *The Complete Guide To The Music Of Fleetwood Mac* (revised ed 2004), 14 Fastforward guitar tutor books; transcribed and arranged over 40 chord songbooks of music by Bob Dylan, Dido, The Stone Roses, David Bowie, Eric Clapton, Travis, The Darkness, and *The Complete Beatles*; and co-authored *100 Years 100 Songs*. He has written articles on rock musicians for the new *D.......ary Of National Biography* (OUP), and published interviews, reviews, articles and ....iptions in magazines such as *Guitar Techniques*, *Total Guitar*, *Guitarist*, *Bassist*, *Bass G......zine*, *The Band*, *Record Collector*, *Sound On Sound*, and *Making Music*, where he ....nthly 'Private Pluck' guitar column. He is a member of the Guild of Internatio..... and Composers, the Sibelius Society, and the Vaughan Williams Society. at www.rikkyrooksby.com.

"Those 12 notes are so mysterious, and each time I sit down at the piano
I can't wait to see where they're going to take me today."
Lamont Dozier